ENERGY AND SECURITY

The Adelphi Library

Energy and Security

THE ADELPHI LIBRARY   1

edited by
GREGORY TREVERTON
Assistant Director, IISS

Published for
THE INTERNATIONAL INSTITUTE FOR
STRATEGIC STUDIES
by

Gower and ALLANHELD, OSMUN

Published by

Gower Publishing Company Limited,
Westmead, Farnborough, Hampshire, England
and
Allanheld, Osmun & Co. Publishers, Inc.
6 South Fullerton Avenue
Montclair, New Jersey 07042, USA

British Library Cataloguing in Publication Data

Energy and Security—
  (Adelphi Library)

1 Energy policy
2 National security

I   Treverton, Gregory   II International
    Institute for Strategic Studies   III Series

    333.7   HD9502.A2

ISBN 0-566-00343-0

0 566 00343 0 (UK)
0/916672/71/9 (US)

Contents

TERMINOLOGY

Absorbers

Low absorbers are producer countries with small populations and high oil production, and consequently high per capita oil revenues (above $1,500 per year). Socio-economic restrictions limit the capacity of these countries to invest revenues productively at home or to spend them on imports. Low absorbers are Saudi Arabia, Kuwait, Abu Dhabi, Qatar, Libya.

High absorbers are producer countries with relatively large populations and per capita oil revenues under $1,500 per year. Depending on their degree of socio-economic development, these countries could invest a large share of their revenues on development and/or imports. High absorbers are Iran, Iraq, Algeria, possibly also Bahrain and Venezuela.

Oman, Nigeria and Indonesia are in a somewhat different position: in all three, infrastructural and socio-economic restrictions limit the speed with which oil revenues can be translated into development. Indonesia and Nigeria will nevertheless be able to absorb large investments and might even still depend on foreign financial assistance.

International Oil Companies

(*a*) The 'majors' or 'seven sisters': Exxon, Texaco, Gulf, Standard Oil of California, Mobil (all American); British Petroleum (British); and Royal Dutch/Shell (Dutch/British).

(*b*) Wholly or partly state-controlled: Compagnie Française des Petroles (40 per cent owned by the French government – often included with the 'majors'), ELF/ERAP (French), ENI (Italian).

(*c*) Other integrated companies ('independents'): Standard Indiana, Atlantic Richfield, Continental, Sun, Occidental, Phillips, Getty, Amerada Hess (all American).

(*d*) ARAMCO: The Arabian-American Oil Company, a consortium of American majors operating the bulk of Saudi Arabia's oil production.

OAPEC

The Organization of Arab Petroleum Exporting Countries, founded in 1968 by Libya, Saudi Arabia and Kuwait. Other members are: Abu Dhabi, Algeria, Bahrain, Egypt, Iraq, Qatar and Syria. Oman and Tunisia have applied for membership.

OPEC

The Organization of Petroleum Exporting Countries, founded in 1960 by Iran, Venezuela, Iraq, Saudi Arabia and Kuwait. Other members, with their year of entry, are: Qatar (1961), Libya and Indonesia (1962), Abu Dhabi (1967), Algeria (1969), Nigeria (1971), Ecuador (1973) and Gabon (1975).

Oil Production/Consumption

Levels are measured in *barrels* and *metric tons*, rates of production in barrels per day (b/d) and metric tons per year. Occasionally, b/d have been converted to t/year, using the approximate conversion rule of 1 million b/d = 50 million t/year. One barrel approximately equals 0·734 tons (the exact conversion depends on the specific gravity of the crude oil type); one ton approximately equals 7·33 barrels.

Persian Gulf

This term has been used throughout this Paper to include Iraq, Kuwait, Saudi Arabia, Bahrain, Qatar, the United Arab Emirates, and Oman.

vii

Introduction

There can now be no doubt that access to and use of energy have clear bearing on the security of nations.

If there were ever any doubt as to the centrality of oil in the general security concerns of the Western nations and Japan, the widespread alarm at the Soviet invasion of Afghanistan has made clear the general perception of threat and underlined the extreme nervousness of the main consumers at any prospect of destabilisation or Soviet penetration into the region.

The oil embargo of 1973 and the subsequent supply shortages suffered by nations that do not produce oil make that point clear. It is equally clear that nuclear energy, despite its drawbacks, will continue to be attractive to countries in both the industrial and the less developed world as a means of diversifying their energy sources, making themselves less dependent on oil from the OPEC nations. Yet many technologies used in producing nuclear energy are also relevant in making nuclear weapons. Thus, the proliferation of nuclear energy technology means that more nations could be in a position to follow India's example and explode a nuclear device. It is no simple matter to separate the peaceful uses of nuclear energy from the acquisition of nuclear weapons. Trying to do so has been and continues to be a major task of the international non-proliferation policy.

The papers in this volume constitute a broad introduction to the issues of energy and security. 'Oil and Influence' examines the possible use of the oil 'weapon' in the light of the 1973 embargo. The analysis underscores continuing features of the relationship between Arab oil-producing states in the Middle East and the industrial nations; the increasing tightness of the global oil market; the growing dependence of all Western states on Middle Eastern oil, despite efforts at energy conservation; the continuing festering of the Arab-Israeli dispute as a possible impetus to use of the oil weapon; and the pivotal role of Saudi Arabia.

'Oil and Security' looks at the other side of the coin, not the possibilities for sucessful use of the oil weapon but the chances that the countries in the industrial world who would be the targets could act to prevent or to protect themselves from it. Too often it is loosely asserted that any reduction in oil imports is a crucial blow to the security of particular countries, and the paper first looks hard at the extent to which oil can legitimately be called a 'national security concern'. Any unanticipated reduction in imports is a nuisance for industrial countries, and it imposes cost, but most of them could suffer up to a 30 per cent reduction in imports with little effect on economic production if the required preparations were in place. Stockpiles of oil could provide months, even years, of insulation from major reductions in supply. However, the oil exporting countries most likely to initiate a reduction for political purposes—

1

Saudi Arabia notably among them—are also those countries that can afford to forego substantial portions of their oil revenues for a considerable period of time.

The Western countries have very different degrees of dependence on imported oil, and that is a crucial factor in any co-operative programme to ensure against disruptions in imports. 'Oil and Security' examines a number of forms of co-operation, as well as the possibility that the oil exporters might counter with the strategy which has proved effective in the past—exploiting the desire of the more vulnerable industrial states to avoid oil losses.

It has long been realised that the widespread use of nuclear energy implied the spread of technology capable of producing nuclear weapons, but that realisation has been dramatised by the continuing oil shortages of the 1970s. The Non-Proliferation Treaty (NPT) of 1967 recognised the link between nuclear energy and weapons but was necessarily based on a sharp differentiation between the existing nuclear-weapon states and those that did not yet possess nuclear devices. It established commitments for both groups of states, and it put heavy reliance on internationally administered safeguards of nuclear facilities in non-nuclear weapons states. 'Prospects for Nuclear Proliferation' is an assessment of the existing non-proliferation regime. It underscores the regime's shortcomings—its discriminatory character, the limited effectiveness of safeguards and the problems imposed by increasing dispersion of nuclear technology. The Indian nuclear explosion in 1974 is an obvious example of what went wrong.

The Indian explosion brought home to the world community the shortcomings of the existing non-proliferation regime, particularly in dealing with states that were not signatories to the NPT. Those shortcomings were all the more evident as states throughout the world accelerated their plans for nuclear power in the wake of the 1973 oil embargo. Those plans have been stepped up only to be cut back a number of times in response to the obvious difficulties in building and operating nuclear reactors, but it is clear that in the short run nuclear energy offers the only realistic way for most countries to reduce their dependence on imported oil. In 1974 the countries that are major suppliers of nuclear technology came together to try to ensure that competition for export orders would not result in export offers being sweetened by the provision of sensitive technologies.

'Nuclear Power and Weapons Proliferation' is a broad introduction to nuclear power and nuclear weapons. It provides a background on the nuclear fuel cycle, and it begins to sketch alternative ways of controlling the proliferation of nuclear technology that might have weapons applications. Yet here, as in the effort by nations to make themselves less vulnerable to interruptions of imported oil, there are no technical 'fixes'. Reportedly, Pakistan was able during 1978, through covert purchases in Western Europe of technologies not on the nuclear suppliers' prescribed list, to acquire the parts for a centrifuge enrichment plant capable of producing weapons-grade uranium. Non-proliferation policy in the future will require a combination of technical instruments and political incentives, and, in the end, an ability to cope with a more complicated and dangerous world once some proliferation occurs.

Gregory Treverton

2

1 Oil and Influence: The Oil Weapon Examined

HANS MAULL

INTRODUCTION

Oil weapon, as used in this Paper, signifies any manipulation of the price and/or supply of oil by exporting nations with the intention of changing the political behaviour of the consumer nations. For reasons given later, the political potential of the oil price is fairly restricted, so that in effect we are mainly concerned with supply interruptions.

Oil power is the power which stems from the dependence of the consumer nations on oil. This forms the basis of any successful application of the oil weapon and includes all factors which allow the producers to influence and control the political behaviour of the consumers. The oil weapon, therefore, is one specific way of using oil power: other ways would be the threat to use the oil weapon, or simply the diplomatic exploitation of consumer dependence.

Two years after the hectic reactions to the first successful application of the oil weapon, the sense of emergency of the energy crisis has widely been replaced by complacency. A cursory glance might seem to justify this complacency: a world-wide recession and unusually mild winters have brought down oil consumption in the industrialized countries and forced the oil producers to reduce their production (and some of them even to lower the price of oil). Besides, the freezing of official oil price levels until September 1975 has meant an effective erosion of the purchasing power of producers' oil revenues, as a consequence of inflationary rises in the cost of imports from the consumer countries.

Yet this seeming return to equilibrium of the international oil system is deceptive. OPEC proved its cohesiveness under pressure, and there is little prospect that a further reduction in demand for oil could reach a level where the organization would come under serious strain and break apart. On the contrary, it looks as if the decrease in oil consumption will soon be replaced by a growing demand for OPEC oil, as the industrialized economies recover from the 1974/75 recession (oil conservation has so far been only marginally policy-induced). A consistent energy policy by the most important actor in the international oil market, the United States, has been blocked by the struggle between President and Congress, and this – together with the decline of American indigenous oil production – has meant that American dependence on Middle Eastern oil imports has not been reduced. The substance of producer power has, therefore, hardly been diminished. What must be even more worrying is the small amount of progress towards a settlement of the Israeli–Arab conflict – for, even though the energy crisis and the Middle East conflict are separate problems, they are strongly linked by the present political situation in the Middle East. Another oil embargo involving production cutbacks is, therefore, a distinct possibility, and has been hinted at repeatedly by Arab oil producers, including Saudi Arabia.

An analysis of the politics of oil and the potential and limitations of the oil weapon in some respects appears more timely now than a year ago, because of a widespread sense that the successful application of the oil weapon in 1973/74 was an event unique in international politics, and that its recurrence is unlikely. In fact, the oil weapon has become, and will continue to be, a force in the international system.

Oil is the raw material most intrinsically interwoven with politics, and oil embargoes and

3

boycotts have repeatedly served as political tools. Even though the political leverage provided by the oil trade has not been used only by countries in the Middle East, this area has been exposed to the politics of oil three times within less than twenty years – each time in connection with Israeli–Arab wars. In 1956 the Suez Canal and the Iraq Petroleum Company pipeline from the Iraqi oilfields to the Mediterranean were closed, and about two-thirds of Middle East exports to Europe had to be re-routed or were cut off. The result was a moderate increase in the price of oil over a short period of time. Some European countries faced temporary shortages, certain industries were affected, but overall production in European countries belonging to the Organization for Economic Co-operation and Development (OECD) continued to grow. In 1967, the Suez Canal was again closed – this time for a long period. Kuwait, Libya, Iraq and Saudi Arabia stopped production after the outbreak of the war – partly as a result of government decisions (Kuwait, Iraq), partly as a result of strikes by oil workers (Libya, Saudi Arabia) – and this stoppage was then replaced by selective embargoes against Britain, the United States and West Germany. Again, the success of the 'oil weapon' was virtually nil and 'hurt the Arabs more than anyone else', in the words of a Saudi Arabian oil minister.[1]

Why did the oil weapon score such a remarkable success in 1973, when only six years earlier it had totally failed? And what exactly is the role the oil weapon will play in future international relations? The substance of the oil weapon and the various forms of its application, as well as the influence producers can derive from it without using it at all, are the main concern of this Paper. This restricts its scope to the political aspects of the international oil market, so that the economic aspects are not considered further than is absolutely necessary for this purpose.

The Paper will first try to establish the essence of oil power by analysing its preconditions on the basis of the 1973/74 crisis. Then it will consider the future development of oil power, with particular reference to the limitations and weaknesses of the oil weapon, as well as possible new dimensions of oil power. Finally, it looks into the politics of some key producer countries to speculate about what possible and probable intentions on the part of these Middle Eastern states could once again lead to the application of the oil weapon.

I. OIL POWER: A POLITICAL REALITY

To find out why oil power has become a political reality since 1967 we have to look at the basis of this power: the trade relationship between producers and consumers. Around 1970 the international oil market was said to have turned from a buyers' to a sellers' market. This was a rather vague way of saying that a fundamental imbalance had developed in the trade relationship between producers and consumers, an imbalance by then no longer offset by outside factors such as political dependence or economic counterweights. This allowed the relationship to be used for political purposes.[2] The leverage inherent in such an imbalance stems from the capability to interrupt trade, and, the larger the difference between the damage the interruption causes to the consumer and that it causes to the supplier, the stronger the leverage.

The damage the target country actually experiences depends on the amount of impoverishment the stoppage or the reduction of supplies inflicts. A good indicator of this is the previous expansion of oil imports, which demonstrates oil's growing importance to the target. The damage experienced is also reflected in the length and costliness of the adjustment process which the supply interruption makes necessary.

One of the main characteristics of the international oil market in recent years has been its rapid expansion. Caused by the parallel boom in all major Western industrialized economies, demand for oil grew at a continuous, and even accelerating, pace to the 1973 peak. This unprecedented rise was the result not only of the 'natural' growth in demand accompanying expanding economies but also of the switch to oil

---

[1] Quoted in Walter Z. Laqueur, *The Struggle for the Middle East: The Soviet Union and the Middle East, 1958–1968* (Harmondsworth: Penguin, 1972), p. 153.
[2] A. O. Hirschmann, *National Power and the Structure of Foreign Trade* (Berkeley and Los Angeles: University of California Press, 1945).

4

Table 1: Oil import dependence – United States, Japan and Western Europe

	Western Europe			Japan			United States		
	1956	1967	1973	1956	1967	1973	1956	1967	1973
Oil imports (million tons)	121·5	443·6	736·2	12·4	116·8	282·5	57·3	116·5	300·7
Imports as % of energy supply	20·7	52·7	62·9	22·9	67·2	85·4	5·6	7·7	17·4
Arab oil imports as % of energy supply	13·4	36·0	45	12·8	33·4	33	1·3	0·6	5

SOURCES: *BP Statistical Review of the World Oil Industry, 1973*; *UN Statistical Papers*, Series J. (Due to difference in the two sources, figures for 1973 are not directly comparable with those of 1956 and 1967.)

as the predominant source of energy supply.[3] Nowhere in the Western world (apart from Canada) was indigenous production sufficient to satisfy the growing demand, so oil had to be imported to fill the gap between supply and demand. Table 1 shows clearly the absolute and relative growth of the significance of imported oil in the energy balance of the Western world. It also shows the strong position of the Arab countries as suppliers; attempts to diversify the sources of imports proved ineffective due to the unique position of the Arab world in terms of oil production (32·8 per cent of world production in 1973) and reserves.

The absolute growth of oil imports shows the increasing damage potential, and the relative growth shows the Arab producers' strong leverage *vis-à-vis* Europe, Japan and – to a lesser extent – the United States. In the case of the United States, dependence on Arab oil accelerated after indigenous production peaked out in 1970.[4]

Since energy is of overwhelming importance for the functioning of all aspects of industrialized economies and societies, the Arab producers' leverage was considerable – unless the consumer economies could adjust to interruptions in supply in such a way as to prevent major disturbances. While they had achieved adjustments at fairly low cost in 1956 and 1967, the situation in 1973 had changed fundamentally. The supply crises in 1956 and 1967 proved manageable because supplies were available from alternative sources, although admittedly at a somewhat higher price: Venezuela, the United States and Iran could step up their production by using excess capacity and divert some of it to European countries affected by the supply interruptions.[5] In 1973, no substantial stand-by capacity was available – certainly nowhere near enough to make up the reduction the Arab oil producers decided upon. Other producers in the Third World also showed no intention of increasing their production, since they, too, profited from the squeeze through its impact on oil prices. Existing stockpiles were hardly more than a temporary cushion against the impact of the Arab oil weapon, and the adjustment had to be achieved by savings in consumption and the limited possibilities of substituting other sources of primary energy for oil.

The European countries, Japan and even the United States, therefore, faced a situation in which the Arab oil producers provided them with a scarce and enormously important raw material for which there was no real substitute –

[3] Cf. OECD Oil Committee, *Oil: the present situation and future prospects* (Paris, 1973), pp. 21–29. The United States, however, was an exception, since she had switched (although generally less impressively) from coal to gas, rather than to oil.

[4] This is clearly demonstrated by comparing July 1972 and July 1973 supply patterns. During the intervening year indigenous production fell by 2·4 per cent, while crude oil imports increased by 62·5 per cent, residual fuel imports by 5·5 per cent and other oil product imports by 27·2 per cent, bringing the total import share to 6 million b/d out of a total supply of 17·5 million b/d (*Financial Times*, 14 September 1973). Between July and August 1973 alone, crude oil imports from the Arab states more than doubled, from 625,000 b/d to 1,285,000 b/d (*Arab Report and Record*, 16–31 October 1973, p. 484).

[5] In 1967 Iran's production increased by 23 per cent while Iraq's fell by 11·5 per cent (Laqueur, p. 153); the United States increased production between May and August 1967 by about 1 million b/d (Sam H. Schurr *et al.*, *Middle Eastern Oil and the Western World: Prospects and Problems*, New York: American Elsevier, 1971, p. 37).

an optimum precondition for the exertion of political pressure, provided there was no countervailing dependence by the producers on stable oil supplies and/or on imports from the consumer countries. We must ask: was the trade relationship between producers and consumers balanced? And, also, was it based upon mutual benefit?

Looking at the structure of trade between producer and consumer countries to establish the degree of balance or imbalance in the relationship, one has to consider two further points. Are oil producers sufficiently dependent on goods supplied by the oil consumers to provide realistic counter-leverage? And are the producers so dependent on the continuation of oil exports that any interruption or reduction would also inflict heavy damage on them?

The Arab countries are indeed to a certain extent dependent on imports from the Western industrialized countries, especially food: for example, in 1972 they imported cereals and cereal products worth at least $297 million from eight industrialized countries (the United States, Canada, West Germany, France, Britain, Italy, the Netherlands and Switzerland).[6] Since the United States has an especially strong position in the world grain market, there appeared to be a possibility of exerting counter-pressure – and indeed this was hinted at by the then Vice-President Ford (8 January 1974). But it appears doubtful whether a counter-embargo could have been organized by Western grain producers; and, even if one assumes such an attempt would have succeeded, the Soviet Union might have derived considerable political advantage from stepping in to make up the shortfall (American grain exports to the Arab countries were about 2 million tons in 1972, while Soviet grain production in 1973 was a record-breaking 222·5 million tons). Some oil producers also possessed large foreign exchange holdings which gave them a good chance of weathering any prolonged trade war and so contributed to their low vulnerability.[7]

As for the other form of dependence mentioned there can be little doubt that the economies of the large-scale oil exporters in the Third World have been largely dependent on oil revenues and the indirect benefits derived from oil production.[8] However, for mutual dependence to exist between producers and consumers, there must be strong incentives for *both* sides to maintain the existing trade relationships. Some producers (the low absorbers) already had more revenue than they could spend, and world-wide inflation and currency devaluations were eroding its value – hence they had no incentive to meet the growing demand by increased oil production.

The Loss of Control

So far we have been dealing with imbalances inherent in the trade structure itself; but to arrive at a more complete picture of the problem, we must consider other aspects of the producer-consumer relationship as well. Though the imbalance of the trade structure was considerably aggravated after about 1970, it can be argued that it existed long before. But in the past, the asymmetries in the consumer–producer relationship enabled the consumer countries to control the behaviour of the producer states. This control had rested on two pillars: the major international oil companies, and Western (first British, then predominantly American) influence in the Middle East oil-producing countries. These allowed the consumers to bring the producers into a world economy working in favour of the industrialized countries (and their oil companies). However, they were gradually eroded by political factors inside and outside the area – most importantly the ascendancy of Arab nationalism and a growing Soviet influence challenging the West, which, in Arab eyes, was compromised by its imperialist heritage and its support for Israel. While the oil producers asserted their independence and sovereignty and

---

[6] *Neue Zürcher Zeitung*, 27 April 1974.
[7] A comparison between foreign exchange holdings at the end of 1971 and figures for total import bills in the same year shows that Kuwait theoretically could pay for 5 years' imports, Libya for 3 years' and Saudi Arabia for 18 months'. See *Petroleum Press Service*, December 1973, p. 452; Charles Issawi, *Oil, The Middle East and The World* (Washington: Center for Strategic and Inter-national Studies, Georgetown University, 1972) Washington Papers No. 4, pp. 41–2.
[8] In the late 1960s dependence on oil exports for gross foreign exchange earnings was around 75 per cent for Iraq, 85–90 per cent for Kuwait, Libya and Saudi Arabia, and close to 100 per cent for the sheikhdoms in the Persian Gulf. At the same time, the oil sector accounted for just under 20 per cent of GNP in Algeria and 33 per cent in Iraq; Saudi Arabia derived 55 per cent, Libya 60 per cent and Kuwait and the smaller sheikhdoms even higher percentages of GNP from the oil sector.

displayed greater confidence in voicing their grievances and demands, not only were the Western consumers simultaneously becoming increasingly dependent on these countries, they also continued to be politically involved in the Middle East area (e.g., through American support for Israel).

This situation made them vulnerable and exposed them to political demands by the oil producers. By 1970 the erosion of consumer bargaining power and the increase in the strength of the producers were well advanced, and the producers only needed to be aware of the full range of their new power. This constitutes another fundamental difference between 1967 and 1973: in 1973 the Arab producers were not only fully aware of their dramatically increased strength but were willing and able to use it.

The catalyst was the revolutionary *élan* of a new regime in Libya, which wanted to establish its nationalist and progressive credentials by taking the lead in the struggle against Western, imperialist influence in the Middle East. In 1970 it put pressure on the oil companies and, in doing so, clearly demonstrated the fundamental shift in bargaining power from the oil companies (which acted for the consumers as well as in their own interests) to the producers. By 1970 Libyan production had been raised to 3·3 million b/d to compensate for the closure of the Suez Canal in 1967, the production lost as a result of the Nigerian civil war of 1967–70 and the prolonged interruption to the supply of Saudi oil along the Trans-Arabian pipeline (sabotaged by guerillas in Syria in May 1970). Europe's increased dependence on Libyan oil (25 per cent) was skilfully exploited: one after the other, companies were forced to accept a large price increase and a revised tax structure. This demonstration of oil power led to a series of negotiations for improved terms for producer countries in the Mediterranean and the Gulf which came to a short-lived standstill with agreements between the oil companies and the producers, reached in Teheran and Tripoli in early 1971.

Higher prices suited the oil companies, which wanted to diversify their sources of supply by developing the reserves in Alaska and the North Sea and unconventional sources of oil, such as tar sands. All these alternatives implied high investment outlays (which had to be financed partly through profits) and higher production costs. But, since higher prices further reduced the incentive for the oil-rich low absorbers to sustain and increase the prevailing production levels, they strengthened the position of the producers even more. However, securing higher prices was not the producers' only strategy. Efforts to gain increased producer participation in, and ultimately total control over, oil production in their own countries dominated the year 1972. This, together with concern about conservation, which led to the introduction of production ceilings in Kuwait and Libya, may have met certain long- and short-term interests of the producers. But they certainly also worked as power-increasing strategies which strengthened the producer's control, increased the squeeze on the international oil market and made any threat involving supply interruptions much more credible than before.

Application of the Oil Weapon

The *intention* to apply the oil weapon in the Israeli–Arab context had long figured prominently in Arab thinking, and President Nasser had proclaimed oil as one of the three components of Arab power.[9] The closer the linkage between the Arab–Israeli conflict and Persian Gulf politics became (and the alignment between Saudi Arabia and Egypt had finally established such a close connection), the greater the temptation to trade stable and sufficient oil supplies against a change in the United States' Middle East policy. The general mood in the Arab world was definitely moving in this direction, and a clear sign of how far it had progressed came when the Saudi oil minister, Sheikh Yamani, declared on a visit to the United States that his country was prepared to supply the quantity of crude oil needed only if the United States created the right political atmosphere.[10] This clear warning, and subsequent confirmations by King Faisal himself, showed that a growing willingness to use economic pressure to force a change in the American attitude to the Israeli–Arab conflict had pervaded the decision-making level of a country considered one of America's staunchest allies, and whose king, less than a year earlier, has still advocated a policy of 'oil and politics don't mix'.

[9] Gamal Abdel Nasser, *The Philosophy of the Revolution* (Cairo: Dar al-Kutub, 1955), pp. 67–69.
[10] *Strategic Survey 1973* (London: IISS, 1974), p. 97.

7

On 17 October 1973 the OAPEC conference in Kuwait (with the exception of Iraq which followed its own policy) decided to cut production by a minimum of five per cent of the September production levels, and thereafter each month by five per cent of the previous month's output.

The agreement was followed by immediate cuts of 10 per cent by Saudi Arabia and Qatar and 5 per cent by Libya, together with an embargo on oil exports to the United States by Libya and Abu Dhabi. Then, on 19 October, President Nixon asked Congress to agree to a $2·2 billion military aid programme for Israel. Saudi Arabia reacted by placing an embargo on all exports to the United States. This was eventually applied by all other Arab producers and was extended to cover other countries, primarily the Netherlands (a move which, whether intentionally or not, aimed at the heart of the European oil distribution system: the port of Rotterdam). Egypt, Syria and Tunisia did not announce any cuts, while Iraq embargoed supplies to the United States and the Netherlands but otherwise tried to restore her output, which had been affected by war damage at the Mediterranean oil terminals in Syria. Iraq dissociated herself from the oil weapon as designed by Saudi Arabia and followed her own line, nationalizing American and Dutch oil interests and urging other producers to break diplomatic and economic relations with the United States and withdraw funds invested there.

On 4 November the Arab oil ministers (again with the exception of Iraq) decided to standardize the level of production cutbacks at 25 per cent of September production; on 24 December production was increased to 85 per cent of the September figure. The OAPEC embargo on the United States was lifted on 18 March 1974 – though Syria and Libya dissociated themselves from this – and Saudi Arabia subsequently increased her production considerably. The embargo against the Netherlands was finally lifted on 10 July, the decision having been delayed by a reluctant Saudi Arabia.

Effectiveness of the Oil Weapon

The objective behind the Arab oil producers' decision of 17 October and the subsequent measures was to use economic pressure to change the consumer states' political attitude to the Israeli–Arab conflict. The system of measures and rules was carefully designed to provide maximum flexibility by means of a range of sanctions and rewards. The United States was, of course, the main target, and the Arab producers expected her to bring pressure to bear on Israel in order to achieve their objectives (return of all territories occupied in the 1967 war, including Jerusalem, and restoration of the legitimate rights of the Palestinians). In theory, the embargo should have been the main weapon, general cutbacks in production being necessary only to prevent its circumvention (even if most-favoured countries had received supplies on the pre-war level, this still would hardly have been sufficient to meet their growing demands). In other words, solidarity was to be made painful for the consumers, who all found themselves with at best the bare minimum of necessary oil supplies and could hardly afford to re-export any of them. In addition, Arab oil ministers also threatened further sanctions against any country which displayed solidarity with an embargoed country.

This system, reportedly elaborated by a group of Arab oil experts long before the October war, was meant to create a shortage in the United States, leading to inconvenience for the final consumer and consequent political pressure on the administration to change its Middle East policy. Other Western consumer countries affected by the oil weapon, were also expected to exert influence on American policy through their governments.

However, even though the Arab oil producers managed to build up economic pressure, they were not totally successful. The embargo did not work properly for two reasons: firstly, some Arab oil evidently 'leaked' to the United States despite the embargo; and, secondly, the international oil distribution system was managed by oil companies in such a way as to spread the damage fairly evenly, by diverting Arab oil away from embargoed ports and replacing it with non-Arab oil. In the case of the United States, total imports of crude and products fell from about 6·6 million b/d in November (when the embargo was not yet effective, due to the time-lag involved in transporting the oil) to about 5·1 million b/d in January. They then increased to around 5·5 million b/d – as opposed to a projected import figure for the first quarter of 1974 of 7·8 million b/d. The shortfall against a projected total oil demand for the first quarter of 19·7 million b/d was thus somewhere between 11 and 14 per cent, not the 17 per cent predicted by the President.[11] Arab oil still reached the United States, though on a small scale; Saudi Arabian imports, 18 million barrels in November, amounted to only 7 million in December, while in January the figure was down to 957,000 barrels and in February to 552,000.[12] Libyan oil also leaked through the embargo (though this cannot be confirmed from American statistics, which do not give the source of oil imports).

The case of the Netherlands was somewhat similar; there, the embargo caused a serious problem only for a short period in December. A good indicator for the Netherlands is re-exports from Rotterdam's refining centre, which fell to 39 per cent of their normal level in the first half of December but recovered to 90 per cent in January – the embargo had become 'almost irrelevant', as the *Petroleum Economist* said, due to the flexibility of the international distribution system. Comparison of the Dutch oil deficit during the last quarter of 1973 with that of other EEC countries and the United States shows that the shortfall was indeed spread fairly evenly, and definitely not in accordance with Arab categorizations of friendly, neutral and hostile. Deficits ranged from 9 per cent (Netherlands) to 25 per cent (Denmark), with the United States, Germany, France and Italy in the 11–14 per cent range.[13]

Approximately equal import deficits do not, however, imply equal damage to the economies concerned. Not only was the shortfall for the embargoed United States no higher than those of other, neutral or even friendly, countries – the United States also was in a favourable position because of her consumption patterns.

First of all, her high per capita energy consumption indicates a large saving potential.

[11] European Community, 'The European Economy in 1973' (Brussels, 1974), p. 65; Petroleum Economist, April 1974, p. 175, June 1974, p. 24.
[12] Times, 10 April 1974.

[13] Petroleum Economist, March 1974, p. 98; European Commission, Energy Balance of the Community (Brussels, 1974).

Table 2: Main consumption sector requirements as % of total oil requirements (1971)
United States, Japan and Western Europe

	Industry (incl. non-energy use)	Transport/residential/ commercial use
United States	24·7	75·3
Japan	55·2	44·8
Western Europe	42·3	57·7

SOURCE: *OECD Observer*, December 1973 p. 24.

Table 3: Consumers' energy saving capacity and energy consumption as % of indigenous production (1971)

Vulnerability	Countries	Saving Capacity indicator*	Indigenous oil production as % of consumption	Indigenous energy production as % of consumption
High	Japan, Italy, Belgium, France	0·6–0·8	0–6·0	11·0–22·0
Medium	Britain, Netherlands, West Germany	0·9–1·1	2·0–7·0	51·0–64·0
Low	USA, Canada	1·1–1·4	74·0–98·0	89·0–110·0

* The saving capacity indicator calculated by *OECD* compares the abilities of consumer countries to absorb reductions in oil supplies. These vary according to the different consumption structures.
SOURCE: *OECD Observer*, December 1973, p. 35.

Secondly, the proportionate dependence of the various consumption sectors differed markedly from that of the other industrialized consumers in Europe and Japan. Since there is considerable flexibility in overall energy consumption (with the possibility of one form of energy being substituted for another), savings in energy can normally be translated into savings in oil, most conveniently and least harmfully in the transport and the commercial/residential sectors. Tables 2 and 3 show the United States' favourable position in this respect, and hence in respect of interruptions in oil supply.

Let us now attempt to assess how the economic pressure exerted on Western consumer countries (despite the apparent partial failure of the embargoes) was translated into political influence. Clearly, the attitudes of Western Europe, Japan and the United States towards the Israeli–Arab conflict have changed significantly since October 1973. However, it seems misleading to attribute these changes solely to the impact of the oil weapon. The most important of them was, of course, the shift in the United States' Middle East policy – but Washington had some very good reasons to put pressure on Israel so as to achieve some progress towards a Middle East settlement, quite apart from the pressure stemming from Arab oil embargoes and cutbacks. First, the Middle East was, and still is, a potential source of super-power conflict (as the events in October 1973 demonstrated) and hence a danger to her détente policy. Secondly, American success in bringing Israel to terms with her Arab neighbours' demands and achieving a stable settlement (or even a serious attempt to do so) would no doubt greatly enhance Washington's position in the Middle East, since the support for Israel constitutes its most important handicap in the Arab world.

On 6 November, the foreign ministers of the EEC agreed on a resolution which also marked a new approach to the Israeli–Arab conflict. The resolution called for Israel to withdraw to the lines she held at the time of the first ceasefire of 22 October (Egypt by that time wanted withdrawal to the same line) and full implementation of UN Security Council resolution 242 in an interpretation which did not differ from the Egyptian one. The inadmissibility of the acquisition of territory by force was set out as one of the principles of the envisaged settlement, and Israel

was urged to end the occupation of the areas she had conquered in 1967. The resolution further called for respect for the territorial integrity, sovereignty and independence of all states in the area and their right to live in peace within secure and recognized boundaries, and stated that any full and lasting agreement would have to take into account the legitimate rights of the Palestinians.

This resolution was widely seen as favourable to the Arabs and provoked bitter criticism in Israel. But, again, it seems an over-simplification to ascribe its content solely to the effectiveness of the oil weapon. Rather, it can be argued that it constituted a new step towards the gradual development of a common Middle East position by the European Community and reflected a slow but clear shift by the British and even West German governments from a pro-Israeli to a more neutral stand. Of course, this shift took into account the Community's high dependence on Arab oil, but the use of the oil weapon speeded up and crystallized the EEC position, rather than fundamentally changing it.

Japan was the most vulnerable of all industrialized consumer countries and the shortfall in oil supplies seemed to affect economic production fairly directly and seriously. At the beginning of December, the Ministry of International Trade and Industry (MITI) calculated the reduction in oil supplies at 16 per cent and predicted the following consequences: steel production would be down by 8–11 per cent, paper and pulp production by 30 per cent, petrochemicals by 20 per cent, cement by 13 per cent, and aluminium by 14 per cent. Furthermore, MITI foresaw a considerable additional push for inflation caused by higher oil prices and shortages.[14] As a result, Japan's modification of her Middle East policy was most marked, even though she finally managed to achieve most-favoured nation status without actually breaking diplomatic relations with Israel. All the same, she had to give up her low-profile, business-first foreign policy, which had achieved neutrality towards the Middle East conflict mainly by being vague. As one official put it, 'our interpretation of the UN resolution 242 has been ambiguous in the past and we are simply modifying it'.[15] The modifications included an appeal to Israel to return to the May

[14] *The Times*, 4 December 1973.
[15] *The Times*, 23 November 1973.

1967 borders and then negotiate a security agreement with the Arab states. Japan also adopted the principle that no territorial gains by military force should be permitted, and the government further explained that it would interpret the Security Council resolution 242 in accordance with the Arab attitude. The Minister of International Trade and Industry, Mr Nakasone, explicitly stated that Japan no longer agreed with the principles of the United States' Middle East policy.

An effect of the oil weapon over and above shifting the policies of consumer governments towards the Israeli–Arab conflict was to produce splits and tensions in the Western alliance and within the EEC. These tensions reflected basic differences in interest between the consumer countries and also, it seems, some mismanagement in dealing with them.

The differences concern, first of all, actual dependence on Arab oil. As pointed out earlier, the United States found herself in a much better position than both Europe and Japan; but even within Western Europe there were marked differences in dependence and vulnerability (see Table 3).

Another fundamental difference involved diverging energy policies. Again, it was France which found herself in a markedly different position from her partners. First, her energy policy had for a long time been marked by the search for stable oil supplies, independent from the 'majors'. This had led to the creation of government-owned, or at least government-influenced, French oil companies which sometimes competed strongly with the majors, and to a large amount of state intervention in energy and oil policies. Secondly, her energy policy since de Gaulle had developed a strong pro-Arab tendency, since it was to the Arab world that France looked for her stable and independent oil supplies. Great Britain and the Netherlands, on the other hand, were both the home of major international oil companies, and therefore refused any kind of interventionist government policy – even more so on a Community level. West Germany, Belgium and Italy fell somewhere between these two poles, the first two leaning towards a liberal policy, the last, through her state company (ENI), following a line similar to France but allowing the international oil companies a greater role.

But the core of the disagreement in the Western alliance and the European community was the issue of security. During the Israeli–Arab war, the United States pursued a policy which took account of American concern for the global balance *vis-à-vis* the Soviet Union and aimed to prevent any shift in Moscow's favour. The European countries, however, were primarily concerned about their oil supplies, and were not prepared to see their economic security put at risk. Apart from Portugal, which allowed the United States to use an air base in the Azores for her airlift to Israel, European governments therefore preferred to take a neutral attitude and to appease the Arabs. Britain declared an embargo on deliveries of arms and spares to all combatant states; this hurt the Israelis more than the Arabs. West Germany protested (after the war was over) against the use of her ports for the transfer of American war material from Germany to Israel. Secretary of Defense Schlesinger's veiled threat that the United States might reconsider her military presence in Germany demonstrated, however, that Germany faced a dilemma: she did not want to antagonize either the Americans or the Arabs.

Within the European Community a basically nationalistic approach prevailed. The problem here was the embargo against the Netherlands. While the Dutch urged the other member countries to show solidarity and arrive at some form of oil-sharing, France and Britain, anxious not to lose their status as friendly countries in Arab eyes, opposed such a move. (Actually, the EEC had no contingency plans for sharing out the oil, since this had been left to the OECD; the OECD oil committee, reportedly under French and British influence, decided not to put its oil-sharing system into action.) Though this did little economic damage (since the oil was shared more or less equally by the companies), the political damage to the idea of European solidarity was considerable: the EEC had to face the hard truth that national interests still had priority over European solidarity.

The oil weapon created a situation where the consumer nations had to react – so that it was no longer possible to gloss over the differences within the Western alliance and the European Community. As problems of oil supply became interwoven with other issues (the essence and character of American–European relations, the

11

size of the Community's Regional Fund), they became increasingly complex and difficult to resolve. This makes it unlikely that the splits and tensions within the West were foreseen and deliberately exploited by the Arab oil producers; it also appears questionable whether they actually served Arab interests. These tensions may have provided an extra incentive for the United States to settle the oil crisis by working for an Israeli–Arab settlement, and the use of the oil weapon did spur the EEC into adopting a united attitude to the Middle East conflict. Nonetheless, despite any independent and active role which the Arab producers may have expected

Europe to play in the process of reaching a settlement, a solution to the conflict still had to be found within the context of super-power bipolarity.

To sum up, it is certainly true that the use of the oil weapon caused a change in the Middle East policies of the main consumer countries, but this change did not constitute a total reversal of previous policies and, at least in the case of the United States, stopped well short of full acceptance of Arab objectives. The fact that the oil weapon was sheathed again before any of the stated Arab objectives had been achieved underlines that its success was not unqualified.

II. OIL POWER: POTENTIAL AND LIMITATIONS IN THE FUTURE

So far, we have been concerned primarily with the supply crisis of 1973–74. The scope of the analysis will now be expanded to take into account some 'guesstimates' about the development of oil power until 1985 – a period for which we possess at least some guidelines, derived from the last crisis, the present situation and factors which will evidently play a significant role over the coming period.

If we want to speculate about the future importance of the oil weapon in international relations, we must first attempt to assess the

future development of oil power in terms of the degree of balance/imbalance in the trade relationship between producers and consumers. Have we already reached the peak of oil power, or is it to grow further?

Development of Oil Power

The strength of oil power depends on the development of the oil import gap of major industrialized countries, which in turn depends on assumptions about supply- and demand-price elasticities (i.e., the responsiveness of changes in

Table 4: Estimated energy consumption and oil imports, 1980 and 1985

	Total energy consumption (million b/d[a])			Total oil imports (million b/d)			Oil imports as % of energy consumption		
	1973[b]	1980	1985	1973[b]	1980	1985	1973[b]	1980	1985
Western Europe	23·4	33·4	41·9	14·7	17	18	63	51	43
Extrapolated targets[c]			36·8			11·1			30
United States	35·2	44·9	54·7	6·0	2	3	17	4·5	5·5
Project Independence targets		42·3	50·0		5·9[d]	0[d]		14[d]	0[d]
Japan	6·6	10·7	14·4	5·6	7	9	85	65	62
Revised official targets		11·8	14·8		7·7	9·8		65	66

[a] Oil equivalent.   [b] Actual figures.
[c] Using EEC Commission targets and assuming the 1973 ratio of EEC to total Western European consumption.
[d] Total energy imports.
SOURCES: Deutsche Gesellschaft für Auswärtige Politik, *Lösungsvorschläge für die Welt-Energieprobleme, Bericht einer Expertengruppe aus Ländern der Europäischen Gemeinschaft, Japan und Nordamerika* (Bonn: 1974), pp. 16, 18 (Arbeitspapiere zur Internationalen Politik); United States Atomic Energy Commission, Report to the President, *The Nations' Energy Future* (Washington, 1973); *Petroleum Economist* May 1974, p. 166, July 1974, p. 254, June 1974, p. 215.

quantities supplied or demanded to price changes) and any orchestrated measures taken towards consumer self-sufficiency. We shall use a set of estimates (see Table 4) based on these two factors and the following assumptions:

1. The price of oil (in constant US $) will be around $7 per barrel for Persian Gulf crude (which is below the present price level).
2. Energy demand will be 10 per cent below pre-October 1973 estimates in areas apart from Western Europe (where it will be 5 per cent lower) and the Third World (where it will be 15 per cent lower). A comparison with preliminary government recalculations of their targets show that these assumptions are reasonable, and in some cases even conservative.
3. In all consumer countries reductions in energy demand can be translated into oil savings.
4. In the United States and Western Europe there will be some substitution of oil by other sources of energy.

On the demand side, these estimates show a total oil import requirement for the three major consumer areas of 26 million b/d in 1980 and 30 million in 1985; world import demand is put at 30 million and 35 million b/d respectively. Let us now contrast these demand estimates with the production potential of the OPEC countries,

particularly the high absorbers. So far these countries have shown a desire to maximize their production in order to fuel their ambitious development programmes and overcome their state of underdevelopment. Present production and future production potential of these producers are listed in Table 5.

Comparison of Tables 4 and 5 shows that the gap to be filled by producers other than those considered as production maximizers is 3·5 million b/d in 1980 and 2 million in 1985. Theoretically, the gap would have to be closed by some or all of the following (all low-absorbers): Libya, Kuwait, Saudi Arabia, the United Arab Emirates and Qatar. These countries would then play the role of marginal suppliers. Of course, such a development is highly unlikely, since it rests on assumptions which cannot all be taken for granted: a very effective energy policy on the part of the consumer nations, and a *laissez faire* policy on the part of the producers (which would be in strong contradiction to their present cartel policies). The producers have a vested interest in high prices and a tight supply/demand situation, and are likely to resort to some measures of market control. Furthermore, the assumption that the high absorbers will continue to keep actual output near to the ceiling of production potential neglects the possibility of price maximization, rather than production maximization. It also ignores the possibility that – given successful industrialization – increased non-oil exports and the replacement of imports by home-produced goods might reduce reliance on oil for export earnings. Iran, Algeria, Venezuela and, possibly, Iraq might well be capable of achieving such an industrial base in the foreseeable future. On the other hand, the low absorbers might find it in their interest to keep production at a fairly high level so long as the present price prevails.

On the consumer side, the developments in the first year after the supply crisis are hardly encouraging. The fall in oil consumption appeared to be almost entirely due to the world-wide recession, and, because of the threat to employment, no energetic and lasting conservation efforts were undertaken. Disillusionment with certain alternative sources of energy (such as nuclear energy and shale oil), for environmental reasons and because of their uncertain profitability prospects, also raised doubts about whether dependence on Middle East oil could

Table 5: High absorbers: present and potential output (million b/d)

	1973	1980	1985
Venezuela	3·5	3	3
Indonesia	1·3	2·5	3
Algeria	1·1	1·5	2
Nigeria	2·1	3	4
Iraq	2·0	3	5
Iran	5·9	9	9
Others	1·5	3	4
Price effect*	—	1·5	3
Total	17·4	26·5	33

* Price effect: allowance for the impact of supply/price elasticity on production. This reflects the fact that higher prices allow more effective (though more costly) extraction techniques.
SOURCES: Deutsche Gesellschaft für Auswärtige Politik, *op. cit.*, p. 19; *BP Statistical Review of the World Oil Industry, 1973, op. cit.*, p. 6.

be significantly reduced within the next ten years. Certainly it will be some years before efforts by international oil companies and consumer governments to develop alternative sources of supply, so as to change the economic framework of producer power, show their impact.

The Problem of Precision: The International Distribution System

The supply crisis of 1973–74 not only revealed the strength of the oil weapon but also exposed some of its weaknesses. Arguably the most important of these is its lack of precision. The producers' handling of the oil weapon, and the rules and regulations that accompanied its use confirm that they aimed at discrimination between the various consumer countries. However, the flexibility of the international oil market (which in terms of distribution, transport and processing is still by and large controlled by the international oil companies[16]) prevailed over attempts to direct the oil weapon only against certain consumers. The very core of the discriminatory strategy, the embargo, therefore failed – a fact which even the producers themselves admitted – so that the only effective sanction the Arab producers possessed was the general cut-back in production.

The flexibility of the international distribution system has two main aspects: the tanker (and pipeline) system and the refineries. The question of whether the flexibility of the international oil market can be upheld in these two areas is of paramount importance for the future of the oil weapon in international relations. If the producers succeeded in destroying this flexibility, they would be able to discriminate against a single consumer, and therefore apply considerably stronger pressure. The oil weapon would thus gain immensely in applicability and could be used for a much wider set of objectives.

The Threat of Precision: Bilateral Arrangements and Power-increasing Strategies

In the aftermath of the October 1973 to March 1974 supply crisis there was a rush by consumer governments to conclude bilateral deals with producers so as to secure oil supplies. For some time this posed the real threat of a fundamental

---

[16] The 'majors' control more than 60 per cent of the world tanker fleet, by ownership or long-term charter, and a similar proportion of world refinery capacity.

change in the international oil market towards strong dependence by single consumers on particular producers. This possibility now appears remote, not least because of a certain reluctance on the part of producers such as Saudi Arabia to enter into agreements of this kind. To be sure there were quite a number of bilateral deals, but they concentrated on assistance by industrialized countries with the problems of economic development of the producer countries, which opened up possibilities for the consumers to offset part of their balance-of-payments deficits by increased exports. There is no evidence of the widespread inclusion of supply guarantees in such deals, even though the hope of achieving security of supplies was clearly among the consumers' motives for concluding them.

Even the present form of bilateral deal, however, appears not to be without political problems. It has been argued repeatedly and convincingly that a strictly nationalistic economic approach to solving the present problems of the consumer countries that centres around bilateral deals would lead to a scramble for markets and competition for the oil producers' revenue surplus. The result would undoubtedly be increased conflict between the consumer countries, and possibly also higher oil prices; the strongest economic powers would prevail, while the weakest would find their problems aggravated. The developing countries without indigenous energy resources would be hardest hit. They would not be able to increase their exports so as to pay their oil bills, and could not hope to attract large capital inflows from the oil producers. Above all they might find their other imports costing more as a consequence of world-wide inflation, due not least to rocketing oil prices.

These drawbacks and limitations would appear to provide strong incentives for finding international solutions to problems such as the orderly transfer of wealth to the producers, the recycling of oil revenue surpluses to consumer countries in need and co-operation in the development of sufficient sources of energy.

While a largely bilateral supply structure is unlikely in the near future, the adoption by some or all the producers of a deliberate power-increasing strategy for purely political reasons could pose a serious threat. Such a strategy could be followed in three ways: the producers could try to increase the dependence of consumer

14

countries on energy under their control; they could attempt to destroy the flexibility of the distribution system by building up a large share in it; or they could simply strengthen their hold on the international oil companies (e.g., by building up large shareholdings).

At the time of writing, there are hardly any signs of such developments, but if they did come about they would clearly lead to a dangerous level of permanent confrontation between producer and consumer countries and/or detrimental economic implications for the producers themselves. For instance, to achieve higher dependence on oil the price would have to be lowered considerably, and even then memories of the last supply crisis would prevent consumers from again relying heavily on imported oil. The producers could also expand their control over energy sources by investing in coal, nuclear energy and conventional and unconventional oil sources outside their area, thereby gaining a substantial foothold in the world energy industries. This might be desirable for economic reasons, but it would hardly contribute to the producers' political power (which stems from the ability to interrupt supplies), since these investments would be outside their effective control and, because the threat of nationalization works both ways, might even serve as hostages in a future supply crisis. Economically, both producers and consumers could gain from such investments, but a necessary precondition would be to develop safeguards against their political use in any form (though most investments made initially for economic reasons would probably take a different form from those made for purely political, power-increasing purposes).

The same holds true for downstream investment by the producers. Expansion of their activities into the tanker and refinery business, and ultimately also into the consumer distribution networks, can be expected for sound economic reasons – indeed for the same reasons which turned the international oil companies into integrated enterprises. However, investments aiming at increased political power, so as to enable the oil weapon to be used in a discriminatory manner, would again take a different form. In essence, the problem appears to be one of thresholds: controlling 5 per cent of the world tanker fleet might not be politically dangerous, but controlling 20 per cent would be.

The oil producers certainly have the potential to acquire a politically dangerous share in the world tanker fleet. Several producers already possess tankers[17] and have ordered a considerable number of new carriers.[18] After the delivery of present orders (which will take until 1979) Kuwait and Iraq, with approximately 2 million and 1·5 million deadweight tons (dwt) respectively, will own the largest fleets among the Arab countries, while Iran has stated her intention to build up a fleet totalling 1 million dwt.[19] With the foundation of the Arab Maritime Petroleum Transport Company (a sub-organization of OAPEC) and its plan to spend $2,000 million over the next five years on tankers, product carriers and liquefied natural gas (LNG) carriers, and with the further expansion by other producers which can be expected, the combined Arab fleet might amount to some 20 million dwt in the early 1980s. For the journey from the Persian Gulf via the Cape route, the amount of oil which by then could be transported annually in producer-owned tankers would be about 100 million tons. However, compared with a world tanker fleet of 246 million dwt (including combined carriers) in 1974 and 221 million dwt on order,[20] these figures for new-built Arab tanker capacity are probably not important enough to pose a real threat to the flexibility of the international distribution system.

The tanker market is a purely competitive business, and although limited shipbuilding capacity may prevent the oil producers from gaining sufficient control by ordering new tankers, the present large tanker surplus could enable them to buy a large second-hand fleet. In a time of tanker surplus private owners might not be assured of full employment of their tankers, and could in any case only expect a low return, but producer governments could probably force employment of their fleets to transport their oil.[21] Costs would be no serious obstacle: if tanker capacity costs $150 per dwt, a fleet of, say, 50

---

[17] Total tonnage in mid-1974 was about 1·5 million dwt in crude, product, and liquefied natural gas (LNG) carriers (*Petroleum Economist*, August 1974, p. 305).
[18] Arab orders amount to 4,783,370 dwt. These orders include 714 million m³ of LNG carriers for Kuwait and Algeria (*ibid.* p. 307).
[19] *Middle East Economic Digest*, 22 March 1974, p. 335.
[20] *Petroleum Economist*, May 1974, p. 181.
[21] Saudi Arabia has already indicated her intention to export 50 per cent of her oil in her own fleet by 1978.

million tons (about one-fifth of the present world tanker fleet) would cost $7·5 billion – a sum definitely within the reach of the oil producers.[22] Another possibility is that they could charter a substantial tanker capacity. This could hardly be done at very short notice, since the capacity available within days is minute, but every year about 14 per cent of the world tanker fleet enters the charter market.[23] In either case, however, the consumer governments would receive clear warning signals well in advance.

Another way for the oil producers to increase their power would be to attempt to gain control over the international oil companies. They could try to acquire large share holdings or, in any future application of the oil weapon, simply to attempt to force the companies to stop *all* deliveries to an embargoed country – not only deliveries of the producers' own oil. The first possibility poses the same kind of problems for the producers as all investments outside their direct territorial control; the second depends on the leverage they possess *vis-à-vis* the companies. This leverage rests on the investments and assets of the companies in the producer countries and their privileges in these countries (they pay lower oil prices than customers without production facilities there). Leverage on both counts has been gradually weakened through participation or nationalization, and, since the producers started to assert themselves and free themselves from the hegemony the companies had long exerted over these countries and their oil industry, the relationship between producers and companies has been moving towards co-existence based on mutual interests: the companies fulfil certain important functions for the producers, which for the time being, they cannot do without.

However, there must be doubts whether in any future supply crisis the oil companies will be as well placed to manage the international distribution system efficiently and share out available supplies as they were in 1973. Apart from the possibility of stronger producer interference, there also is the question of consumer government involvement: the companies have been

heavily criticized for their management in the last crisis.

The emergency programme of the International Energy Agency[24] might help the companies to destroy the flexibility of the oil weapon once more by allocating available oil supplies fairly, since it provides them with the necessary governmental approval. Moreover, it would (if effective) provide another barrier to discriminatory application of the oil weapon, since the scheme obliges every member to maintain an emergency oil reserve of 60 (later 90) days' consumption and to have contingency plans for reducing oil consumption. If one or more member countries suffer a reduction in supplies of 7 per cent or more, or can be expected to experience such a shortfall, the affected countries will have to activate measures to save 7 per cent of oil consumption. If the shortfall exceeds 12 per cent of demand a 10 per cent saving will be required, the rest being made up by other members. If this cannot be done the available oil will be shared between member countries.

The scheme therefore provides an institutionalized device to prevent discriminatory application of the oil weapon against a single member of the IEA. Whether it stands the test of application or could be circumvented or invalidated by the producers remains to be seen. It is certainly true that the scheme depends on the oil companies' control over the international distribution system, since the companies will be in charge of the management of the allocation. Sufficient producer control over the international tanker fleet would therefore most likely invalidate the scheme, or at least require additional measures.

The Ceiling of the Oil Weapon: World Economic Crisis and Fundamental Political Change

If we assume that the future international oil market will retain its present flexibility and that discrimination will be impossible, then the damage caused by supply interruptions will be distributed more or less evenly, and it will be the most vulnerable consumers which suffer most. In the last supply crisis, these were Japan and

---

[22] M. A. Adelmann, *The World Petroleum Market* (Baltimore and London: Johns Hopkins U.P. 1972), p. 126, quotes prices between $100 and $138 per dwt for VLCC (very large crude carriers) from Japanese shipyards in early 1971.
[23] *Ibid.*, pp. 104–60.

[24] At the time of writing member countries are Belgium, Canada, Denmark, Germany, Ireland, Italy, Japan, Luxembourg, the Netherlands, New Zealand, Spain, Sweden, Switzerland, Turkey and Britain. Norway has a special associated status with the IEA.

16

those developing countries with either little or no indigenous energy resources and/or heavy dependence on imported oil; next in vulnerability came some of the European consumers. The producers, therefore, faced a choice of either taking into consideration the impact of the oil weapon on the weaker consumers, or else pressing ahead in order to exert pressure on the main target, in that case the United States. If in future the producers take into account the situation of the weaker consumers, then this sets a fairly low ceiling for overall cutbacks, and it looks as if the oil weapon's lack of discriminatory capability actually gives any target a whole group of hostages – consumer countries weaker than itself. In applying the oil weapon, therefore, the producers not only risk political alienation of non-target countries but also turmoil and unpredictable developments in and around those countries. Once a major industrialized country was caught in a serious economic crisis triggered by shortage of oil supplies, a chain reaction throughout the world economy would probably be inevitable, the consequences of which would be unpredictable and uncontrollable and might backfire on the producers themselves. Economic crises in the consumer countries would lead to social tensions and political unrest, and dramatic changes could not be ruled out. New radical governments, in the face of tremendous domestic pressure, might decide to try solving the supply crisis by military force – desperate and irrational as such a move might be.

But the producers operate not only within the context of a rather sensitive world economy but also in an international political system, and they have to consider the impact of the oil weapon on this – and especially on the super-power balance. The conservative Arab oil producers cannot be interested in weakening the Western alliance, and more precisely the position of the United States, either on a global or a regional level. In the last crisis the United States was clearly given carrot and stick treatment; not only was she subjected to an embargo, she was also invited to play a more prominent role in the Middle East. In future, if a producer thinks an alignment with the United States desirable, he will probably not press too hard and will rely on rewards as well as sanctions, since in the long run an alignment has to be based on mutuality of interest and predictable behaviour by both

sides. If the United States were antagonized she would try to reduce her dependence on the producers as quickly as possible and would look for other allies to pursue her interests; these allies might be found within the producer society (perhaps an opposition group which could be helped to power) or in the area. So long as rational behaviour prevails among producer governments, therefore, consideration for the regional and global political context, as well as for the functioning of the world economic system, sets a limit to the pressure which could be exerted through the oil weapon.

However, even within the limits of this pressure, the built-in time lag of the oil weapon appears to constitute another problem for the producers. There is a lag in the transport system which means that tankers loaded before the decision to interrupt supplies was taken will still be arriving in the consumer countries for some weeks afterwards – the exact time depending on the distance to the destination. This lag might be increased by the consumer countries' use of stocks and stand-by capacity, possibly within the framework of the IEA. All this means that the oil weapon is a somewhat awkward instrument of political coercion, with a tendency to draw out a crisis situation. On the one hand, this gives decision-makers time, reducing the psychological pressures of an acute crisis and consequently also some of the dangers of irrational behaviour. On the other hand, the time-lag inherent in supply interruptions might devalue the oil weapon in certain kinds of crises and could be used by consumers to decide on countermeasures or to try to respond in other areas: e.g., by threatening the producer's allies or shifting support to his regional rivals.

It appears, then, that the political and economic effects of using the oil weapon cannot be separated – indeed its power is derived from the economic damage it can inflict. But the economic consequences of a serious supply interruption stretch over years and are hardly controllable by the producers. Oil supply shortages cause fertilizer shortages, which in turn affect the grain harvests months after the oil weapon has been sheathed. Higher oil prices speed up inflation and trigger off a wage–price spiral. Insofar as the oil weapon aims at the basic functions of a society, the decision to apply it resembles the decision to go to war: once it is made, the exact course of events and the consequences might get out of control. This does not exclude the possibility of a further application of the oil weapon, but it is not going to be an instrument frequently used for exerting political pressure. The implication also might be that the producers will look for new ways and means to use their oil power.

The Impact of Applying the Oil Weapon

What has been the impact of the first successful application of the oil weapon? Will it enhance or reduce its power? There is some contradiction in the answers to these questions. Certainly, the future application of the oil weapon has now become more credible, since the Arab producers have actually shown the will to use it. On the other hand, it is to be hoped that the consumers will have learned from the 1973–74 crisis: the political risks of relying heavily on energy imported from producers who have little economic incentive to continue the prevailing level of production, and who could easily afford to reduce it, or even halt it for some time, has now become obvious. This awareness should trigger off a whole series of processes aimed at reducing this insecurity. In the longer run, these will probably result in a situation similar to that outlined in Table 4, with the consumer countries' dependence on imported oil significantly diminished. However, even in the shorter run the consumer countries could reduce the impact of the oil weapon. The 1973–74 crisis demonstrated that the shortfall of oil which can be absorbed without serious consequences is higher than expected, and that, as long as industrial production and vital transport functions can be upheld, the immediate effect of the oil weapon is limited. By preparing emergency allocation plans, increasing the flexibility of the internal distribution and refining systems and by co-ordinating consumer policies the impact of any future oil shortage could be reduced. This might partly be offset, however, by greater economy in the use of oil during the period between now and any future use of the oil weapon, due to attempts to reduce the impact of higher oil prices. Reductions in non-essential oil use and deliberate measures and contingency plans to improve the capacity to absorb shortages might thus have a roughly balancing effect. But, even so, the psychological climate has changed: consumer governments should now be less inclined to panic and resort to *sauve qui peut*

policies. While in 1973 no government seemed to know exactly what the oil embargoes and cutbacks really meant for them, the oil weapon and its impact should now be a known quantity.

The net effect, it seems, is that the producers' freedom of manoeuvre will become more restricted. In order to bring substantial pressure to bear on consumers, they may have to resort to much higher initial pressure, bringing them dangerously near to the limits at which the oil weapon becomes counter-productive.

Producer Solidarity

The solidarity of Arab oil producers proved their greatest strength in 1973–74, but at the same time the crisis revealed the fragility of this solidarity; differences of interest, mistrust and concern about the future balance within the Arab world soon created cracks. Producer solidarity will continue to be an important factor in the success of any future application of the oil weapon – and indeed might be the decisive factor.

One of the differences of interest that would have to be overcome is economic. Some of the oil producers urgently need every penny of their oil revenue to meet their expenditures and might suffer heavily from a substantial loss of revenues over a long period (though in 1973–74 the producers more than made up for the reduction in output by the increase in prices). This possibility did concern OAPEC states, as witness the introduction into the important resolutions of 17 October and 28 November of damage-limiting clauses which set a floor to production cutbacks. Indeed one country – Iraq – refrained from *any* general cutbacks, most likely for fear of just such losses of vital revenue. As a consequence of the prolonged struggle with the Iraq Petroleum Company, Iraq had never experienced the same degree of production expansion as the Gulf states. The leadership – already set on a course of rapid economic growth and fundamental social and economic change – therefore decided to adopt a different policy against the United States and the Netherlands: nationalizing their oil interests and declaring embargoes against them, but without reducing Iraq's overall production. Algeria and some of the small Gulf sheikhdoms also needed all the oil revenues they could get, and the Algerian Head of State, Houari Boumedienne, actually stressed in an

18

interview with a Lebanese newspaper that his country suffered from the general production restrictions since it did not possess large foreign exchange reserves.[25] Algeria's position also reveals another difference of economic interest: as Boumedienne pointed out in his interview, the Algerian economy is closely linked with the European area and is bound to suffer from adverse developments there.

The first difference could be overcome by designing a production cut-back scheme according to each producer's degree of vulnerability to losses of revenue, rather than according to a general margin of production cutbacks for all producers (countries like Saudi Arabia, Kuwait, Abu Dhabi and Libya would then bear the main burden of reductions). For the second difference, which depends on the amount of integration into and sensitivity to, the industrialized economies, there is no simple solution.

Producer solidarity would always have to face the problem of a common political objective. Even Arab hostility to Israel in the last crisis did not produce a really unified position, for a rift within the Arab world and within the producer action group soon became evident. Egypt pressed for a political solution based on compromises and co-operation with the United States, while Libya and Iraq refused any kind of negotiated settlement in advance and protested against the conclusion of a cease-fire. Syria's leadership had decided to fight the war along Egyptian lines but faced constant pressure from more radical groups inside the power elite, especially the army,

and the tactical moves necessary for President Assad to retain his position resulted in a Syrian course wavering between negotiation and obstruction. This rift between conservatives and progressives and between moderate and radical attitudes towards the Israeli–Arab conflict was bound to reappear over the question of how and when the oil restrictions were to be eased, if at all.

Political moves also indicated the growing dissension in the Arab oil producer group. Libya tried to bridge the rift between herself and Egypt and press for closer co-operation between the two countries, and it seems likely that this was meant as a move to counterbalance Saudi Arabian influence. The decision to lift the embargo against the United States was repeatedly postponed – allegedly because of opposing views about its desirability among the Arab producers. When the lifting was finally declared on 17 March, Libya and Syria did not join the Saudi-Egyptian leadership. Arab disunity was probably fostered by the Soviet Union, whose past success in the Middle East was largely due to the conservative–progressive confrontation and the conflict with Israel, and in a direct attack on Egypt, Moscow warned of any premature relaxation in the economic pressure on the United States. Similarly, the decision to lift the embargo against the Netherlands led to a split in OAPEC, with Saudi Arabia (reportedly influenced by the United States) delaying the lifting, and Algeria strongly advocating – and then unilaterally declaring – an end to the embargo.

III. OIL POWER: THE WIDER CONTEXT

If it is possible to draw any conclusions about oil power (and with the host of factors influencing the future development of oil power, they must be very tentative indeed), then they could be summed up as follows: oil power as the result of an imbalanced trade relationship will continue, but it may well have reached its peak and could lessen in the medium term. The only real qualitative increase which might come about in the future would be the possibility of being able to use the oil weapon selectively. This possibility

[25] Clyde H. Farnsworth, 'Mideast rivalries push oil prices', *International Herald Tribune*, 2 January 1974.

cannot be ruled out but, even if it is realized, oil power is not unlimited except in the sense that it could trigger a vicious circle of growing and uncontrollable damage.

As long as rational behaviour prevails, there appear to be various restraints and ceilings on the amount of pressure which could be exerted. But, assuming that the producers do not want to cause uncontrollable and rapidly spreading damage to the world economy, they do nevertheless have some freedom of action and the ability to impose sanctions. They can exert disintegrative economic pressure on alliances and create conflict and tensions within and among industrialized nations. They could exacerbate the differences between developed and less-developed countries or mitigate them. They might be able to draw other states into regional conflicts, and even influence the global balance of power – although admittedly only indirectly and in a way which could hardly be called 'controlled'. It is unlikely that the producers could exert a direct influence on the strategic and security balance (even though the world-wide naval operations of the West, and probably also the Soviet Union, are to a limited extent dependent on Middle East oil for bunkering and are therefore somewhat vulnerable), since the backbone of the strategic balance, the nuclear deterrent, would not be affected; even serious restriction of the operational capacity of conventional forces seems unlikely, since stockpiling and a flexible supply system could probably cushion the impact of regional shortages. On balance, however, the oil weapon would seem to be a weapon of last resort. Its problems of control and precision, the inherent time-lag and the difficulty of organizing an action group sufficiently coherent to guarantee success make it unlikely to be frequently used for comparatively minor objectives. Producers might therefore try to substitute other forms of rewards and sanctions derived from their oil power which would give them political influence and leverage. Before we turn to this problem, however, we have to consider briefly who will actually have the power to use the oil weapon.

Who Could Apply the Oil Weapon?

A precondition for using the oil weapon successfully would be the ability to cause real and serious damage to the consumer countries. This is the very essence of oil power, since leverage sufficient to cause only inconvenience would not be very effective. The 'more' in damage potential, even though it might never be used, is at the heart of real power.

There are four theoretical cases to consider: the application of the oil weapon by one producer against one consumer; by one producer against all consumers; by a group of producers against one consumer; and, finally, the application of the oil weapon by a group of producers against all consumers.

We already are in a situation of substantial production capacity surplus,[26] so the first possibility can largely be discounted, on the grounds that there would be sufficient stand-by capacity in other producing areas to make up the shortfall in deliveries from one producer to one consumer. The only single consumer with a demand so large as to pose a potential problem is Japan, and as long as she keeps her sources of supply sufficiently diversified, there is no real threat. Only if sources of supply were insufficiently diversified and all other producers were unable or unwilling to make up one producer's shortfall would there be a real political problem. Assuming that in 1985 Japan depended on a single producer for one-third of an import demand of 9 million b/d, the producer would have to cut production by 3 million b/d in order to exploit that dependence for political purposes. Such a cut would be feasible for countries such as Saudi Arabia or Iran but, in the absence of special arrangements among producers, it should be possible for Japan to make up the losses from other sources.

If the oil weapon could be directed against an individual target country separately, then the further possibility arises of its unilateral use by one producer against any country which is heavily dependent both on few sources of supply and on tankers owned by the producer in question. In the case of an embargo, surplus capacity from other areas might not reach such consumers because of lack of alternative tanker capacity. Apart from availability of surplus production and spare tanker capacity, a further key variable in such a situation would be the behaviour of other producers.

Looking now at the possibilities of a non-discriminatory use of the oil weapon by a single producer (the more likely case), we first have to make a tentative assessment of the damage threshold. If we assume a world net import demand of 30 million b/d in 1980 and 35 million b/d in 1985 (in line with the estimates put forward on p. 11) and postulate a 20 per cent shortfall as the damage threshold for the most dependent consumer countries, then this produces figures of 6 million b/d in 1980 and 7 million b/d in 1985.

[26] According to the report of a group of experts submitted to the Energy Co-ordinating Committee set up by the Washington Energy Conference, OPEC had unused capacity of 4·5 million b/d in April 1974. By the end of 1974 this surplus had reached over 6·2 million b/d.

Looking at the production potential of the producer countries (Table 5), we can conclude that Iran is one of the countries which could afford unilateral production cut-backs of this order, while Iraq, whose reserves are said to be potentially very large, might also be very nearly in a position to do so. But it is Saudi Arabia, a low absorber with a production potential of up to 20 million b/d, which is least vulnerable to losses of income even over a prolonged period. Saudi Arabia, then, if one considers her capabilities alone (without allowing for intentions) is by far the most likely to apply the oil weapon unilaterally.

The most dangerous case would be action by a group of producers against one consumer. This assumes that the flexibility of the international distribution system would be destroyed. Again, however, such action could only be successful if there were no stand-by capacity outside the action group and no consumer solidarity. Obviously, not all countries will be vulnerable even to a total embargo (this would be true, for example, of the United States if she faced an Arab action group), and it is difficult to see a target other than the United States, which could arouse a sufficient degree of hostility in several producer countries. However, if there were such a country, the political leverage producers could apply to it would be enormous.

The fourth possibility is co-ordinated producer action against all consumers. Given the political and economic differences in OPEC it is hard to imagine a general application of the oil weapon by that organization for political reasons. The greatest potential for producer solidarity no doubt exists, and will continue to exist, in the Middle East and North Africa, among Arab producers organized in OAPEC. Co-ordinated Arab action will continue to constitute the most real threat to consumer states. But solidarity is difficult to obtain and could be mobilized only in a limited number of cases – and solidarity inevitably makes the application of the oil weapon more complicated, since the producers' various policies have to be accommodated and combined into a single policy.

So long as a strong faction among the producers favours a course of moderation, therefore, a common application of the oil weapon will most likely be based on the mildest of the possible options. The various ceilings on the use of the oil weapon will doubtless also come into play, particularly as group action raises the level of potential damage. That potential would, however, be greatly enhanced by Saudi participation. Indeed, given Saudi Arabia's strong influence in Kuwait and the Persian Gulf sheikhdoms, any attempt to create an Arab oil action group without her would face considerable difficulties. Even if she did not attempt to make up the losses caused by the Arab producer group, her abstention would mean a considerable reduction in the damage the group could inflict, since the only other country with a strong bargaining position and low vulnerability would probably be Libya. Actual Saudi opposition would probably cause such a use of the oil weapon to fail – though, since this would imply an open clash between 'progressive' and 'conservative' Arab countries, oil supplies might be interrupted by sabotage and guerilla activity in the Persian Gulf.

Price as a Weapon
In the definition of the term 'oil weapon' already given, it has been said that the weapon consists of the manipulation of oil supplies and/or price for political purposes, and it has been noted that both will most likely go together in any future interference with supplies. But could the price of oil alone also be used as a political tool?

Manipulating price does, of course, in principle offer the possibilities of both conferring rewards and inflicting sanctions. Some consumers might be sold oil on preferential terms (indeed this already has happened in the case of developing countries), and preferential prices and the threat of their withdrawal could constitute considerable leverage *vis-à-vis* weak consumer countries, and might be used to achieve political and economic influence. Apart from these limited possibilities, however, the price of oil can probably not be used as a negative sanction.

The producers having gradually become fully aware of their market bargaining power and raised prices accordingly, the price of oil is presumably now not too far off the ceiling imposed by the cost of developing other sources of oil and energy and by the vulnerability of the consumer states. For the future, it can be expected that OPEC will keep the price of crude near this ceiling for purely economic reasons. Price is the only interest common to all OPEC members, and those countries which are still concerned about

Table 6: Estimated production and revenues of OPEC countries (1974)

Country	Est. production (million b/d)[a]	Average export earnings per barrel ($)[b]	Est. oil revenues ($ million)
Saudi Arabia	8·643	9·25	29,181
Iran	6·128	9·30	20,801
Kuwait	2·843	8·93	9,267
Iraq	1·829	10·47	6,990
Abu Dhabi	1·750	9·82	6,272
Qatar	0·546	10·00	1,993
Oman	0·297	9·60	1,041
Dubai	0·232	9·17	766
Bahrain	0·068	9·08	225
SUBTOTAL	22·336		76,536
Libya	1·700	12·27	7,613
Algeria	0·889	12·26	3,978
Venezuela	3·025	9·50	10,489
Nigeria	2·300	10·71	8,991
Indonesia	1·457	9·10	4,839
Ecuador	0·232	8·77	743
TOTAL	31·939		113,189

Oil revenue estimates are based on the assumption that total production is exported. Due to indigenous consumption, and to fluctuation in prices, these figures give only an approximate impression of OPEC oil revenues.

[a] SOURCE: *Oil and Gas Journal*, 30 December 1974.
[b] SOURCE: *Middle East Economic Survey*, 31 May 1974.

securing maximum income will resist, and already have resisted, any attempts to bring prices down. There will therefore be little room for using higher prices as a lever for political purposes – quite apart from the fact that oil prices by themselves are probably very difficult to handle as a purely political weapon, since market factors and economic interests still play an important role in their formation. Prices will therefore probably only be important in connection with another attempt to use production cutbacks for political leverage; they might well shoot up again in such a situation of shortage, though this might be detrimental to the longer-term economic interests of the producers.

Oil Revenues: The Monetary Dimension of Oil Power

The quadrupling of oil prices during 1973, combined with the continuing demand for oil, has brought forward a new form of oil power: enormous revenue surpluses. Estimates of the actual amount of future surplus in the longer-term vary but give an impression of the dimen-

sions of the oil producers' financial power.[27] Table 6 gives some estimates of OPEC oil income in 1974.

The amount of revenue surplus in the more distant future depends on a variety of economic and political factors, such as the pace of economic development in the producer countries, the development of Arab politics[28] and the development of consumption and the terms of trade with the industrialized countries. But there will be vast surpluses for some time, and this money can and will be used politically.

One use would be to shift foreign exchange

[27] An early 1975 World Bank estimate puts the accumulated OPEC surplus in 1980 at $460 billion at current prices ($248 billion at constant prices), of which Saudi Arabia, Kuwait, Qatar and the United Arab Emirates alone account for $335 billion. American government sources and estimates by the Chase Manhattan Bank project a lower figure for 1980.
[28] Including the possibility of federations or alliances between producer and non-producer countries. Egypt alone will attract large sums simply because her political friendship is a key to influence in the Arab world as a whole.

holdings from one currency into another.[29] However, unless the oil producers transfer their surplus into the Soviet Union or store it under their beds, they cannot avoid circulating it in the international monetary system. Within this system, provisions to avoid drastic fluctuations of exchange rates already exist in the form of swap arrangements among central banks, and, if necessary, these could be improved or new ones designed. If such measures failed there would still be the possibility of international agreements to control and restrict large currency movements and, as a last resort, the freezing of oil producers' assets. (Ironically, while the industrialized countries worry about the disruptive potential of Arab revenue surpluses, the Arab countries worry about their assets being frozen.[30]) The use of foreign exchange holdings as a weapon therefore does not appear very likely, since the consumer countries would have better methods of protecting themselves against this than against oil supply interruptions.

Other applications of the producers' financial power for political ends are much more likely. Most of the Arab producers are politically and militarily vulnerable, and so will be under strong pressure to buy their security by appeasing the Arab have-nots. If they are not seen to share at least some of their wealth with these have-nots, and to throw some of their weight behind them, the result could be a new confrontation in the Arab world. For this reason development assistance, grants, payment for arms and similar projects in the Arab world will swallow a large slice of the oil revenue surplus.

Similarly, money could be used to cement political alignments, so as to give the oil-producers greater influence in inter-Arab rela-tions, and to weaken countries hostile to the producers by financing opposition groups and subversive movements or by bribing politicians and army officers. Rivalries and divisions among the producers themselves (such as those between Saudi Arabia and Libya) might even result in competition among producers for influence in other countries, with the accompanying beneficial effects for the target.

In a wider geographical context, oil money could be used as a reward for political ends, as well. Clearly, the attractiveness of large-scale Arab investment provides strong leverage on both developed and developing countries, but particularly on the latter, and the same goes for grants and cheap loans. Libya and Saudi Arabia have already used their wealth in this way: both of them offering credits and grants for African countries willing to break diplomatic relations with Israel, and Saudi Arabia attempt-ing to offset Libyan influence in black Africa. Libya also is said to finance opposition groups and guerilla movements both inside and outside the Arab world.[31]

Spin-off of Oil Power

If the producers exploit their current position skilfully, they could become very influential indeed, because of the combination of their ability to manipulate the price and supply of oil with the ability to deploy their financial capacity for political ends. Saudi Arabia is well placed in both respects, while Iran, too, stands to gain diplomatically by virtue of both her oil produc-tion rate and the economic and military power which she can now develop rapidly.

Apart from the deliberate exploitation of oil power for specific purposes, however, the Arab producers and Iran will play a more important role in international relations in general – simply because they constitute a factor to be taken into account by foreign policy decision-makers throughout the world. This influence will be

[29] The Arab countries have repeatedly threatened to use their revenue surpluses as a weapon, and after 1967 there was a shift of Arab money from Sterling into other currencies, mainly Francs. Libya also resorted to this method to punish Britain for her alleged complicity in the Iranian occupation of a few small islands in the Persian Gulf in November 1971. The Iraqi version, an appeal to withdraw all Arab funds from the United States, met with little approval. See Gerd Junne, 'Währungsspekulationen der Ölscheiche und Ölkonzerne', in H. Elsenhans (ed.), Erdöl für Europa (Hamburg: Hoffmann & Campe, 1974) pp. 277–302.

[30] Kuwait, for example, keeps a large amount of her financial reserves as liquid as possible, to protect herself against such a measure (The Economist, 5 May 1973, p. 44).

[31] According to a report in The Times, (4 January 1974), Libya finances its own Palestinian underground movement and also contributes to Black September (£35 million), other Palestinian organizations (£20 million) and the Eritrean Liberation Front (£10 million), as well as opposition groups in Syria (£1·3 million), South Yemen (£1 million), Chad (£1·2 million), Morocco (£2 million), Tunisia (£1 million), Philippines (£2 million), Panama (£1·5 million), and Thailand (£300,000). See also Arab Report and Record, 5 January 1974, p. 7.

achieved without great effort simply because of the present and likely future state of the international oil market and the political implications which result from it. These implications, which give oil power a day-to-day pay-off aspect, are the following:

a. The oil-producing countries, or most of them, will command vast financial reserves and surpluses. In order to attract oil producers' investible funds, other countries will make considerable efforts and offer advantages. These will result, directly or indirectly, in even more oil power and political influence, because economic assistance and development will create new capabilities, and because political concessions can be expected to form part of any package offered to obtain a share in Arab wealth. It will be very difficult not to be on good terms with the oil-producing countries.

b. The predicted rise in oil demand has to be met by Arab oil production beyond a level which would result in full absorption of oil revenues by the producer country. Even if there were an arrangement which solved some of the problems of investing the revenue surpluses generated by extracting more oil, rather than leaving it in the ground, it still seems likely that the economic incentives to increase production will not be sufficient to ensure that the demand is met. This clearly brings in other forms of incentives – political incentives. These could be handed out both on a bilateral basis and internationally. The first would involve policies of appeasement: i.e., conceding the oil producers' demand and supporting their policies. The second would imply a general upgrading of the role of oil producers in international organizations and processes; this could apply above all to financial institutions, where the oil producers will be directly involved on a major scale, but it could also apply to political organizations, such as the United Nations.

c. Finally, and most importantly, the very possibility of application of the oil weapon can be politically exploited. Like military power, it does not actually have to be applied to provide political leverage. The rhetoric of the oil weapon, oil diplomacy (possibly including the use of symbolic stoppages and embargoes to show that the producers mean business) and accommodation of consumers' policies to producer objectives even before these have been formulated as demands – these will all be important aspects of future international politics, and almost certainly the most salient expression of oil power.

The daily pay-off of oil power, then, will constitute one of the ever-present factors in future international relations. So could the forms of power derived from oil power as such: economic and military power.

To the degree that the oil producers succeed in building and developing modern industrialized societies, some of them will become economic powers large enough to overshadow their regions. To be sure, the difficulties of leap-frogging modernization are enormous: shortage of skilled labour, technicians and administrators; lack of infrastructure; shortage of raw materials other than oil in many countries; divisions between rural and urban and between traditional and modern sectors and the consequent cultural lags in way of life and attitudes. Furthermore, there are also problems caused by the fact that the ability of underdeveloped countries to industrialize is constrained by the pre-existence of large-scale industries in the developed countries. The oil-producers do, however, have two advantages: capital and the power, exploiting consumer dependence on oil, to gain entrance into new markets for their industrial products and to secure themselves a privileged position in those markets. The real transformation of oil power into economic power, however, can probably only take place through the development of the internal markets. To achieve this, the producers must meet two preconditions: there must be a sufficiently large population, and the standard of living and spending power of all classes (not only the small upper and middle classes) must be increased. The latter in turn requires fundamental changes in the social (and ultimately also the political) structure, since the rural masses, which still largely live in poverty and caught in pre-industrial cultural patterns, must be enabled effectively to improve their lot. In the light of this, one could expect that Algeria, Iran, Venezuela and possibly Iraq might become economic powers of regional importance within the period under consideration. The other oil producers will probably still be struggling with the problems and difficulties of development, though some of them could use their financial power to acquire a share in industrial production abroad.

A second form of power derived from oil power is military strength, and the amount of military expenditure and of large-scale arms imports from industrialized countries has risen recently on an unprecedented scale, especially in the case of Arab producers and Iran.[32] The reasons for these huge deals are manifold – considerations of internal and external security, prestige and status, and interstate rivalries – but they have introduced, or are about to introduce, extremely sophisticated modern weapon systems (such as the F-14 or MiG-23 fighters, 'smart' bombs and missiles) to the Persian Gulf and the Israeli–Arab zone. Effectively, the gap in conventional military technology between the industrialized countries and this Third World area has been closed. Nonetheless, it seems doubtful whether this increase in hardware can be translated into an equivalent increase in military power. The vast amount of sophisticated weapons now pouring into these countries poses enormous problems of absorption in training, service and maintenance, and shortage of skilled personnel will mean both heavy dependence on foreign assistance and a considerable delay before fighting power increases to match the equipment inventory. The impact of these large purchases on the importers will also be considerable in economic and political terms. Manning the new systems will constitute a heavy drain on trained technicians and specialists in their societies, while the large military expenditures and the huge amounts of hardware will further strengthen the political influence of the army officers.

The main consideration appears to be whether the increased military power of the states involved leads to fundamental imbalances. Iran is striving for military superiority in the Persian Gulf and for an influential role beyond it, with the intention of stabilizing the *status quo*, and her growing power might indeed have such a stabilizing effect in the Indian subcontinent. In the Gulf itself, however, the Arab states (and especially Saudi Arabia and Iraq) seem unwilling to accept Iranian military hegemony and will try to increase their own military power to prevent it as far as possible. Given the now well-established link between the Persian Gulf and Israeli–Arab zone, this in turn could lead to a conventional imbalance in the latter area. Here, and possibly also in the Gulf, the result might be that some countries would look to nuclear weapons to re-establish the balance. Israel already at least possesses the capacity to build nuclear devices in a very short time, and other countries might follow. The spread of nuclear technology for peaceful purposes to Iran, Egypt, Libya and Saudi Arabia opens vast possibilities for nuclear proliferation.[33]

IV. INTENTIONS BEHIND THE OIL WEAPON

Having tentatively assessed the damage potential and the capabilities which the oil weapon provides and the limitations and preconditions for its successful application, we will now try to outline possible intentions and objectives, as well as situations which might lead one or more producers to use the oil weapon again.

It is assumed that intentions are shaped by two sets of factors: internal and external. Internal factors include the interests of the decision-makers and influences and pressures on them from within their society, including ideologies and perceptions. Ideologies are thought to correspond at least loosely with the interests

[32] For instance, Iran's recent purchase of 80 F-14 fighters from the United States, worth $1,800 million, far exceeds the total value of Iranian arms imports over the decade 1961–71. For further details on the arms trade, see Hanns Maull, 'The Arms Trade with the Middle East and North Africa', in *The Middle East and North Africa 1974/75* (London: Europa Publications, 1974), pp. 94–9.

[33] Egypt might be provided with nuclear reactors and fuel by the United States and France, and Egyptian scientists are also working in Indian nuclear centres. Iran has its own Atomic Energy Commission, with an Argentinian adviser. She will receive two nuclear reactors and the necessary fuel from the United States (according to a provisional agreement) and two nuclear power stations are to be provided by France, which will also provide nuclear fuel and set up a nuclear research centre. Negotiations and agreements about nuclear co-operation exist between Iran and India, Canada, South Africa and possibly the Soviet Union. Saudi Arabia and Libya have also voiced interest in nuclear power plants. See *Middle East Economic Digest*, 5 July 1974, p. 764, 31 May 1974, p. 625; *Arab Report and Record*, 1–15 June 1974, p. 220.

of the political and economic elites and counter-elites but might develop their own momentum and are therefore worth separate consideration. Foreign policy factors include any producer's regional and global relationships and the alliances and foreign policy objectives of the other countries. It is also assumed that the behaviour of the producer states will not be guided by outside powers (at least not where this would interfere with the interests of the producer country or, more precisely, its leadership). It seems unlikely that the West will regain its previous degree of control over the oil producers (even though closer economic interaction might lead the producers into considerable dependence on the West and therefore restrict their freedom of action), and the hypothesis of 'Soviet hands on the tap' is highly improbable for the same reasons which apply to the West (strength of Arab nationalism, awareness of power, declining value of military force as a means of control) and because the Soviet Union faces certain additional weaknesses (her limited economic potential, the fact that Soviet goods and technology are often non-competitive with the West's, and the fact that the Soviet bloc cannot provide an alternative market for Middle East oil).

Let us first consider the internal and external setting of three producers – Iran, Iraq, and Saudi Arabia. These are the three countries which, during the period under consideration (or at least the latter half of it), might be able to cut back production sufficiently to cause considerable damage to consumers. They are also to a certain extent representative of the producers in general, since they cover two Arab regimes, one progressive and one conservative, and one non-Arab producer. Furthermore, all three states border on the Persian Gulf and are linked by a variety of coinciding and conflicting interests.

Iran

Iran is definitely the most powerful of the three states. Her population now numbers about 32 million people, during the last decade she has rapidly developed an industrial sector which is not dependent on oil, and the country contains rich natural resources apart from oil. She is also one of Asia's biggest importers and, last but not least, is a formidable military power with a modern army, navy and air force.

Iran's rapid development into a state of regional-power status during the last decade was the result of a process of determined reform (the White Revolution) initiated from the top, without any participation by the population in the political and economic decision making. The Shah is still the main, overwhelmingly important political factor, and he controls the political process by a variety of means. Political opposition is virtually eliminated by co-opting potential counter-elites into the present system and by suppression. In a broader perspective, the Shah's power rests on two pillars: the combined support of the old upper class, which his land reform programme turned from a feudal, land-based group into an industrially-based group, and the growing middle class in the cities; and, secondly, the loyalty of the armed forces (and specifically the officer corps). These groups also profited most from the White Revolution.

Political stability and economic progress are still closely interconnected. To assure the survival of his regime, the Shah has to accommodate the demands of his main supporters and also to defuse the potential for social conflict by substantially raising the living standard of hitherto neglected groups and classes. The pledge of further rapid economic growth and development is therefore based not only on economic but also on political reasons. Both are reflected in the main objectives of the new 1973–78 development plan, which aims for rapid economic growth, equitable distribution of income and wealth, a better socio-economic balance between rural and urban areas, administrative reform and stronger national defence, as well as expanded industrial output and international trade.

This programme clearly shows Iran's capacity to absorb even higher oil revenues to a large extent. Moreover, her comparatively limited oil reserves allow her to go for higher crude oil prices, since she does not have to be concerned about the eventual substitution of Middle East oil by other sources. By the time this substitution is reasonably advanced Iran can hope to have an economic base which will allow her to halt any crude exports and concentrate on goods produced with her own oil as a raw material and a source of cheap energy.

A large portion of future oil revenues will be absorbed by defence. The 1973–74 budget allocated slightly more than $2 billion for that purpose, and the defence budget is expected to run at 25 per cent or more of each national budget during the five-year period of the development plan.[34] Iranian defence expenditure helps to ensure the loyalty of the officer corps, which might be the only possible threat to the present political system, and strengthen the army, which has the potential to crush any internal opposition to the present order. But defence expenditure also serves various external functions – mainly, it seems, as an instrument of an ambitious foreign policy designed to increase Iran's influence in the region and to provide an integrative force, a common focus for nationalist sentiments of the whole Iranian people. The impressive arms build-up can therefore be expected to continue, and might also be reinforced by an indigenous arms industry.

Iran's foreign policy unfolds mainly in two spheres: global and regional. The global setting is dominated by Iran's long border with Russia, by past experience of Russian interference in Iran's internal affairs and by the Russian objective of securing access to warm-water ports in the Indian Ocean. The underlying pattern of Iran's relations with the super-powers is therefore clearly pro-Western – mistrust of Soviet intentions and reliance on the United States as the main ally – and a fundamental reversal of the pattern seems unlikely as long as the present regime remains in power. In the day-to-day aspects of diplomacy, however, Iran sets out formally to accord strictly equal treatment to both the United States and the Soviet Union; a state visit by the Shah to Washington is consequently balanced by one to Moscow. Iran has a wide range of trade and economic relations with the Soviet Union and has even bought some weapons there since 1967, when she concluded a small-arms deal worth some $110 million. She has recently also introduced China into this balancing act (Peking supports Iran's arms build-up and her claim that only littoral states should be responsible for the security in the Persian Gulf).

Iran justifies her concern about the Persian Gulf as a defensive precaution against possible encirclement by hostile, pro-Soviet states. Iraq has been her main source of anxiety, since the 1958 revolution there, because the progressive governments which followed the fall of the Hashemite monarchy have all proved more or less hostile to Iran. The main bone of contention has been the dispute over the Shatt el-Arab waterway. There have also been tensions between the two over alleged Iranian interference in the Kurdish problem in Iraq and over the expulsion of Iranians from Iraq; sporadic border incidents occurred, the last in 1974, and both sides tried to foster internal problems of the other country.

The Iraqi–Soviet treaty of friendship in 1972 and Soviet diplomatic progress in India and Afghanistan intensified Iranian fear of encirclement by Soviet allies, as did the danger to Persian Gulf stability posed by the South Yemen and by the Popular Front for the Liberation of Oman (PFLO), a group supported mainly by the South Yemen, and probably also Iraq, which has been conducting a guerilla war in the Omani province of Dhofar.

Against this potential threat to her vital trade links in the Persian Gulf, Iran tried to establish her predominance there, using a combination of military superiority and diplomatic moves. She imposed a military solution on the dispute over the Tumb Islands with the Sheikhdoms of Sharjah and Ras al Khaimah by simply occupying the islands, and she gave military assistance to the Sultan of Oman in his fight against the rebellion in Dhofar. On the other hand the patronage she is exerting over the sheikhdoms on the west coast of the Gulf builds on close ties between the two Gulf coasts and on educational and health assistance Iran has made available for the United Arab Emirates. Iran also dropped her claim to Bahrain as a gesture of goodwill when Britain withdrew her presence in the Gulf, and it seems that she has effectively taken over from Britain the role of guaranteeing the *status quo* in the Gulf. The existence of the conservative sheikhdoms prevents closer co-operation by the radical forces in the Persian Gulf, although a fundamental change in one of them (as opposed to a palace revolt) might well trigger a similar development in others, eventually turning the

---

[34] Keith McLachlan, 'Strength through Growth: Iran on the March', *New Middle East*, June 1973, pp. 20–23.

whole west coast of the Gulf into a progressive, nationalistic and possibly united front, hostile to Iranian influence in the area.

To promote stability in the Persian Gulf and prevent an Arab–Iranian confrontation, Iran tried to improve her relations with the Arab world after the October war, using both economic assistance and diplomatic support. This strategy proved successful, and it reached its climax in the announcement in March 1975 of the outlines of an overall agreement with Iraq to settle all disputes between the two countries which traded Iraqi concessions in the Shatt el-Arab conflict for discontinuation of Iranian support for the Kurdish rebellion in Iraq. Whether this agreement will prove durable, remains to be seen.

In an attempt to secure Iran's trade interests and foster her importance in the wider region, the Shah directed his attention to the Indian Ocean. Again his main interest seemed to lie in preserving the *status quo*. After the Indo-Pakistani war Iran made it clear that she could not tolerate a further disintegration of Pakistan, but at the same time tried to achieve friendly relations with India. She also offered to mediate in the conflict between Pakistan and Afghanistan. Since Pakistan takes a growing interest in fostering her relations with the Arab world (the air forces of Abu Dhabi and Libya employ Pakistani pilots, and Pakistan would obviously be interested in forging close economic links with the Arab states), Iran can also hope to contribute indirectly to stability in the region by close co-operation with Pakistan. The same objective can also be assumed to underlie Iran's new interest in the Central Treaty Organization (CENTO) and in the Regional Co-operation for Development Programme with Turkey and Pakistan (which ultimately envisages a customs union comparable to the European Free Trade Association or the early European Community).

Here, another fundamental concern of Iranian foreign policy becomes visible. If Iran is to press on with her industrialization programmes her own domestic market might soon be insufficient to absorb the increased industrial production, and the country will look for new markets in the region. Indeed, it looks as if economic considerations might constitute a very important motive behind Iran's foreign policy – and probably also the only 'offensive' motive, the pursuit of which needs political

stability and appears to be linked to the present *status quo* in the area.[35]

To sum up, one can make the following points about the Iranian attitudes towards the use of oil power and the oil weapon. Assuming internal political stability – and indeed as one prerequisite of such stability – Iran's oil revenues will be used largely for development and social change, economic growth and the diversification of oil power. Oil power and the economic strength and military influence derived from it will be used to secure the regional *status quo* in the Persian Gulf and the Indian Ocean, probably accompanied by an expansion of Iranian economic and political influence which would render the country a regional power centre. The use of the oil weapon seems highly unlikely and would probably only occur in a situation where Iran felt some fundamental interest was threatened in a way which it was beyond the scope of her other – considerable – capabilities to cope with.

Iraq

Like Iran, Iraq is a country with considerable potential for economic growth – mainly in the agricultural, but also to some extent in the industrial sector. She possesses a vast area of potentially fertile land and rich, if still not fully exploited, water resources. The population of about ten million includes many skilled and professional people. However, Iraq's overall performance in the economic field lagged behind Iran's; between 1964 and 1969 her annual average growth in Gross National Product only reached some 5·8 per cent. While the performance has improved since then, a comparison of her potential and actual achievements leads one to conclude that in the past Iraq has missed a chance of economic development.

---

[35] Iran has proposed a common market of the littoral states of the Indian Ocean which, according to an interview with the Shah in a Bombay weekly, should be built around a closer Indian–Iranian economic co-operation. Iran promised India considerable aid and arranged for oil deals at very favourable terms. Pakistan also will receive Iranian oil 'at a price we can afford', according to a Pakistani spokesman. Iran also negotiated large loans to, and economic co-operation projects with, Arab countries such as Egypt, Syria and Morocco. The agreement with Egypt provides *inter alia* for joint ventures in Egypt and Egyptian purchases of machinery, equipment and buses. See *Middle East Economic Digest*, 31 May 1974, p. 623; *The Economist*, 4 May 1974, p. 52.

The present government has therefore opted for an economic policy of rapid growth through effective exploitation of oil reserves. It is intended to create a diversified industrial base of a non-capitalist nature (i.e., a mixed economy heavily relying on the public sector) and to use agrarian reform as the chosen way to achieve social justice and more equal income distribution. As in the case of Iran, the military forms a strong pressure group which will have to be accommodated and controlled if the present regime is to survive, but it does also look as if survival will be possible in the long run only if the government succeeds in raising the standard of living throughout the country.

Between 1961 and 1970, the Kurdish revolt and the consequent almost continuous state of civil war in the north of the country contributed to the relatively poor performance of the Iraqi economy (according to one estimate, the war absorbed 90 per cent of annual oil revenues[36]). In 1970, it looked as if a settlement was finally in sight: Baghdad and the Kurdish leaders agreed on a 15-point programme for Kurdish autonomy to be implemented by 1974. However, relations between Baghdad and the Kurds gradually deteriorated, and in March 1974, after the central government's unilateral declaration of an 'autonomy law' unacceptable to the Kurds, renewed fighting broke out. The agreement with Iran in March 1975, which resulted in the withdrawal of Iranian support (in hardware, logistics and troops), allowed Baghdad to launch a decisive military offensive which, in combination with strong Iranian pressure on the Kurdish leadership, succeeded in forcing the Pesh Merga (Kurdish irregulars) to leave Iraq or surrender. Whether this is the end of the long Kurdish fight for autonomy within Iraq remains to be seen, but for the time being another obstacle to rapid internal development and economic growth has been removed.

There can be no doubt that Iraq does desperately need a decisive new development effort, especially in the rural areas which hold the majority of the population. The country has a great deal of potentially fertile land, but in order to develop it a large and expensive system, of drainage and irrigation is needed to bring down the high water table level and reverse the process of salinization which affects large areas. Current plans provide for the reclamation of no less than one million hectares at a cost of £2,000 million, but even this represents only one-fifth of the land which needs improvement. A system of dams and irrigation channels to control and utilize the rich water resources of the Euphrates and the Tigris needs huge investments – and so do the government's plans to transform agriculture into a largely mechanized sector based on co-operatives.

Industrialization is less urgent in Iraq than in other developing countries, since the country is basically agrarian, and her agriculture could probably accommodate twice her present population. But while the 1970–74 development plan gave high priority to agriculture, industrialization was also an important objective. Iraq already has a small industrial base (employing roughly 10 per cent of the labour force in 1971) which she plans to extend rapidly, and she is well off for raw materials other than oil (deposits of iron ore, chromite, copper, lead and zinc have been found in the north, and test drilling is now being carried out). The 1970–74 development plan envisaged a total investment of some $4,700 million, and the present plan (1974–79) has provisionally allocated $7,500 million, so that the greater part of any increased oil revenues could be absorbed. The government seems aware of the country's present opportunities and has decided to exploit them fully by expanding the oil sector as quickly as possible; production, currently running at 2·2 million b/d, is to increase to 6 million b/d in 1981.[37]

Iraq's foreign policy setting may be described on two levels: that of her relationships with the great powers, and that of her relationships with other countries in the region. With regard to the former, Iraq's close alliance with Moscow, formalized in the treaty of friendship in 1972, is the outstanding feature. The Baghdad regime's hostility to 'Imperialism' and 'Zionism', its socialist convictions and the need for assistance in the 'battle of endurance' against the Western oil companies made the government almost naturally turn to the Soviet Union, which became the main supplier of arms and economic assis-

---

[36] Jean Gueyras, 'Les Dirigeants de Baghdad ont besoin de stabilité pour consolider leur succès dans le pays', *Le Monde Diplomatique*, July 1973, pp. 21, 28.

[37] *The Middle East and North Africa 1972/3*, (London: Europa Publications, 1973), p. 553; *Middle East Economic Digest*, 24 May 1974, p. 600.

tance. Furthermore, the need for a powerful ally to balance Iran's overwhelming military power and Iraq's isolation in the Arab world further enhanced the need for outside support. This isolation was felt increasingly in Baghdad as developments in other Arab countries turned in a conservative direction – for example with the ousting of the Ali Sabri group by President Sadat in Egypt and the abortive Sudanese *coup* by a left-wing coalition with strong Communist support (the short-lived government in Khartoum was immediately recognized by Baghdad). After the 1973 war, Iraq again diverged from the mainstream of Arab opinion concerning the Israeli–Arab conflict, rejecting any political solution and declaring full support for the Palestinians and later, when differences of opinion arose in the Palestinian Liberation Organization about the future approach towards the conflict, she stood by the hard-liners of the 'Palestinian Rejection Front'.

Internal reasons also favoured a closer link with Moscow: the Ba'th regime wanted to integrate the Communist Party into government and, while relaxation of earlier tough suppression of the Communists helped rapprochement with Moscow, the Soviet Union presumably also used her influence to achieve accommodation between Ba'thists and Iraqi Communists. Finally, Baghdad hoped to isolate the Kurds, who in the past received some support from the Soviet Union and from the Iraqi Communists.

Even though the Soviet Union is undoubtedly Baghdad's main ally, in recent times Iraq has repeatedly shown a desire to improve relations with the West.[38] This is probably because economic relations with the West are more profitable than support from the Soviet Union and her allies in Eastern Europe, and the Iraqi government was reportedly not very happy with the latter's economic assistance (a Czech refinery at Basrah, for instance, was not completed to schedule). Big contracts in the oil sector are now expected to go mostly to Western companies, and there is a clear desire to get on better terms with European countries. Iraq's short- and medium-term need for Western assistance and know-how as well as the need

for long-term export markets for her vast potential oil production make such co-operation attractive for her.

On the regional level, Iraq's position is characterized by her isolation in the Arab world and her policy of opposing the *status quo* in the Gulf. Saudi Arabia and Iran, both allied to the United States and linked to the Western capitalist economy, are deeply suspicious of the radical government in Baghdad and its claim to a bigger say in Gulf politics. One of the bones of contention has repeatedly been Kuwait. In 1961 President Qasem claimed Iraqi sovereignty over this small but oil-rich state, but was thwarted by British and Arab military support to Kuwait. After Kuwait refused an Iraqi demand for a loan in December 1972 tensions and border clashes occurred. The underlying reasons for the dispute with Kuwait, however, are more complicated and reflect economic issues (Iraq's need for a new, large oil terminal in view of her small coastline and her dependence on access to the Gulf via the Shatt el-Arab, and disputes over the potentially very rich sea-bed in the north of the Gulf) as well as fear of Iran's predominance and the threat it posed to Iraqi sea communications through the Gulf. Iraq's 1973 demand for parts of Kuwait territory met with the opposition not only of Iran, but also Saudi Arabia; Iran's offer of military assistance to Kuwait was in fact turned down, but a later offer by Saudi Arabia was accepted, and Saudi troops moved into Kuwait to protect the border with Iraq.

An analysis of probable future intentions suggests that Iraq is much more likely to resort to the oil weapon than Iran. Internal factors tend to produce radical and revolutionary external policies, and the country is basically striving to change the present regional *status quo*. The leadership might therefore feel threatened by external forces and react aggressively against these – real or perceived – threats. Once involved in a regional conflict, however, Iraq might quickly find herself in a position of inferiority which could only be coped with either by relying on massive Soviet support or alternatively by using the oil weapon to influence the behaviour of her immediate opponents via pressure on their Western allies. On the other hand, one has to bear in mind that Iraq's capabilities are restricted, first because the oil weapon could probably

---

[38] See Gueyras, *op. cit.* and Robert Graham, 'Iraq: rising expectations', *Middle East International*, October 1973, pp. 9–11. See also the interview with the Iraqi oil minister, Saadoun Hudammi, in *Le Monde*, 19 December 1973.

only be applied effectively in the context of a producer action group, and secondly because she will need a large amount of her oil revenue to sustain and expand her programme of rapid economic growth and social change. Since economic success is probably also an important factor for the internal stability of the present order, this would work as a moderating influence on her foreign policy and reduce the incentive to use the oil weapon.

Iraq's foreign policy in the first months of 1975 did indeed show a marked swing towards more moderate policies and towards improving relations both with other Arab countries (except Syria) and with Iran. This would appear to reflect a concentration on domestic affairs and rapid internal development, and possibly also a desire not to become too dependent on the Soviet Union. The March 1975 outline agreement on settling all her disputes with Iran highlights this change in Iraqi foreign policy.

Saudi Arabia

In Saudi Arabia the present leadership must above all be concerned about the potential danger of a radical nationalist opposition at home. This would most likely stem from the officer corps, and unrest and attempts to overthrow the monarchy reported in 1969, followed by drastic purges in the air force, demonstrate that a Libyan-type *coup* is a distinct possibility within the rest of this decade. A fundamental change in the political system seems more likely in Saudi Arabia than in either of the other two countries discussed here. The survival of the regime probably depends on its capacity to avoid alienation of the officer corps and accommodate and integrate it. This group asks not only for material privileges (which will be easy to provide) but probably also for a gradual expansion of political participation and of consideration of the political mood within the army (which is likely to be more nationalist and moderate than the present leadership). A return to the previous regional isolation of the 1960s, therefore, seems improbable: Saudi Arabia will further try to play an important role in Arab affairs, designed to accommodate or isolate potential external adversaries. This trend is likely to gain momentum when the political elite is extended to include the army officers and the technocrats; these groups will become more important as the formerly direct relationship between ruler and ruled in the traditional structure is gradually eroded – a process which has already started. Should the present leadership succeed in satisfying these potential counter-elites and integrating them into the political and economic structure by giving them special privileges, more influence and some say in foreign policy, and should the monarchy effectively manage social and economic change without losing control over the side-effects of that process, there is probably a good chance for the survival of the present order.

As for super-power relations, the Soviet Union seems to be excluded as a potential ally under present circumstances for ideological as well as political reasons. If regional considerations allow (i.e., if the United States is acceptable within the Arab world as an ally), Saudi Arabia can be expected to continue to rely on American support but in a looser relationship than in the past. Economic links with Japan and Western Europe will be accompanied by political relations of greater importance, and the country will probably develop a rather diffuse foreign policy via involvement in various international organizations dealing with the recycling and investment of Saudi oil revenues and economic assistance to the Third World. This will probably also result in various bilateral agreements.

In the regional arena Saudi Arabia at the moment seems to be basically satisfied with the *status quo* in the Persian Gulf, though there is a certain amount of suspicion about Iranian intentions.[39] These are unlikely to lead to serious conflicts, however, and Saudi Arabia will probably concentrate on the task of spending her oil surplus.

Saudi Arabia's economic position is somewhat different from other oil producing states, since the sheer magnitude of her oil reserves places the country in a separate category: she may be able to produce crude oil well into the twenty-first century, and possibly even into the twenty-second (i.e., into a period when oil might have lost its importance). It also looks doubtful

---

[39] The immediacy of these conflicts has been considerably reduced in 1974/5, as highlighted by an agreement between Saudi Arabia and Abu Dhabi which settled the territorial disputes between the two countries: Saudi Arabia accepted Abu Dhabi's claim to the Buraimi oasis in exchange for a potentially oil-rich strip of land.

whether she will be able to build up, to a degree sufficient to sustain the country's standard of living, an industrial base capable of using all her oil to produce goods based on cheap oil both as a source of energy and as a raw material. Any further disruption of the international oil market, therefore, would increase the danger of making the Saudi oil worthless. For this reason the country cannot be interested in further disturbances of supplies and price increases; a stable relationship with consumer countries would serve her interest best. Undoubtedly Saudi Arabia will do a lot to create an economic base and diversify her sources of income, and there thus is some potential for oil revenue absorption. But the enormous revenues which have been predicted for her will to a considerable extent have to be directed into investments outside the country, and even outside the region – which again will probably contribute to a search for stable consumer–producer relations.

Capabilities mark Saudi Arabia as the country most likely to use the oil weapon. Given the present political order, however, an analysis of possible intentions seems to indicate that, while the decision-makers might be pressed into using their powerful leverage, they are not very likely to use it as an active instrument of their foreign policy. For various reasons, Saudi Arabia would probably prefer a stable producer–consumer relationship, and she seems satisfied with the present *status quo*. On the other hand, the Saudi government would appear to be more exposed to pressures both from inside and outside the country than Iraq. The present regime's vulnerability not only to internal challenges but also to radical Arab opposition from outside is considerable, and to accommodate these forces the government might have to adopt policies much more radical than it would like. The assassination of King Faisal and the smooth transition of power demonstrated the relative strength of the Saudi regime, which rests basically on the vast royal family and its omnipresent influence within society and politics. On the other hand, the loss of Faisal's unique position of strength both in Saudi Arabia and in the Arab world could well lead to the new regime being more strongly exposed to the various pressures from within and outside – pressures, which will often be contradictory, therefore complicating predictions

about the future course of the policies of King Khalid and Crown Prince Fahd.

Other possibilities that might lead Saudi Arabia once more to unsheath her oil weapon could stem from a fundamental change in the present social and political order. This would create a new type of situation, or, as an intermediate possibility, might lead to a more adventurous foreign policy in the Persian Gulf designed to reduce the Iranian influence (which in itself would constitute a challenge to the *status quo*).

The Role of Ideology: Nationalism and its Future importance

Modern Arab nationalism played a significant part in the erosion of Western influence and control over the Arab world. It is made up of strong anti-Western sentiment, inclination towards various forms of socialism (public ownership of industry and the nationalization of foreign interests as a means to rapid social and economic modernization and greater equality) and, last but not least, fervent opposition to the state of Israel. It will be of some significance in the future, though most likely with considerable changes. Further successes by radical Arab nationalism will have to be achieved against conditions less favourable than during the last two decades. In the past this nationalism has been the ideology of a new class pressing for political power against a traditional order often marked by inefficiency, corruption and inability to fulfil the growing expectations of the peoples concerned. The vast oil revenues available to the oil-producing countries (which are largely governed by conservative regimes) might now reverse that precondition. There is a good chance that these regimes might not only succeed in maintaining the political and social *status quo* within their own societies against the background of social and economic change; they might even be able to reverse the swing of the 1960s towards the Left in the Arab world (indeed they have already started to do so).

The most important ideological factors of the future will probably be strong nationalism (mainly local but on some issues also pan-Arab – e.g., *vis-à-vis* Israel), independence from foreign interference and influence, and social justice (which, given the enormous resources of the oil-producers, could be achieved through a purely 'capitalist' approach). Arab nationalism could be conveniently married with Islamic tradition, which might as easily result in a radical as in a conservative orientation (cf. the different, but equally 'Islamic', ideologies of Saudi Arabia and Libya). Another trend, which could actually tend to erode the importance of ideologies, is a pragmatic and technocratic orientation towards solving the various problems accompanying social change. Such an approach will more and more replace the ideological approach, since social tensions and conflict will diminish as the oil wealth spreads throughout the Arab countries, and the problem changes from sharing scarce resources into effectively allocating and managing vast resources.

Overall, then, a gradual decline in the importance of ideology can be expected, though some relics will undoubtedly remain. Among them will be strong antagonism towards any attempt by outside powers to interfere with the sovereignty of the states in the area, and some degree of common opposition against Israel – the actual degree depending largely on the progress made towards an Israeli–Arab settlement.

Possible Future Application of the Oil Weapon

Like other weapons, the oil weapon has offensive and defensive capabilities. The threat and the application of the oil weapon for defensive purposes would aim at securing vital interests of an oil-producer country (or, more precisely, its incumbent regime). The offensive use would aim to increase power and influence and would involve a change in the *status quo*. In this section we shall briefly consider three possibilities: the defensive use of the oil weapon against consumer countries; defensive and offensive use of the oil weapon in a regional context, with the consumer countries being used as targets (but only to further the ultimate purpose of achieving objectives against other countries in the Middle East) and the offensive use of the oil weapon in a global context.

The most obvious contingency in which the oil weapon would be used is a threat to the sovereignty and integrity of a producer or one of its allies by a consumer state attempting to intervene militarily or by subversive means. The fundamental nature of the threat posed to a producer by such intervention would remove many of the restraints and limitations of the

oil weapon discussed earlier. The supply interruption would probably take the form of destruction of oil installations, since immediate concern for the survival of the present regime in the producer country would override consideration of future consequences for consumers or even the producers themselves. (Such a situation is equivalent to a typical escalation process in warfare, which increases the damage for both sides.) Such an attack would also create considerable pressure for producer solidarity and vastly improve the chances of co-ordinated producer action. This contingency is thereforeun likely.

Oil power and the oil weapon could, of course, also be used in the defence of important economic interests of the producer countries: e.g., stability of the terms of trade (the ratio of oil price to the price of goods imported by producers), pursuit of economic development and modernization, and a stable return on foreign investments. The various forms of oil power could also be used to prevent erosion of the producers' present power by consumer co-operation in sharing out oil supplies in a crisis or by diversifying away from OPEC oil.

Looking at the regional setting, any future application of the oil weapon seems unlikely, except in two contexts: the Israeli–Arab conflict and a clash in the Persian Gulf. The Israeli–Arab conflict is the most likely contingency; should fighting break out again on a large scale, or the present negotiations for a settlement end in a stalemate without further prospect of at least some progress along the lines desired by the Arab states, then a new application of the oil weapon seems almost inevitable. This issue provides a framework for common action by Arab producers, and they would be under considerable pressure both from within and outside their own countries to repeat the past success in using the oil weapon; besides, the Arab producers have committed themselves to a solution of the Israeli–Arab conflict.

In the Persian Gulf, all the three states thought to be potential unilateral users of the oil weapon are littoral states and involved in the various actual or possible conflict constellations in the area, each involving a clash between two or more large producing countries: anti-*status quo* powers (Iraq, South Yemen) against *status quo* powers (Iran, Saudi Arabia); Iran against Saudi Arabia; and Iraq against Iran.

33

As for the first possibility (which could, but need not, involve South Yemen and other revolutionary forces, like the Popular Front for the Liberation of Oman), the basic intention and the driving force would be Iraq's desire for greater influence in the Persian Gulf. She might rely on other countries or groups in the Gulf for support and, even though such an alliance would not appear very stable, it might serve her purposes in the phase of common struggle against the *status quo*. She could also hope for Soviet support in such an attempt to expand her influence and change the balance of power in the Gulf. Various arguments seem to indicate, though, that the possibility of such a conflict is fairly remote. First, the overwhelming military superiority of Iran and (potentially) the even greater superiority of Iran and Saudi Arabia together would not allow Iraq openly to challenge those two states without Soviet support – but such support would inevitably lead to super-power conflict. Besides, the Soviet Union appears interested in good relations with Iran and could probably not be brought to take sides openly and exclusively. The same argument might even apply to China, which anyway would be unable to lend sufficient military support. The success of clandestine attempts to overthrow the regimes in Saudi Arabia and Iran will depend largely on the internal state of affairs in these countries, but the chances do not appear very promising. Still, open conflict between the groups espousing and attacking the *status quo* in the Gulf might result from an escalation process, without either side really intending to go to war, or from Iran just using a pretext to try to rid herself of the hostile regime in Baghdad.

Iraq might also try to confront the conservative powers separately. The success of an attempt against Saudi Arabia would depend partly on the state of the Iranian–Saudi relations, but even if Iran were not involved in the confrontation, Saudi Arabia would still be a formidable opponent. One bone of contention which could produce such a clash might be Iraq's claim to Kuwait, or parts of Kuwaiti territory; on this point Iraq could feel compelled, for internal reasons, to take risks rather than lose face and retreat. If Saudi Arabia were unable to cope with the Iraqi threat, Kuwait could expect some Arab support (military and/or political) and probably also Western assistance in the form of strong pressure on Moscow to restrain Iraq, or perhaps direct intervention with arms deliveries and even troops. Should the West be reluctant to give assistance Saudi Arabia and Kuwait might threaten to use their oil weapon in order to secure it. In such a conflict, and if there were a largely bilateral market structure, Iraq could use the leverage of her oil power against, say, France to force her to support Iraq politically and with arms deliveries, thereby creating a rift in the Western alliance.

The same issue of leadership and influence in the Gulf might also lead to a confrontation between Iraq and Iran, and Iraq might even be able to enlist the support of other Arab countries against Iran. There could be a danger of super-power confrontation arising out of an Iraqi–Iranian conflict, depending on what attitude Moscow took. Once again, the balance of power in the Gulf makes such a conflict unlikely – it would only be possible as 'accidental war', the consequence of hazardous brinkmanship. Nonetheless, if a conflict between Iraq and Saudi Arabia and/or Iran did occur, it would lead to serious disruption of oil supplies, since fighting would affect the trade routes in the Gulf.

At the moment, such a clash appears rather remote, given the recent improvement of relations between Iraq and the conservative states in the Gulf. However, a potential for conflict does exist, due not only to the already mentioned bones of contention between Iraq and Iran, but also to the ethnic differences and historical distrust between Arabs and Persians. Indeed the Iran–Iraq détente appears very vulnerable to any change in leadership, especially in Baghdad (Iraq's settlement with Iran has already come under severe attack from some Arab countries, especially Syria). In addition, a fall in demand for OPEC oil could be caused by consumers developing alternative sources of oil and energy supplies, and this could lead to a need to allocate production quotas among OPEC countries. Such a situation might find Iraq in an awkward position, since she has very good prospects of substantially raising production and also needs revenues urgently. She might then decide to adopt an aggressive export policy of undercutting, which would be mainly directed against Iran and Saudi Arabia.

34

Saudi Arabia and Iran could possibly clash if the United Arab Emirates and other small sheikhdoms on the west coast of the Gulf weakened and disintegrated. Both countries might then be tempted to establish their control over that area, since a *status quo* policy would no longer be possible. A similar development could result from an 'imperial' attitude by Saudi Arabia towards the sheikhdoms, possibly as a consequence of internal change in Saudi Arabia. It seems, however, that such a conflict would be counter-productive for both parties, so long as they intend to contain Iraqi and Soviet influence, and the incentive to reach agreement would be strong. Furthermore, the fact that the United States is the main supplier of arms and the principal ally of both countries would act as a restraint, as would the fact that war between them could not result in a decisive victory for either but might weaken both. The possibility of such a conflict appears remote; nevertheless, if it did occur disruption in the flow of oil would be likely. Besides the impact of military actions in the Gulf, supplies might be affected by the fact that Saudi Arabia, as the weaker side, would probably be tempted to resort to the oil weapon if she feared a decisive Iranian success.

A fundamentally new situation could result from a radical military *coup* in Saudi Arabia. If Iraq succeeded in engineering a Ba'thist-inspired *putsch* in Riyadh, a common front of Arab Gulf states against Iran could develop. But, given the potential for internal conflict and tension within such a grouping, it would probably not last for very long and would soon change into Saudi–Iraqi rivalry. The outcome might be the same if an independent military regime took power in Riyadh. Such a government would probably steer an independent course, opposed to Iran and her predominance in the Gulf (which it would definitely try to challenge, the bone of contention again being the small west-coast sheikhdoms), but also opposed to Iraq and her claim to leadership at least of the Arab side of the Gulf. Such a development in Saudi Arabia would almost certainly intensify the tripolarity in the Gulf and lead on to new possibilities for great-power confrontation. The Soviet Union would either be reluctant to take sides at all and would try to accommodate both parties in order to avoid

conflict, or would vote for one side and (if the United States were not accepted for ideological reasons) leave the other without an ally. This might lead Iraq or Saudi Arabia to try to use China as a great-power ally. Alternatively, Europe or some European states could be drawn in as a balancing factor, again with serious consequences for great-power relations in other areas. The threat of the oil weapon would loom large, since a radical and ideologically dedicated Saudi government would possess enormous damage potential as long as the imbalance of bargaining power between this producer and the consumers prevails.

The possibilities discussed so far have concentrated on oil power being used mainly to involve consumers in regional conflicts to achieve producer objectives. Oil power and the oil weapon could also, in some circumstances, be used to minimize consumer involvement: the producers might try, by using the various sanctions and rewards oil power provides, to reduce consumer links with Israel and other countries considered hostile. A strategy of isolating Israel has been applied before, in Africa and with the economic boycott organized against companies investing in Israel. Japan, for instance, would find it difficult to resist sustained pressure to break diplomatic relations with Israel, and the only reason for the Arabs not to demand this is that such a development would have hardly any impact on the Israeli–Arab conflict.

Regional objectives or defence of vital interests are not the only possible motives for the application of oil power, however. The Arab producers might strive to become the leaders of the Third World. Some countries (Libya, Algeria) have indeed voiced such aspirations, but in practical terms oil power has not yet been used systematically for this purpose. Economically, only a limited part of Arab financial resources has been made available for the Third World, which has suffered most from higher oil prices. In principle, the oil producers could try to achieve the gradual redistribution of wealth on a global scale and the reversal of the trend towards consistently growing inequality between developed and less-developed countries. This would, however, require an extremely skilful application of all aspects of oil power and its derivatives – especially price and cash.

A starting point for such a strategy, which

would aim at a controlled conflict between developed and less-developed countries, would be a two-tier price system for oil, giving developing countries a specially favourable price. This could be accompanied by a quota system favouring supplies to developing countries and keeping deliveries to developed countries scarce and expensive (withdrawal of the special status for Third World countries could block any attempts to re-export the cheap oil to developed countries). The vast oil reserve surplus which would probably prevail when the market was split into a large 'seller's' market and a small and artificial 'buyer's' market could be used as an additional means of encouraging industrialization and rapid development in the Third World. Not all the money would have to come from the oil producers, since they could use oil power to bring the developed countries to take an equal share in the institutions designed to finance the Third World development plans. The result of such a co-ordinated effort would be to impose low growth-rates on at least some consuming countries, while the economic development of the Third World would be speeded up. It would become very attractive for developed countries to invest 'upstream', where raw materials and cheap energy would provide favourable conditions and new large markets would be within reach, and one could imagine some consequent transfer of industrial production into the Third World. This would not necessarily be opposed to the long-term interest of the developed world, since it would defuse the potentially explosive aspects of the world class-structure, and the developed countries would probably still be in control of the world economy through their superior know-how, research and development capacity, and control of the world-wide communication and information systems.

The economic co-operation between the Arab states and the Third World countries would then have to be institutionalized politically. The first step might be an Organization of Raw Material Exporting Countries. Present institutions, like the United Nations and its affiliates, also could provide a framework for co-ordination, and no doubt the Arab states would have a very influential voice in any such institution. But they would have to be prepared not to seek dominance: they could only be successful if they stressed the basic unity of a

Third World polarized against, but not in confrontation with, the developed countries.

Events in 1974–75 demonstrated that the OPEC countries will indeed strive for a leading role in the Third World. This became especially obvious in the discussion at the OPEC summit in Algiers and at the tripartite Paris meeting for the preparation of a producer/consumer conference. On both occasions OPEC states rallied behind the Algerian demand for a reform of the international economic order, which means above all a reorganization of the whole raw material trade between the Third World and the industrialized countries by means of producer cartels, so as to ensure stable returns for the producer countries. This would probably mean some form of index-linking of raw material prices, as already suggested in the case of oil. OPEC's attempts to act as the *avant-garde* of the Third World would seem to be, at least in part, a power-increasing strategy adopted in the light of the United States' policy of non-cooperation in dealing with OPEC (though at the end of 1974 this policy changed somewhat towards a more co-operative approach). All the same, in 1974 the OPEC producers repeatedly managed to rally a substantial majority of Third World countries behind their policies, thereby asserting their intention of becoming a leading force in world politics as advocates of the less-developed countries.

The desirability of such a development could only be assessed after further detailed discussion, but it is unlikely to be realized fully. First, the degree of Arab unity required seems difficult to achieve. Since splits into various camps seem likely to continue (most notably a progressive–conservation division), various rivalries, on Third World strategies and on other matters, might emerge and partly offset each other (for instance, the competition between Libya and Saudi Arabia for political influence in certain African countries). Second, the Arab states seem to lack the capabilities required for leadership of the Third World. They do not have numbers of highly-educated people with specialist training, they do not have the planning and research capabilities for such a strategy of effectively assuming leadership in the manner outlined, and (considering the enormous amount of money needed to promote Third-World economic development) they might even lack the

36

resources. The Arab states' oil wealth must be limited in duration, and they do not possess other resources sufficient to this task. They would also have to sacrifice some of their own interests (the reluctance to resort to a two-tier price system shows how difficult that is) and would probably have to increase production, so as to make sufficient amounts of oil available, without greatly increasing their revenues. Finally, they would have to resist the temptation to create a clientele of dependent states which could also serve as markets for Arab products.

It seems more likely that certain aspects of this development will become reality, but in a different framework. The international system will be more differentiated. The developed states will be divided into the largely oil self-sufficient (possibly even oil-exporting) states, like the super-powers, Canada or Australia, and heavily dependent consumer states, like Japan and parts of Europe – and this would contradict predictions of various poles of more or less equal influence and importance. The developing countries will also be divided into the rich oil-exporting countries, a 'middle class' of countries with large raw material resources and some degree of self-sufficiency in oil, and, finally, the countries without significant natural resources of any kind. Simultaneously with this stratification of world society a network of linkages, based on various degrees of interdependence and imbalanced dependence will develop between various centres like the super-powers, Western Europe, Japan, China, the Arab countries and possibly other oil-producing countries, such as Iran or Venezuela. In particular, the Arab countries might function as a centre of the Islamic world or of parts of the African continent.

V. CONCLUSIONS

The picture emerging from our assessment of strength and weaknesses of the oil weapon is a complex one. Under present circumstances, its applicability would appear to be rather restricted; developments in the Israeli–Arab conflict still constitute the contingency most likely to lead the Arab oil producers once more to use the oil weapon, though open clashes in the Persian Gulf (which are in any case bound to lead to major supply interruptions) might also involve its deliberate application. Any analysis, however, cannot simply be based on present conditions, since oil power is derived from the state of the international oil market. This market is, in turn, subject to a wide range of influences, predominantly the strategies of major actors like producer and consumer governments and oil companies, and its dynamics are bound to influence strongly the ability of the producers to use their resource as a political instrument. The balance of power might swing back to the consumers or further towards the producers. In the short and medium term, the most essential and sensitive area appears to be the international distribution system; in the longer term, the geographical redistribution of supply–demand patterns might turn out to be the overriding element of change.

Should the producers acquire a sufficient share of the world tanker fleet to allow the discriminate application of the oil weapon, the range of this new factor in international relations could be expanded considerably. Under these circumstances it might be some developing countries which could be the most vulnerable consumers, for not only are they often dependent on one or two oil producers for substantial amounts of their energy supplies, but they might be the first to rely on rigid bilateral trade structures involving the tanker fleets of the oil producers. This vulnerability will no doubt be reflected in the foreign policies of such countries.

Leaving aside the possibility of such bilateral structures developing between oil producers and consumers, the result of our analysis might appear somewhat paradoxical. While the future possibilities for the application of the oil weapon seem very restricted, it will nonetheless be of very considerable importance in future international politics. This paradox is explained by the fact that the oil weapon, which is simply the ultimate sanction of oil power, is a sanction that will not be lightly resorted to but will nevertheless, by its very existence, constitute an omnipresent factor in international relations. Oil diplomacy will replace the actual use of the oil weapon because, while the latter is a relatively awkward and costly political instrument of last resort, oil diplomacy can make full

37

use of all dimensions of oil power and the forms of power derived from it: threats, symbolic sanctions (embargoes without cutbacks, stoppages), wealth, military power and, finally, economic power. Already the influence of oil diplomacy can be felt in international organizations such as the United Nations, UNESCO, the IMF and the World Bank and in many areas of international economics, not to mention the Israeli–Arab conflict. Like other forms of power, oil power is diffuse and not quantifiable (it rather resembles credit-worthiness) and does not necessarily have to be congruent with the actual capabilities which back it: the oil producers are at the moment 'credited' with a power which could well exceed their actual capabilities.

The net result of the oil crisis in 1973–4 was a fundamental change in the international political system. A new group of actors has achieved prominence and begun to exert its influence in world politics. These powers will assume a mediating position between the highly developed countries and the majority of the Third World. They will in many aspects still be dependent on their great-power ally and their economic partners among developed countries, but their economic leverage will allow them to build a considerable and diversified power base, attracting surrounding states and areas which will then serve as raw material suppliers, markets and receivers of capital investment. The economic dependence and possible inferior military power of those countries would also open them to the political influence of the regional power.

Possible candidates for the regional power role are Iran (for parts of the Middle East and for the Indian sub-continent), Iraq (Arab world?), Saudi Arabia (Arab world, Africa), Algeria (Africa, Maghreb), Venezuela (Caribbean), Nigeria (West Africa), Indonesia (South-East Asia). The super-powers might use regional powers as substitutes for direct control and influence in certain areas of the Third World (as the United States has already been trying to do with Iran), but the regional powers will in the future probably strive for a higher degree of independence in which mutuality of interest will be paramount, and other forms of dependence will diminish in significance. This implies that regional powers might clash without their allies being able to prevent it (the foregoing discussion of Persian Gulf politics tried to speculate about such possibilities). Under the heading of mutuality of interest the consumer states will be asked to assist in the economic development of the oil-producing countries and in the building up of their power base by arms deliveries, technological assistance and political support. The producing governments might also want some help in the field of intelligence and counter-subversion capacities – in securing the internal order of their states against opposition groups.

One final point: our analysis of oil producers' possible intentions and the limited range of conflicts which might cause the oil weapon to be used again are largely based on the assumption of rational behaviour by the producer governments. While this assumption could be questioned, it would appear justified. First, the past behaviour of the oil producers has showed considerable skill and circumspection in their application of the oil weapon, and, second, successful application of the oil weapon requires co-operation between two or more producers to achieve sufficient damage potential (and potentially also sufficient control over the world tanker fleet). The assumption of irrationality would therefore demand joint irrationality by more than one producer government (this would even apply to Saudi Arabia, provided her production and her share of the international market do not increase significantly).

Nevertheless, a cataclysmic oil war cannot totally be ruled out. If the producers – or some of them – do not see any other option open to them and feel desperate enough to cause world-wide chaos, then 'total' oil war might break out. So long as the oil producers continue to supply the world with a vital share of its energy supply, the result would be a suicidal spiral of escalation and destruction on a world-wide scale.

APPENDIXES

Statistical Profile of Main Middle Eastern and Third World Oil Exporters

Appendix I: Oil Power 1974

	Published proven reserves (end-1974)		Production		Estimated revenues ($m)	Foreign exchange holdings ($m end-1974)
	million barrels	% of world total	million b/d	% of world total		
Saudi Arabia*	173,150	24·2	8·64	15·2	29,181	13,424
Iran	66,000	9·2	6·13	10·8	20,801	7,653
Kuwait*	81,450	11·4	2·84	5·0	9,262	933
Iraq	35,000	4·9	1·83	3·2	6,990	3,036
United Arab Emirates	33,920	4·7	2·03	3·6	7,200	n.a.
Qatar	6,000	0·8	0·55	1·0	1,993	n.a.
Oman	6,000	0·8	0·30	0·5	1,041	200
Bahrain	336	0·05	0·07	0·1	225	n.a.
Libya	26,600	3·7	1·70	3·0	7,613	3,504
Algeria	7,700	1·1	0·89	1·6	3,978	1,362
Venezuela	15,000	2·1	3·03	5·3	10,489	5,412
Nigeria	20,800	2·9	2·30	4·1	8,991	5,506
Indonesia	15,000	2·1	1·46	2·6	4,839	1,386

* Including share of Neutral Zone.

Appendix II: Absorption Capacity 1974

	Imports ($m)	Estimated per capita oil revenue ($)	Estimated population	Development expenditure ($m)[a]
Saudi Arabia	3,473	5,305	5,500	DP 1975–80: 140,000
Iran	5,974	642	32,410	DP 1973–8: 42,800[b]
Kuwait	1,529	8,424	1,100	DB 1974–5: 340
Iraq	1,176[c]	651	10,740	DP 1974–9: 7,500
United Arab Emirates	800 (1973)	22,154	325	DP 1968–73: 740
Qatar	195 (1973)	22,144	90	DB 1974–5: 154
Oman	134 (1972)	1,407	740	n.a.
Bahrain	450	937	240	DB 1975: 100·9
Libya	3,140	3,399	2,240	DP 1972–5: 7,421
Algeria	3,715	243	16,350	DP 1974–7: 23,529
Venezuela	4,042	894	11,730	—
Nigeria	2,734	148	60,860	DP 1970–4: 2,371[b]
Indonesia	2,597[c]	38	126,780	DP 1974–9: 11,708

[a] DB – Development Budget; DP – Development Plan.
[b] Figures include only government expenditure as envisaged in Plan.
[c] First three quarters only.

2 Oil and Security:
Problems and Prospects of Importing Countries

EDWARD N. KRAPELS

INTRODUCTION

More than one hundred nations import energy resources, and in order to maintain their economic and social activities these imports must be both continuous and sufficient.

On three occasions since World War II, Arab members of the Organization of Petroleum Exporting Countries (OPEC)[1] have deliberately reduced their outflow of oil in order to influence the settlement of their dispute with Israel. The last reduction was the longest and largest: it lasted five months, and Arab oil supplies were reduced from the September 1973 level by 24 per cent in November 1973, 23 per cent in December 1973, 16 per cent in January 1974, 14 per cent in February 1974, and 12 per cent in March 1974.[2]

These supply reductions affected nearly every country that relied on imports from OPEC and the major oil companies,[3] despite the fact only the United States, the Netherlands, and a few other nations were specifically embargoed. In response, many governments declared they would make major changes in their nations' energy systems in order to reduce their need for imported oil. The United States was most ambitious, asserting that she would meet her energy needs from domestic resources by 1980.

Today, it has become apparent that this will not come about; on the contrary, the volume of imports demanded is expected to increase through the next decade.[4] With the exception of a few new energy producers, such as Britain, Norway and Zaire, the degree of oil import dependence of most countries will not be reduced significantly either by increased domestic production of energy resources or by decreased consumption of imported oil. As a result, governments must find other ways to safeguard continuity and sufficiency of their supplies. They may build larger oil stockpiles, establish new companies, join new multilateral organizations, establish closer relations with their oil suppliers, and modify their foreign policies in order to decrease the probability that they will be targeted in future reductions of oil supplies for political purposes.

Oil is, of course, only one of the primary energy resources; natural gas, coal, and nuclear fuels are also traded between nations. Nonetheless, the focus here will be on oil, because it is by far the most important fuel and will remain so through the 1980s. The concern of this Paper is to re-evaluate the problems of energy dependence in

---

[1] The Arab members of OPEC are Algeria, Iraq, Kuwait, Libya, Qatar, Saudi Arabia and the United Arab Emirates (UAE). The other members are Ecuador, Gabon, Indonesia, Iran, Nigeria and Venezuela.
[2] Estimates from US Senate, Committee on Foreign Relations, Subcommittee on Multi-national Corporations, *US Oil Companies and the Arab Oil Embargo: The International Allocation of Constricted Supplies*, a report prepared by the Federal Energy Administration's Office of International Energy Affairs, 94th Congress, 1st session, 27 January 1975 (Washington DC: USGPO, 1975), p. 7.
[3] Exxon, Texaco, Mobil, Standard Oil of California, Gulf, British Petroleum (BP), and Shell.

[4] Leading forecasts of energy supply and demand, though differing in specific estimates, agree in this respect. See Commission of the European Communities *Reports on the Achievements of the Community Objectives for 1985* (Luxembourg: Publications of the European Communities, January 1976); Organization for Economic Co-operation and Development, *World Energy Outlook* (Paris: OECD, 1977); US Federal Energy Administration, *National Energy Outlook* (Washington DC: USGPO, February 1976); and International Bank for Reconstruction and Developments, *Energy and Petroleum in non-OPEC Developing Countries, 1974–1980*, Staff Paper No. 229 (Washington DC: World Bank, February 1976).

the light of this continuing need for oil imports, and to determine whether oil import dependence can properly be considered a 'national security concern' (and, if so, under what circumstances).

Countries that import oil face two related threats: increases in the price of oil and reductions in supply. The price set by OPEC in December 1973 created widespread fears that many countries would simply be unable to pay for the oil imports required to fuel their domestic economies, or that they would amass such large payment deficits that they would slide into bankruptcy. At the same time, the reduction in the supply of Arab oil created the fear that the quantity of oil on the market would be insufficient to support the desired national production and employment levels.

The price and supply problems are thus clearly related. If OPEC were to raise the price to $40 per barrel, many of their customers would 'lose' a certain amount of oil, simply because they could not afford it. Conversely, a reduction in supply creates pressure on price as the consumers compete for such oil as is available. Supply reductions, however, have been used in the past to apply direct political pressure on the importers because they have a quicker impact and can be used more discriminately than price increases. In 1973 the reduction of supplies was intended to achieve satisfaction of Arab political demands, while the OPEC price increase was intended to be a permanent economic change, unrelated to particular political issues.[5] The emphasis of this discussion, therefore, will be on the security implications of energy supply reductions, because they are more immediate and overtly political threats to importing states.

An energy supply disruption should be considered a security threat when it hinders 'the capacity of a society to cultivate its culture and values'.[6] Chapter I attempts to describe the magnitude of energy supply losses required to cross this threshold, concentrating on the vulnerabilities of states that have become accustomed to a given level of energy supply. However, since energy export reductions tend to be distributed internationally, as the 1973 crisis showed, Chapters II and III consider the energy security problems of the developing nations, the Communist importers, and 'outsiders' like Israel and South Africa.

Vulnerability is a function not only of the domestic energy system but also of the international forces that affect trade: the international oil industry and the political relations among and between oil importers and exporters. Chapter IV therefore combines the domestic and international determinants of vulnerability to reach an understanding of the differences in national interests, and national anxieties, among the oil importing nations. Chapter V then focuses on these differences. Now that oil supplies must be regarded as a political weapon, the differences in vulnerability must be regarded as an important factor in the 'strategy' of conflicts, and Chapter VI examines various strategies in order to identify the implications for security of energy dependence.

I. ECONOMIC VULNERABILITY OF INDUSTRIAL NATIONS

The history of the world's evolution towards energy import dependence is now available in scores of publications. The current energy situation in the major countries of the Organization for Economic Co-operation and Development (OECD), who demand the bulk of the world's energy exports, is as follows:

1. The United States and Canada use oil for about 45 per cent of their energy requirements. In 1975 the United States had to import about 37 per cent of her oil supplies. Canada produced almost as much as she consumed, but shipped about half her own oil to the United States, leaving the Eastern Canadian provinces to import almost all their oil needs. A

---

[5] For a comprehensive discussion of the effects of oil prices, see Edward R. Fried and Charles L. Schultze (eds), *Higher Oil Prices and the World Economy* (Washington DC: Brookings Institution, 1975). The study concludes that, with proper economic management, the price increases of 1973 should be manageable for most countries.

[6] Richard N. Cooper, 'National Resources and National Security' in *The Middle East and the International System: Part II: Security and the Energy Crisis*, Adelphi Paper No. 115 (London: IISS, 1974), p. 8.

recent projection[7] of future import demand indicates that the United States' import needs will change from 6 million b/d in 1975 to 7·8 to 9·3 million b/d in 1980, and will be in the range 4·3–10·9 million b/d in 1985.[8]

2. In Europe, northern countries – Britain, West Germany, the Netherlands and Belgium – can be distinguished from southern Europe by their lower dependence on oil (48, 55, 44 and 57 per cent respectively), and by their domestic coal and gas production. The North Sea will enable Britain to be self-sufficient in oil in 1980, and Norway (an insignificant consumer of oil) to export close to one million b/d. Official projections of future import demand for these four countries show a decrease from 4·9 million b/d in 1975 to 4·4 million b/d in 1980, and an increase to 5·1 million b/d in 1985.

3. France, Italy and Japan use imported oil for 70 per cent or more of their energy needs and do not produce significant quantities of oil or gas. Official projections show future oil import demand increasing from 9·2 million b/d in 1975 to 10·8 million b/d in 1980, and to 12·5 million b/d in 1985.

In these projections, the aggregate demand for imports is not expected to decrease in the coming decade. Thus, accidental or deliberate disruptions in oil trade will continue to be of major concern to the industrial states.

The international political and security implications of this dependence and vulnerability can be viewed in two ways. First, dependence on imported oil can be reduced only gradually. It takes years to find new oil supplies or to develop alternative energy sources, and, in addition, most energy analysts do not believe it is possible to reduce the level of energy consumption without retarding, or stopping, overall economic growth.

However, the problem of the long-term sufficiency of energy resources is overwhelmed when oil exports are disrupted. The problems of short-term oil shortages and vulnerability at a particular point in time, and thus exposure to the pressures which oil suppliers can exert, have been largely neglected. One analyst, Richard Cooper, asks, 'Are we not vulnerable in the very short run, perhaps to the point of threatening our security?', and answers that 'To some extent we are . . . but even the short-term adaptability of modern economies is surprisingly great, especially when a crisis is widely perceived to be a crisis and thereby evokes co-operative behaviour'.[9] But, if it were 'great' enough, dependence would not be a major concern. Therefore, it is necessary to consider the conditions or circumstances in which concern, or lack of concern, about short-term disruptions is warranted.

Vulnerability Estimates by the US Government
On 21 November 1973 Secretary of State Kissinger warned the Arab nations that 'the United States would consider counter-measures if the oil embargo is continued indefinitely or unreasonably'.[10] This remark, made when the duration and severity of the Arab oil curtailments were unknown and frightening factors, implied that there was a breaking point in the American economy's short-term ability and willingness to adjust to an oil loss. Kissinger did not state where that point might lie, although in January 1975 he partially clarified the purpose of his comment. 'Some of my remarks have created a certain hysteria . . . about the possible use of force by the United States. . . . It is important to understand what I said . . . in case of actual strangulation of the industrialized world, we would reserve our position. Now, if you analysed this, no Secretary of State could say less. We cannot take the position that no matter what the producing countries do, we will acquiesce.'[11] Nevertheless, even hinting at the possibility of using armed force to secure oil supplies poses in a fundamental way the question of the relationship between energy and security. At what point do oil shortages create sufficient problems to justify armed retaliation?

---

[7] Projections by the International Energy Agency (IEA) as reported in *The Economist*, 10 April 1976. The estimates assume (a) an OECD economic growth rate of 4·3 per cent per year from 1974 to 1980 and 4 per cent per year from 1980 to 1985; and (b) no fall in the real price of oil. These projections, like others, must be viewed with caution. The IEA projections are used under these three points solely because they are most likely to represent governments' best estimates.

[8] Levels of production and consumption are expressed in barrels per day (b/d). President Carter's new energy programme, announced as this Paper was going to press, aims to limit US oil imports to 8 million b/d by 1985.

[9] *Op. cit.* in note 6, p. 11.
[10] *International Herald Tribune*, 22 November 1973.
[11] Address to *Time* magazine luncheon, 17 January 1975, declassified State Department transcript.

There are only rough guesses, no detailed and systematic analyses, of the ability of industrial economies to adjust to oil losses in the short term. For example, in early 1975 the US Treasury Secretary submitted to President Ford an assessment of the relationship between dependence on oil imports and national security: 'Any sudden disruption in excess [of 1 million b/d] would have a prompt substantial effect upon our economic well-being, and, considering the close relation between this nation's economic welfare and our national security, would clearly threaten to impair our national security. Furthermore, [in the event of a complete loss of oil imports] the total US production of about 11 million barrels per day[12] might well be insufficient to supply adequately a war-time economy. As a result, the national security would not merely be threatened, but could be immediately, directly and adversely affected.' The Department of Defense stated in the same report: 'The degree of our energy self-sufficiency must be such that any potential supply denial will be sustainable for an extended period without degradation of military readiness or operations, and without significant impact on industrial output or the welfare of the populace.'[13]

The Treasury's estimates are similar to those previously presented in the *Project Independence Report* of the Federal Energy Administration.[14] The report states that if supplies are lost for one year, the first million barrels of daily oil supplies lost (about 6 per cent of total oil supplies) would not produce significant economic losses. The second million barrels lost would produce an economic (GNP) loss of about $30 billion (less than 3 per cent of GNP). Additional losses of oil would produce increasing economic losses: that is, the ratio of economic to oil loss would increase. According to this estimate, a total loss of American oil imports for one year would result in a GNP loss of more than $150 billion in the crisis year,

which would dribble on, with decreasing force, in subsequent years. This would, of course, be an economic disaster of 1930s proportions.

These estimates, however, do not explicitly account for the manner in which the energy consumers, with appropriate government encouragement, might be able to prevent or minimize economic losses. They are derived in a fashion that may overstate in particular the costs of the initial oil losses, so leaving an impression of extreme sensitivity. Other observers have made generous estimates of the ability of industrial countries to adjust to oil supply disruptions. Cooper, for instance, said that short-term adaptability is 'surprisingly great', although he does not give evidence to support his opinion. More significantly, the experience of the United States in World War II suggests that an industrial economy can digest a big energy loss and still achieve a healthy growth rate, if the 'necessary measures' are made known and accepted by the populace.[15]

An investigation of vulnerability should include two factors: the technical aspects of oil use – the amount the consumer can save without reducing his economic contribution to the society – and his willingness to make such an effort, which will depend on the political circumstances surrounding the oil loss. The technical dimension of this problem is immensely complicated and will vary from country to country (and regionally within most countries as well). The social and political dimension is as complex. It has been necessary to simplify the discussion of these problems in order to move on to the international factors that are another pertinent focus of this Paper.

An Examination of Vulnerability

Oil is needed for four primary purposes: transport, manufacturing, heating and electricity generation. The value of the oil used by each of these sectors differs (for instance, the production of steel adds more value to the economy than a weekend trip to a resort), and this distinction

---

[12] American oil production is declining: in 1973 it was 10·9 million b/d, in 1974 10·5 million b/d, in 1975 10·0 million b/d. This will continue until Alaskan oil becomes available in 1977–8.
[13] David R. McDonald, US Department of Treasury Memorandum, 'Report of Investigation of the Effects of Petroleum Imports and Petroleum Products on the National Security pursuant to sec. 232 of the Trade Expansion Act, as amended', 13 January 1975.
[14] US Federal Energy Administration, *Project Independence Report* (Washington DC: USGPO, November 1974), pp. 364–9.
[15] See, for instance, Mansfield, *A Short History of OPA*, Office of Temporary Controls, Office of Price Administration, 1948, cited in National Petroleum Council, *Emergency Preparation for Interruption of Petroleum Imports into the United States*, Supplemental Papers to Interim Report of 15 November 1973 (Washington DC: NPC, 21 December 1973), p. 87.

becomes important when supplies are inadequate to meet demand. In order to minimize economic losses, governments will grant more oil to those uses which are deemed to have the higher economic and social values. Using Germany and France we can provide an illustration of the effects of a severe curtailment of oil supplies on each sector and then consider more specifically the nature of the consequences. Table 1 shows surprisingly

Table 1: French and West German Sector Oil Consumption as Percentage of Total Oil Consumption

	France	Germany
Agriculture	2·9	1·1
Heavy Industry	14·7	22·1
Power Plants	12·4	5·7
Light Industry	23·0	15·7
Heating	23·7	34·2
Transport	23·3	21·1

SOURCE: Appendix 1, p. 31.

small differences in the percentage of total oil supplies demanded by the various sectors in the two countries, indicating that an equivalent loss of oil might have a relatively similar effect on their economies. However, when one looks at each sector's utilization of oil in relation to other

Table 2: Percentage of French and West German Sector Energy Demand Met by Oil

	France	Germany
Agriculture	n.a.	n.a.
All Industry	61·1	49·6
Power plants	59·2	8·9
Heating	65·8	62·2
Transport	100·0	100·0

n.a. = not available.
SOURCE: *Statistics of Energy, 1959–1973* (Paris: Economic Statistics and National Accounts Division, OECD, 1974).

energy sources (Table 2) several striking differences become apparent. In the case of the two important productive sectors – industry and power – France relies more heavily on oil, and imported oil at that, than Germany. This is particularly evident in the electric power industry. The difference results from the decisions by the German government over the past two decades to maintain domestic coal production, whereas French governments allowed coal production to

decay to give way to cheaper imported oil. Equivalent disruptions of oil imports would, therefore, be more damaging to the French economy than to the German.

We can get some idea of the impact of oil losses by considering how a hypothetical disruption could be allocated among the sectors. If both countries lost 40 per cent of their oil supplies for an undetermined period, one possible allocation of the shortage is shown in Table 3. Although

Table 3: Possible Allocation of 40 per cent Reduction in French and West German Oil Supplies

Sector	% Reduction in sector supplies	% Contribution to reduction in overall supplies	
		France	Germany
Agriculture	10	0·3	0·1
Heavy industry	30	4·4	6·6
Power plants	35	4·3	2·0
Light industry	40	9·2	6·3
Heating	45	10·7	15·4
Transport	55	12·8	11·6
Total		41·7	42·0

this is but one of many potential allocation schemes, it does illustrate the nature of the problem governments face. The agricultural sector uses little oil, but its supplies are clearly vital. The extent to which oil can be conserved in the industrial and electric sectors is relatively fixed, since governments would be extremely reluctant to allow any oil supply disruption to cause a decline in industrial production. The greatest potential for conservation therefore lies in the heating and transport sectors.

Each sector responds differently to reductions in oil supplies. In the private transport sector the 55 per cent supply loss would require drastic changes in individuals' life-styles. There are various ways to take advantage of the potential conservation in this sector: for instance, to prevent maldistribution of supply a 'white market' could be created. Petrol ration coupons could be issued in equivalent numbers to all motorists, and those who needed more petrol would be allowed to purchase coupons from others willing to sell them. However, the ability of an industrial society to adjust to such changes has not really been tested, not even in 1973. But it does seem

44

possible that even a 50 per cent cut in fuel could be achieved in this sector without severe economic effects, because there are substitutes for automobile uses (especially in Europe, where there are extensive train services) and because much automobile travel can be temporarily curtailed without directly affecting employment and production – except, of course in the car service industry.[16]

The same cannot be said for the heating sector. The time of year when the supply reduction occurred and the weather would be complicating factors. Curtailing heating oil requirements by 45 per cent has more of a differential impact on consumers than petrol curtailments, because those who do not use oil for heating would not be affected at all. Furthermore, any government would come under severe pressure to prevent suffering, and, although curtailing 45 per cent of a consumer's heating oil does not mean he would necessarily be 45 per cent less warm, the unpredictability of the weather and the nature of the consequences of heating oil shortages make it difficult to take advantage of the considerable potential that exists.

The differences in vulnerability between France and Germany are more pronounced in the industrial sector than in transport and heating. An oil loss of 35 per cent would not affect Germany's overall electricity production severely, since it is substantially based on coal, but would have a very significant effect on the French electric power system and might even require electricity to be rationed, as occurred in Britain in 1973/4.

Indeed, the actions of the British government in the face of a miners' strike provide a good case study of the short-term potential of an industrial economy to adjust to an energy loss. Drastic changes were instituted: British industry went on a three-day working week, some companies were limited to 60 per cent of their normal working hours, and others were allocated only 65 per cent of their normal electricity supply. A study conducted for the government afterwards concluded that 'what would appear to have happened . . . is an increase in the awareness of management of the dynamic elements of . . . manufacturing activities. The emergency provided the pressure, and thereby the confidence to change, in some cases dramatically. . . . Increased output per hour worked was almost universally experienced.'[17] It must be mentioned, however, that the crisis only lasted three months, and the study did not hazard a guess about the consequences of a longer shortage.

The adaptability of industry to energy shortages is a key to the overall vulnerability of the economy. Within the manufacturing sector some industries are more vulnerable than others; and within industries some firms are more vulnerable than others. A company's vulnerability is largely a matter of whether it uses oil as a direct feedstock, as in chemicals; for process heating, as in glass; or for space heating, as in engineering or assembly plants.

Despite the ability of most industries to make some adjustment, a 30 per cent oil loss to the heavy industries (including those which use oil as a feedstock or for process heating) would be almost certain to result in production losses. Many of these industries have already increased their efficiency in response to the 1973 price increases. If the iron and steel, chemical, textile and cement industries, which provide the basic goods of the industrial societies, had to be deprived of oil supplies because the other sectors were already being stretched to their limits, an oil import reduction would become more than an inconvenience. Industrial output would fall, orders would have to be met from inventories until, when these were exhausted, the inability of subsidiary or 'down-stream' industries to get the basic elements of their operations would cause *their* output to decline. As a consequence, production and employment losses would rise very quickly.

Quantified estimates of the level of economic loss resulting from various levels and duration of

[16] Several studies have concluded, however, that the 'psychological' reaction to the curtailments of petrol can have a substantial economic effect. For example, during the 1973–4 embargo American car sales declined sharply, apparently as a result of the consumer's fear of continuing petrol shortages. However, more detailed studies reveal that, while demand for large automobiles dropped sharply, the demand for compacts actually increased beyond the capability of companies to supply them. See US Federal Energy Administration, *The Short-term Microeconomic Impact of the Oil Embargo* (Washington DC: USGPO, n.d.).

[17] 'Preliminary Study into the Effects of the Three-Day Working Week' (MCH Consultants Ltd for the National Economic Development Office, April 1974, unpublished paper).

oil loss are not available in the public literature. Nevertheless, it is safe to conclude from this discussion that a 40 per cent reduction in supplies to France and Germany would cause a considerable loss in production. In theory, one might be able to identify a level and duration of oil supply loss that could be labelled 'tolerable', or 'less than severe', and argue that anything less should not be considered a security threat. Conversely, somewhere there exists a 'zone' where the economic effects begin to pile on top of one another, and where production and employment begin to decrease exponentially and, no doubt, alarmingly. Governments cannot be certain where this zone lies, since previous energy disruptions (in peacetime) have not reached it. Opinions on where it lies vary from government to government, and even ministry to ministry, and this uncertainty is part of the overall political problem created by dependence on energy supplies that can be disrupted for political reasons.

This 'technical uncertainty' is compounded by the uncertainties about public reaction to the crisis. That reaction is bound to be influenced by variables – such as attitudes towards the issue responsible for the crisis and towards the government, the time of year (a winter shortage would be physically more uncomfortable than a summer one), and the overall health of the economy. In the 1973–4 crisis, various governments' support for Israeli actions led to the Arab oil curtailments. These occurred in the autumn and winter but – as a result of mild weather and, in most countries, effective allocation of supplies by industry and government – the people of the industrial states did not suffer from the cold. In most countries the economic downturn which lasted until 1976 was beginning. Finally, the curtailments were suspended in part in January 1974, and in full in March. As a result, the supply reduction did not actually cause severe problems. Moreover, there was no strong groundswell of public reaction against the Arab countries, Israel, the United States or the other parties that various schools of thought held responsible for the curtailments. In short, public tolerance was not really tested. We simply do not know how much longer the crisis would have been endured, nor in what policy direction 'non-endurance' would have pushed governments.

One analyst has recently noted that 'a threat to economic security is not only a function of the magnitude of an external economic influence, but also of the strength of the socio-political systems which are confronted by such a challenge.'[18] It seems likely that a 40 per cent loss of oil would lead, in time, to a collective 'loss of temper' in almost every importing country, but the 1973–4 crisis (in which many countries lost 10 to 15 per cent of their oil supplies for four or five months) did not do so. Somewhere in between these levels of loss, therefore, there must lie a zone of rapidly decreasing tolerance. In the remainder of this discussion, it will be assumed, somewhat arbitrarily, that this zone lies at a level of 20 to 30 per cent loss (the critical zone for duration, which will be discussed below, is even more difficult to approximate). But it should be emphasized that little is known about this problem. Much depends upon the political circumstances surrounding the event. Subsequent sections will consider those circumstances and use the 20 to 30 per cent estimate as a means to translate the 'technical uncertainties' into the political problems that are the next focus of the study.

The Role of Oil Stockpiles
In addition to restraints on domestic energy demand, energy stockpiles – which exist in every country, though at substantially different levels (see Appendix 3) – can help to offset oil import losses. Their utility for emergency purposes, however, is limited by several factors. To illustrate, we can once again contrast France and Germany. In France, where the government regulates the minimum stock level, an average oil stockpile of 214 million barrels, or 113 days of oil consumption requirement, was maintained in 1975; and in Germany, where the government imposed a lower requirement, 169 million barrels, or 73 days of oil consumption requirements, were held.[19]

Assuming for the moment that the minimum oil stock level required by the industry to provide the economy with the necessary kinds and amounts of products is 50 days of consumption, and that a 40 per cent reduction of oil imports occurs, it is possible to determine the

---

[18] Wolfgang Hager, *Europe's Economic Security* (Paris: Atlantic Institute, February 1976), pp. 15–16.
[19] Taken from US Central Intelligence Agency, *International Oil Developments: Statistical Survey* (Washington DC: USGPO, 12 August 1976). The report does not cite the source of the data.

Table 4: Possible Duration of French and West German Oil Emergency Reserves Under Various Management Assumptions (1975 Data)

	France	West Germany
'Emergency reserves' (stocks in excess of 50 days' consumption, 000 barrels)	102,606	48,160
Oil imports with 40% reduction (000 b/d)	1,344	1,530
Government oil consumption target levels (000 b/d):		
Plan A 90%	2,016	2,398
Plan B 80%	1,792	2,132
Plan C 70%	1,568	1,865
Oil supply shortfall (000 b/d) under:		
Plan A	672	868
Plan B	448	602
Plan C	224	335
Duration of emergency reserves (days):		
Plan A	152	55
Plan B	229	80
Plan C	458	144

SOURCES: Stock data from Appendix 3. Consumption data from *BP Statistical Review of the World Oil Industry, 1975* (London: British Petroleum Company, 1976).
See note in Appendix 3 for qualifications on the use of stock estimates.

number of days the government can use stocks to maintain a given level of oil consumption.[20] Table 4 shows that the higher levels of stocks might enable France to maintain a given level of consumption longer than Germany. However, due to the greater vulnerability of the French economy, the French government might maintain a higher level of oil consumption (Plan A), thus reducing the difference between the two countries in the duration of emergency reserves.

Oil stocks, as this example illustrates, can even out differences in economic vulnerability among industrial countries. This apparently lies behind the pattern which to some extent already exists of some countries (e.g. France, Italy and Japan) maintaining higher stock levels, measured against consumption, than others (e.g. Germany and the Netherlands). Whether the stock levels are

adequate, however, depends upon the level and duration of a supply reduction: the higher the level of oil stocks, the more severe and protracted a disruption of oil imports an economy can withstand. Thus, oil stocks are simply a kind of insurance policy. There is financial risk involved in under- or over-insuring (though it is seldom possible to know the appropriateness of cover beforehand), and the fear of over-insuring prevents many governments from building the really massive stockpiles that would materially increase their security against even the most dire prospects.[21]

While it is true that many nations plan to increase their stock levels, many of them to comply with the obligations of the IEA and the EEC, the United States and Japan appear determined to make the largest increases. In 1975 US Congress authorized the early stages of a programme which could lead to a 1,000-million-barrel 'National Strategic Petroleum Reserve' by 1981. In 1976 the Japanese government announced its intention to build up 180 days of stocks by 1980.[22]

Such massive reserves would protect the United States and Japan against a variety of reductions in oil imports. Suppose, for instance, that in 1980 America imports 10 million b/d and consumes 20 million b/d; and that somehow imports fall by six million b/d as a result of a deliberate supply curtailment by a group of oil exporters. The life of the 1,000-million-barrel American reserve under various demand restraint programmes can be shown as follows:

Replace all lost imports with oil from reserve	167 days
Replace half lost imports with demand restraint, half from reserve	333 days
Replace lost oil with maximum demand restraint (25% of consumption), the rest from reserve	1,000 days

[20] For discussion of minimum stock levels needed to assure adequate operation of the distribution system, see p.49.

[21] The costs of creating facilities for storing oil are estimated at $0·85–$1·55 per barrel for underground (salt dome) storage and $6–$12 per barrel for aboveground storage. In addition, of course, there is the cost of the oil itself and the cost of tying up the capital required for the project. Source: National Petroleum Council, *Petroleum Storage for National Security* (Washington DC: NPC, August 1975).

[22] Platt's *Oilgram*, 23 June 1976. A 100-million-barrel stockpile in Italy, for example, could involve an initial outlay of $1·6 billion, and carrying costs of $100 million per year.

This simple arithmetic shows that if the United States Government were willing to cut demand to the bone before drawing down stocks, it would greatly prolong the period over which a deliberate curtailment would have to be maintained before the American economy would be seriously affected.

Stocks in Europe will apparently not be built up to the proposed American level. At best, all the other major countries except France will build up to only 90 days of consumption (which for these countries, excepting Britain, is equivalent to imports). Even if demand were curtailed by 20 per cent, their emergency reserves would be used up in about six months in the event of a major (40 per cent) reduction of imports.[23]

Are such stocks sufficient against a determined adversary? Most proponents of the security benefits of stockpiles argue that producers could not afford to curtail production long enough to exhaust such reserves. But the countries most likely to curtail production are also those which are generating funds in excess of their immediate requirements, and much of the oil that will be used to fill the storage tanks will come from their fields. In any case, though, stocks are valuable because they 'buy time', creating a lag between the day of the export reduction and the day the import shortage cannot be replaced. Nonetheless it should not be thought that they provide absolute security against deliberate supply reductions. Rather, they should be considered an element which disrupters of oil supplies must take into account when they are planning their strategies.

The International Energy Programme

The preceding discussion described the problem a reduction in oil supplies creates for individual economies. It is now necessary to consider the international factors which determine how a world disruption of oil supplies affects distribution to importers. This involves international agreements, the multi-national oil companies and the actions of the oil producers.

The starting point for this discussion is the International Energy Programme (IEP). In response to the 1973–4 oil crisis, the United States called the Washington Energy Conference in February 1974. The conference created the Energy Co-ordinating Group and charged it with designing a collective energy position on the various problems the governments had identified. The outcome was an agreement to set up the International Energy Agency, with an emergency programme establishing rules to deal with future supply disruptions. The IEP was similar to the programme which had existed in the OECD Oil Committee, but the full participation of the United States, and the establishment of a framework in which the oil companies would be required to participate, have given the IEP a greater potential influence in the management of oil supply curtailments.[24]

The objectives of the emergency programme of the IEP are quite simple. When a reduction in oil imports occurs, supplies will be allocated according to predetermined formulae. When only one or more members lose over 7 per cent of their normal oil supplies (measured against supplies in a recent base period) the rest of the members will share any additional loss that may occur. An individual country, therefore, can anticipate losing no more than 7 per cent of its oil supplies up to the point where the whole group loses that amount. When the supplies of the whole group fall by more than 7 per cent, each member's loss will be determined as follows: first, all members will lose 7 per cent of their normal oil supplies if the group shortfall is between 7 and 10 per cent, and 10 per cent of normal supplies if the group shortfall is greater than 12 per cent; second, any remaining deficit will be distributed on the basis of import shares. Countries which produce oil internally (the United States, Canada, West Germany, Austria, Turkey and Britain) naturally have a smaller import share than consumption share. In this manner, the programme gives 'credit' to countries which produce some of their own oil. Appendix 2 on p. 71 illustrates the effect of the allocation programme. Note that the five producing countries (Britain was not producing oil in 1975) have a higher ratio of supply rights to normal consumption.

---

[23] Both governments and oil companies are uncertain what really happens as stocks are drawn down below the various 'working levels'. For that very reason they will be reluctant to approach these thresholds.

[24] A list of IEA members can be found in Appendix 5. The text of the agreement, as well as an extensive discussion of its implications, can be found in *The International Energy Program: Hearings before The Senate Committee on Interior and Insular Affairs* (Washington DC: USGPO, 1975).

The programme allows countries to make up the shortfall in energy supplies in any way they choose. For most of them, however, the choice will be between reducing supplies to their consumers and drawing on oil stocks. Thus, most countries will have to rely on oil stocks to avoid having to curtail consumption more than 10 per cent. This naturally requires that sufficient stocks should be available.

As implied in the previous discussion, estimates of the availability of stocks for use in emergencies have varied widely. In the initial discussions of the IEP, it was decided to use the standard OECD definition of stock levels (formulated for reporting purposes), to deduct from this figure the oil used to fill pipelines and held in various other industrial facilities, deduct an additional 10 per cent, and then call the remainder an 'emergency reserve'.[25] It was quickly noted by other observers that these estimates created an unrealistic picture of the situation. As Senator Henry Jackson said, 'we are giving the appearance of a strategic reserve – what we are really doing is talking about the oil that is in the pipeline system'.[26] The United States National Petroleum Council (NPC) studied the utilization of existing industry stocks in the United States and concluded the American emergency reserve base was only 150 million barrels (23 days of imports) rather than the 977 million barrels (158 days) calculated by using the IEA definition. The essential difference between the NPC and IEA estimates is that the latter considered oil in working stocks as part of the emergency reserve; the NPC did not, stating that this supply would be needed to 'keep the oil logistic system operating efficiently' and recommending that it should not be included in calculations of American reserves.[27] The NPC recommendation that the United States build a 'real' emergency reserve of 500 million barrels got wide support from both branches of government and from political parties, and funding was authorized in 1975. The new American reserve, however, will not be in place before 1981.

The stock situation in Europe is even more complex. The European Economic Community, the IEA and various national governments have imposed stock guidelines and requirements, but the definitions of stocks differ, and an estimate of how much of them could be used without replacement in an emergency is not available. It is generally agreed that the IEA definition of 'emergency reserves' overstates the amount that can be withdrawn, and oil industry specialists believe that, as a rule, 40 to 50 days of oil supplies must be held in stock to allow smooth operation of the distribution system. Thus, the amount of time purchased for importers by the IEP and its stock drawdown policies is more limited than a superficial examination suggests (see final column in Appendix 2). And once emergency reserves are depleted, there is little the IEA members can do to help one another cope with large import losses.

The IEP has not yet had to be implemented; at the time of writing, only its technical ability to process the data and run the allocation system had just been tested after two years of work by the Agency. During this technical 'start-up' period, the IEP has been touted, particularly by the US State Department, primarily as a deterrent against the imposition of supply curtailments and as a tool to encourage a joint political approach by the importers. A State Department official said: 'By agreeing in advance how we will prepare for and respond to another supply cut-off, we have greatly reduced the risk that another embargo will result in the type of conflict and strain in our overall relationship which occurred in the last crisis – and by demonstrating our collective determination to increase our ability to withstand the economic impact of a supply interruption, we have limited the effectiveness of the so-called oil weapon.'[28]

However, in the light of factors discussed earlier, it is clear that there are some obstacles to such success. First of all, some countries are clearly more vulnerable to oil losses than others. Among IEA members, the United States, Canada, Britain, the Netherlands and West Germany would suffer less from a given oil shortage than Japan, Italy, Belgium, Spain, Sweden, Denmark, Switzerland and the other minor members, because oil constitutes a smaller percentage of their total energy requirement. Secondly, although stocks could reduce the differences in vulnerability between the two groups, only Japan and Switzerland in the more vulnerable category

[25] *Ibid.*, pp. 36, 94.
[26] *Ibid.*, p. 33.
[27] *Op. cit.* in note 21, p. 11.

[28] *Op. cit.* in note 24, p. 23.

seem committed to increasing stocks significantly. Although the IEA members have agreed to attain 90 days of oil consumption in stock by 1980, which would increase the length of time the group could withstand a given level of oil loss, the conclusion that this 'greatly reduces' the risk of another embargo assumes that the oil producers would be deterred simply because they would have to hold a given reduction in exports a few months longer. This conclusion would be more easily justified if many more IEA members committed themselves to accumulating really substantial emergency reserves. On the record to date this does not seem likely. The unwillingness to agree to substantial increases in stocks is the Achilles' heel of the Agreement, and it implies that many members do not take seriously the

threat of a significant reduction in supplies. As a result, should such a reduction occur, there is a substantial risk that the more vulnerable and the 'understocked' will find it difficult to go along with their IEA partners.

Finally, the will to co-operate in meeting an oil shortage must also be questioned. It is unlikely that IEA members will agree in advance on a common political view on the next Arab–Israeli dispute. But if such a common political ground is not found when the next crisis occurs, can the IEP work? Would consuming countries whose views differ from the IEA leader, the United States, want it to work? This is the most difficult problem of all, and one to which we shall be returning after completing the survey of other energy importers.

II. ECONOMIC VULNERABILITY OF DEVELOPING COUNTRIES

So far, we have discussed only the vulnerability and supply security measures of the major countries, because they dominate the world energy import market. There are, however, some eighty other countries that also import oil and are vulnerable to disruptions.

The developing countries, like the OECD members, have differing degrees of dependence and vulnerability. People often distinguish three kinds of non-industrial states: the lower-income countries, e.g. Uganda; the middle-income countries, e.g. Liberia; and the higher-income countries, e.g. Zambia. Most developing countries have two distinct economic sectors. Energy use in the urban sector approximates that of developed countries, and oil and electricity are the primary fuels; in the rural sector heat is simply obtained from the combustion of wood or coal. A disruption of oil imports would primarily affect the urban areas. In the lower-income countries, therefore, a very small segment of the population would be affected while in the higher-income countries the energy loss might affect a large number, depending on the extent to which the economies are integrated. The vulnerability of Brazil, for instance, which imports more than 500,000 b/d, is more comparable with that of developed than developing economies.

Aside from differences in economic structure, the vulnerability of developing countries also varies as a result of their petroleum industries and

the manner in which oil supplies are transported into the country. Many countries do not have any domestic fossil fuel production. A smaller number have no refineries and must rely on neighbouring countries or distant refiners for their products. Landlocked nations must rely on their neighbours' willingness to allow oil to pass through, and many countries that do have access to the sea have only one port at which oil can be loaded.

Table 5 categorizes developing countries according to their vulnerability to disruption of oil imports. The countries in each category face different security threats. The 'most vulnerable' can have their oil imports disrupted by the oil producer, the supplying company and the transit state. Since the volumes involved are so small, most states in this category rely on a single exporter and a single company. At the same time, however, the amount of oil is so small that it is easy for a company, especially a major oil company, to replace the oil should the producer decide to embargo the country.

A more serious source of concern is the ability of a neighbouring country to block the flow of imports. When conflicts occur between the landlocked state and a neighbour through which oil normally passes, international conventions and the economic loss of transit fees forgone may not be sufficient to deter the transit state from blocking the flow of oil. In the summer of 1976 an

Table 5: Developing Countries, by Vulnerability of Oil Supplies

Most vulnerable

Latin America
Paraguay

Near East
Afghanistan

Africa
Mali
Upper Volta
Niger
Chad
Central African Republic
Botswana
Rhodesia
Malawi
Zambia
Uganda

Highly vulnerable

Latin America and Caribbean
Haiti
Cuba
Dominican Republic
Panama
Belize
Uruguay
The Guianas

Near East
Pakistan

Far East
Hong Kong
Laos
Cambodia
Vietnam
North Korea

Africa
Mauritania
Gambia
Port Guinea
Guinea
Togo
Dahomey
Cameroon
Equatorial Guinea
Somalia
Ethiopia

Moderately vulnerable

Latin America
Costa Rica
Guatemala
Honduras
El Salvador
Nicaragua
Barbados
Netherlands Antilles
Jamaica
Bahamas
Chile
Brazil

Middle East
Jordan
Lebanon
Israel
Turkey

Near East
Bangladesh
Sri Lanka
India

Far East
South Korea
Taiwan
The Philippines

Africa
Morocco
Senegal
Sierra Leone
Ivory Coast
Ghana
South Africa
Mozambique
Tanzania
Kenya
Sudan
Malagasy Republic

Least vulnerable

Latin America
Peru
Argentina

Most vulnerable: landlocked countries with little or no domestic oil production and little or no refinery capacity.

Highly vulnerable: coastal states with little or no domestic oil production and little or no refinery capacity.

Moderately vulnerable: countries with little or no domestic production and sufficient domestic refinery capacity.

Least vulnerable: countries with substantial domestic oil production.

instance of disruption by a transit state occurred when oil bound for Uganda was stopped by Kenya. This 'embargo' affected Uganda almost immediately, because she has no domestic refinery and consequently very few oil stocks. To compound the difficulty, there was no alternative route by which Uganda could acquire oil, except possibly by air in tanker planes, which few countries have. An oil shortage would not have affected the activities of most Ugandans, but it did have a significant effect on Uganda's military capability. Had a war with Kenya broken out, it is quite possible that the Ugandan armed forces would not have had sufficient oil to defend the country. Kenya's embargo was thus clearly a threat to Uganda's national security, and President Amin's willingness to accede to Kenyan demands, after several weeks of the embargo, is evidence that the use of the oil weapon in this instance was highly effective.[29]

'Highly vulnerable' countries are less likely to suffer at the hands of their neighbours – though, in the case of war, countries with only one port still have a problem if the port facilities are destroyed. In peacetime these countries are vulnerable also to the actions of their refiners. Guyana, for instance, receives her petroleum products from Venezuela and, should supplies from this source no longer be available, would have to find another refiner. Under most conceivable circumstances, this should not be difficult, since the amount needed is so small; the lack of a domestic refinery, however, means there is probably little oil stored, so replacement oil would have to be found rapidly.

'Moderately vulnerable' countries, which have sufficient refining capacity for domestic needs, could not be deprived of their oil supplies by neighbouring countries' actions, short of destruction of refining facilities; their vulnerability is to the oil suppliers and the oil companies. The two countries in this category whose political situation makes their energy vulnerability most interesting are Israel and South Africa. In 1975 Israel returned part of the Sinai Peninsula to Egypt and she also lost control over the Abu Rudeis oil field, which had been producing 70,000 b/d, and without it she produces less than 1,000 b/d.[30] South Africa has been officially embargoed by

the Organization of Arab Petroleum Exporting Countries since 1973. However, she continues to receive oil from other sources at about 250,000 b/d, and, as in the case of Israel, the embargo does not result in a chronic shortage of imported oil.

If the oil companies are observing the Arab embargo, they must be shipping Iranian, Nigerian, Indonesian or Venezuelan crude supplies to the two countries. Iran seems the most likely source, since the Shah has repeatedly stated that his government does not care to determine the destination of its oil. In addition, the National Iranian Oil Company is a partner in at least one South African refinery, and supplies crude oil to South Africa.[30] In both cases, the relationships of the governments with the international oil companies and with a single producing country are sufficient to provide the needed oil imports. Should all the OPEC countries order their companies to suspend shipments, Israel and South Africa might face real difficulties, and in anticipation of this possibility, both regimes have taken measures to minimize their dependence on oil imports and to build up large stocks. They may also be able to replenish their supplies in part by purchasing oil in various 'spot markets', where individual cargoes are available and where it is possible to camouflage both the source of the oil and its destination. Since neither country uses vast quantities of oil, such purchases – in addition to demand restraint and stocks – would probably enable both to survive a determined OPEC embargo indefinitely. It would appear that dependence on oil imports, even though creating complex problems, does not pose an effective threat to national survival.

The 'least vulnerable' countries, with considerable domestic oil production (though short of self-sufficiency), may temporarily increase production, use up their petroleum stocks, or reduce demand should their imports be curtailed.

In all four categories, the vulnerability of a specific non-OECD nation to direct action by OPEC is less than that of the industrial states. The oil companies and the various spot markets could provide easy alternatives, since the supply needs of most of these countries are so small. Of course, the greater the import dependence, the more difficult it may be: Brazil, which imports 600,000 b/d, would have a more difficult time than the Ivory Coast.

---

[29] See the *Financial Times*, 22 July 1976.
[30] *International Petroleum Encyclopedia, 1976* (Tulsa, Okla.: Petroleum Publishing Co., 1976), p. 132.

The developing countries, individually and as a group, face a more serious threat when OPEC reduces oil supplies in a conflict with the OECD. A general shortage creates greater competition for the available supplies, and can lead to higher prices, as it did in 1973. Many poorer countries found it difficult to afford the oil, and a price-induced 'shortage' resulted. In addition, the strain of having to pay the higher prices set back the development programmes in many countries and led to a real reduction in national income.[31]

The IEA's emergency programme tries to take the vulnerability of the developing countries into account. Article 11 of the Agreement states that 'it is not the objective of the Programme to seek to increase in an emergency, the share of world supply that the group had under normal market conditions . . . due account should be taken of the position of the individual non-participating countries'. However, although the IEA will not try to increase its share, even maintaining its share of a smaller supply will cause the non-participating countries to lose some oil. In addition, some countries are bound to do worse than others in the competition for available supplies. The primary source of security in this event will be the oil companies. Holding vast quantities of oil in transit, their willingness to provide particular shipments of oil will determine whether the individual countries will suffer or not.

III. ENERGY PROSPECTS OF THE COMMUNIST COUNTRIES

The position of energy affairs in the East–West balance has been overshadowed by the conflicts between OPEC and the OECD. This is not surprising in the light of the near self-sufficiency of the Communist group and, as a consequence, their extremely minor involvement in world energy trade.

Appendix 4 on p. 72 presents statistics on the oil situation in the Soviet Union, Eastern Europe and China. The European Communist countries consume significant quantities of energy – on a per capita basis, as much as many OECD countries – but they still rely on coal to a far greater extent and are only gradually shifting to oil. Indeed, Italy alone consumes as much oil as all the East European states together; the total oil imports of the Council for Mutual Economic Assistance (COMECON) in 1975 could have been met by Abu Dhabi alone; and Soviet oil exports to the West were only 5 per cent of OECD total imports. In the OECD the leading importer of Soviet oil was Italy, and she received only 135 thousand b/d, or 6 per cent of her total imports.[32]

As with the OECD, there is uncertainty and much speculation regarding the energy future of the Communist countries. Most forecasters predict that the current relationship between the Communist and non-Communist energy systems will not change significantly before 1980.[33] COMECON will not significantly increase its purchases of OPEC oil, in large part because it cannot easily muster the required foreign currency; the Soviet Union has agreed to continue shipments of most of her oil exports to Eastern Europe,[34] in large part to maintain the economic structure of the alliance; and China, according to most analysts and the most recent evidence, will not be able to become a major exporter before 1980.

Observers of energy matters in Communist countries are in wide disagreement about prospects beyond 1980. There has been speculation that Soviet oil production could 'take-off',[35] and also that COMECON will face an 'energy crisis'.[36] To get an idea of the range of potential changes, we can examine the most pessimistic projection about rates of growth of COMECON's energy pro-

---

[31] *Energy and Petroleum in non-OPEC Developing Countries* (op. cit. in note 4).
[32] British Petroleum Company, *BP Statistical Review of the World Oil Industry – 1975* (London: British Petroleum Company, 1976).

[33] For full discussion see Jeremy Russell, *Energy as a Factor in Soviet Foreign Policy* (Farnborough, Hants: Saxon House, 1975) and Iain F. Elliot, *The Soviet Energy Balance* (London: Praeger, 1974).
[34] This is evident in the Soviet Union's 1976–80 plan, as presented in *Guidelines for the Development of the National Economy of the USSR for 1976–1980* (Moscow: Novosti Press Agency, Vol. XI 17, No. 12 (1890) 12 March 1976), p. 20.
[35] See, for instance, letter from D. Rigassi of *Russian Petroleum Press Review* to *The Middle East*, December 1975, citing the 'enormous potential of the USSR, possibly to exceed that of the Middle East within the relatively near future'.
[36] *Christian Science Monitor*, 28 May 1974.

duction and consumption (zero growth in production and an annual 4 per cent growth in consumption): total COMECON import requirements would be only 1 million b/d in 1980 and 4 million b/d in 1985. According to a contrasting projection, to maintain the Communist bloc's energy autarchy, the Soviet Union's East Siberian onshore and Far East off-shore deposits must be developed and transported to the Western Soviet Union. This will be a tremendous undertaking. The difficulties of operating in the hostile environment nearly as far from the industrial centres of the Soviet Union as it is possible to go, requiring thousands of miles of pipelines, a vast number of pumping stations and much money, have moved some to conclude the Soviet Union must have Western assistance in technology, oil company involvement and credit.[37]

It must be noted, however, that the Soviet oil industry has developed to the position of the world's leading producer of oil without large-scale Western involvement, so it would be an unwise assumption that it is incapable of going it alone. Nevertheless, it is true that Western involvement could help, and this fact poses an interesting question for Western policy-makers. Is it in the OECD's energy, economic and security interests to help the Soviet Union increase energy production? Would the West prefer an energy-autarchic COMECON, or one involved in the world markets? In essence, these are 'strategic' questions, in that they influence the military capability and political flexibility of the Communist states, and they raise several important issues.

First, it is interesting to observe that Secretary of State Kissinger and other officials have stated that the United States is developing a 'trade strategy' as a part of America's overall policy towards the Soviet Union: 'We have seen trade as a set of instrumentalities to address the set of problems we face with the Soviets. We have to find a way to develop a coherent trade strategy that goes beyond the commercial views of individual firms'.[38] In the light of the Soviet Union's own objective 'to realize measures aimed at the SU's wider participation in the international division of labour',[39] it is possible that energy trade will be affected by the increased importance and political flavour of Soviet–American trade.

In the context of increased East–West economic interaction, the Soviet energy objective will be to use Western assistance to help increase oil and gas production, while it appears that the American objective will be to make that help conditional upon proper Soviet behaviour. The 'strategic' outcome, in terms of effectiveness in channelling Soviet behaviour, will depend upon how much the Soviet Union needs help, and how adeptly the United States implements her trade strategy. Neither of these is clear at this time, but several observations can nevertheless be made.

Energy technology will not be easy to include in a deliberate American trade strategy. For one thing, it could be argued that the most experienced company in both off-shore and cold-climate oil operations is the British Petroleum Company. The Soviet Union could get much of the technology she needs from BP if American companies were barred from dealing with her, unless the United States could induce Britain to apply similar restrictions on her companies' activities. In addition, the concept of a Soviet technological deficiency is conspicuously absent from two of the recent major studies of Soviet energy affairs,[40] which characterize Soviet energy problems as infrastructure deficiencies and capital constraints, rather than critical technological gaps. Western assistance, therefore, may not be essential but, rather, desirable and helpful.

The second question concerns Eastern Europe and its relationship with the Soviet Union, OPEC

---

[37] For example, 'The hoped for *deus ex machina* is the foreign capitalist. The feat required . . . is such that only United States and Canadian technology can help'. From Joseph Yaeger and Eleanor Steinberg, *Energy and US Foreign Policy* (Cambridge, Mass: Ballinger, 1974).
[38] US State Department, 'Text of Sonnenfeldt's remarks on Eastern Europe', and 'Kissinger on managing the emergence of Russia as a super-power', official non-verbatim summaries of remarks made at a meeting in December 1975; *International Herald Tribune*, 26 April 1976. Kissinger does not appear to consider the long-standing US government restrictions, dating from the Export Control Act of 1949, a sufficient strategy. For detailed discussions of US economic policy towards the Communist countries see US Senate, Committee on Foreign Relations, Subcommittee on Multi-national Corporations, *Multi-national Corporations and United States Foreign Policy*, Part 10 (Washington DC: USGPO, 1975); US Senate, Committee on Foreign Relations, *Investments by Multi-national Companies in the Communist Bloc Countries* (Washington DC: USGPO, June 1974); and Gunnar Adler-Karlsson, *Western Economic Warfare, 1947–67* (Stockholm: Almquist and Wiksell, 1968).
[39] *Op. cit.* in note 34, p. 79.
[40] By Russell and Elliot (see note 33).

and the OECD. Soviet energy supply has been one of the building blocks of the COMECON. For years, Soviet oil has been utilized by every East European country except Romania, and the oil has been available on 'soft terms'; that is, requiring no foreign currency payment and at a low price. The Soviet Union has already agreed to continue to provide oil through the remainder of this decade. In this energy relationship, the East Europeans find themselves even more vulnerable to reductions in energy imports than the OECD countries. They resemble the landlocked developing countries in having a single supplier, and most of the oil comes in by pipeline, which could easily be cut by the Soviet Union. The political situation, of course, is different: the purpose of COMECON is to develop a mutually beneficial economic interdependence, and the Soviet Union has never used the direct threat of an oil embargo to change or prevent change in the behaviour of one of her allies. However, the possibility does exist, and the potential for causing damage is considerable.

In the 1980s, it is possible that a significant change will occur in the COMECON energy system. If Soviet oil production is lower than expected, or if demand grows faster than expected, it will be necessary to import oil. The upper limit on this demand, as stated previously, should be about four million b/d, in 1985.[41] If the East Europeans are forced to turn to OPEC oil, they will probably have to earn several times the current levels of foreign currency to pay for it,[42] and therefore will have to gear their economies to produce more goods for export to members of the OECD and OPEC. If so, this would be a serious retreat from the COMECON ideal of an economic market, and the trade links with OECD and OPEC could halt or hinder the further development of the Communist regional economy. As an alternative, the Soviet Union could choose to import oil herself

and continue to send her own petroleum to East Europe. In this case, as a buyer for her bloc, she would be dealing with the oil producers as the third largest customer for oil imports. Western governments might prefer East European countries to deal individually with the OPEC states.

There is a third possibility, that neither the Soviet Union nor the East European governments will be able to develop adequate oil trade relationships with the OPEC states, or raise enough foreign exchange to buy the desired quantity of imports. To avoid this, the Soviet Union may feel it is important to develop political relations with several major oil producers long before the dependence on imports grows to major proportions. Saudi Arabia and Iran are obvious targets. However, although both are bound to want cordial relations with the Soviet Union, they also prefer to pattern their new industries on, and purchase most of their imports from, the OECD states. Iraq and Algeria have been willing to barter oil for Soviet goods and assistance, but they still deal largely with the hard currency areas. Given OPEC's general preference for Western trade and technology, the Soviet leaders must worry about their source of future oil imports, should they be necessary. A client state in the Middle East willing to deal largely with the Communist countries may become a major requirement in Soviet foreign policy.

Finally, there are two possibilities which could enable the OECD's energy dependence to be exploited by the Soviet Union. The first concerns the possibility that the Soviet Union could cut the OECD's seaborne oil supply lines. This is an old problem. Tankers are difficult to defend against attack by submarine, aircraft or cruise missile, and the Straits of Hormuz, the most important oil transit bottleneck, can be blocked or mined. The Soviet capability for this, however, is more properly analysed in a military assessment of the relationship between NATO and the Warsaw Pact. Action against oil supply lines would occur only in a general war, or would be sufficient provocation to start a war, and NATO's response would not be solely on the seas but would be aimed at the Pact's particular weak points. One other observation is apt. The interdiction of oil supplies does not create an immediate strategic advantage: as in the case of an OPEC embargo, oil stocks could be used to keep the economy going for some months, and in the crisis atmosphere

---

[41] It could be much higher if the Communist countries are on the verge of a period of very rapid economic growth. Almost all forecasts in the early 1960s underestimated the OECD's energy requirements for this same reason. Oil was cheap in those days, however, and it may not be possible to reach such high growth rates at current energy prices.

[42] On 6 September 1976, according to the *Financial Times*, the Czechoslovak government announced that Czech purchases of Soviet crude would fall short of the agreement negotiated for the period 1976–80 by an unspecified amount.

created by the outbreak of war civilian consumption could be drastically cut.

The second possibility concerns the Soviet–OPEC relationship. One of the roles the Soviet Union has been able to play successfully is that of the disinterested but concerned party in OPEC's dispute with the industrial states. This role becomes useful when an OPEC government takes action that is unpopular in the OECD (e.g. Iraqi and Libyan expropriations of oil company assets) and faces actual or threatened reprisals. The Soviet Union has provided political, military and economic support to oil countries in these circumstances. Political assistance came in the form of declarations of support, and military assistance in the form of military goods and, in the case of Iraq, a security guarantee; economic support came in the form of purchases of oil, primarily by means of barter deals. These gains could be illusory – in oil affairs, for instance, neither Libya nor Iraq has shunned oil exports to the OECD – but the Soviet support may have been very helpful in enabling them to withstand the initial fears of the consequences of their actions. Such Soviet support would be very important if the OPEC country involved were Saudi Arabia. Although it is unlikely that the conservative Saudi regime would seek an overt alliance with the Soviet Union, it is possible that in the face of strong pressure from the OECD the Saudi government would welcome discreet assurances that the Soviet Union would be prepared to render economic, political or military assistance.

The energy prospects of China are unclear, and there have been widely conflicting estimates of her oil production potential in the 1980s.[43] It is worth noting that China's exports for 1976 did not show significant increases over 1975. Furthermore, the Japanese government, China's primary customer, has apparently set a maximum planning target for Chinese imports in 1981 of only 300,000 b/d.[44] However, if the reserves and technology allow, China may increase production so as to discourage Japan from involvement in the Soviet East Siberian oil development projects. Moving that oil west to the Soviet Union or east to the Sea of Japan will require establishing a network of pipelines, roads and service communities in some of the prime areas of potential Sino–Soviet clashes. If she has not done so already, China may try to entice Japan away from involvement in this project with offers of future oil supplies, and the offer will be all the more attractive because, by virtue of government policy and more favourable geographic location, Chinese oil development will not require large-scale financial or technological involvement for Japan.

There is no other area of the world where energy decisions so directly affect purely strategic considerations, and this puts Japan in a difficult position. She clearly wants to reduce her extreme dependence on the Persian Gulf, and both Communist sources provide welcome diversification of energy supply. She may consider Soviet oil more secure than Chinese oil, but Soviet oil requires much capital, and providing the capital may sour relations with China. For Japan, therefore, energy complicates an already difficult political situation.

IV. THE WORLD OIL MARKET

Having surveyed the vulnerability of the three groups of importers, it is necessary to examine the links in the international system that tie them to the oil exporters, for these relationships influence to a great extent the circumstances in which energy supplies can be threatened, and also the extent to which energy security can influence other international relationships. In effect, this section is a description of the world oil 'market', and since the industrial states and their companies dominate the market, the developing and Communist countries will not figure prominently. The OECD emphasis leads to the role of energy strategies in international politics, in Section V.

Geographical Factors

Table 6 shows the flow of oil from the world's export centres to the importers. By scanning the

[43] For the conservative view, see Vaclav Smith, 'Energy in China: Achievements and Prospects', *China Quarterly*, March 1976. For the optimistic view, see Selig Harrison, 'China, the Next Oil Giant', *Foreign Policy*, Fall 1975.

[44] *Neue Zürcher Zeitung*, 4 February 1976; *Far Eastern Economic Review*, 23 January 1976.

Table 6: World Oil Flows 1975 (000 b/d)

Exports from:	United States	Canada	Latin America	Western Europe	Africa	South-East Asia	Japan	Australia	Other eastern hemisphere	Total exports
United States	—	20	65	70	5	—	30	10	10	210
Canada	800	—	—	—	—	—	—	—	—	800
Latin America	2,270ᵃ	270	120	380	40	—	20	—	75	3,175
Western Europe	45	—	—	—	165	—	—	—	35	245
Middle East	1,140	540	1,525	8,815	475	1,450	3,675	255	630	18,505
North Africa	500	—	140	1,530	—	—	70	—	165	2,405
Other Africa	—	—	—	—	—	35	—	—	—	35
South Asia	—	—	—	5	—	—	—	—	—	5
South-East Asia	400	—	80	—	10	—	885	80	—	1,455
Japan	—	—	—	5	—	—	—	—	—	5
Australia	5	—	—	—	—	10	35	—	—	50
USSR, East Europe and China	15	—	210	970	15	70	160	—	30	1,470
Total imports	6,025	850	2,340	12,610	710	1,565	4,945	345	945	30,335

ᵃ This includes oil from other parts of the world refined for export to the United States.

DEFINITIONS: *Latin America* includes Mexico, the Caribbean and South America. *Western Europe* includes European members of OECD, Yugoslavia, Cyprus, Gibraltar and Malta. *Middle East* includes the Arabian peninsula, Iran, Iraq, Israel, Lebanon and Syria. *North Africa* includes territories on the north coast from Egypt to Spanish Sahara. *Other Africa* includes those territories on the west coast from Mauritania to Angola, and also includes territories on the east coast from Sudan to the Republic of South Africa, South West Africa, Malawi, Zambia, Rhodesia, Uganda, Malagasy Republic. *South Asia* includes Afghanistan, Bangladesh, Burma, India, Pakistan and Sri Lanka. *South-East Asia* includes Brunei, Cambodia, East Malaysia, Indonesia, Hong Kong, Korea, Laos, Philippines, Singapore, Thailand, Taiwan and Vietnam.

SOURCE: *BP Statistical Review of the World Oil Industry – 1975.*

table horizontally, one can see that the Middle East dominates supply; by scanning vertically, one can see that the OECD (the United States, Europe, Japan and Canada) dominates demand. Among the industrial nations, the United States has the most diverse sources, with about 35 per cent of her imports coming from the Middle East, 35 per cent from Latin America, and 12 per cent from Canada. Europe and Japan rely on Middle East oil for about 70 per cent of their imports.

The geographic pattern of oil trade is among the most closely watched variables of the energy problem. The fact that average daily imports into the United States from the Arab countries increased from 1,120 thousand b/d in 1974 to 1,770 thousand b/d in 1975 is given prominent coverage in newspapers and is made use of by government officials as an indication that the United States energy security position is gradually deteriorating.

Since the Arab countries have been the only exporters to curtail oil supplies for political purposes, it is thought that countries most dependent on them are most vulnerable, and that countries relying more on Indonesian, Venezuelan, Nigerian and Iranian oil are least vulnerable. It is certainly clear that the Arab states can best afford to use oil reductions for political purposes, because Saudi Arabia, Kuwait, the UAE and Libya do not need their immediate revenues to purchase imports; they have amassed sufficient foreign exchange surpluses to do with less oil revenues for months, if not years, if need be. However, it is not necessarily true that countries which do not rely on Arab oil are less likely to suffer import losses if Arab oil were to be curtailed.

The 1973–4 Arab oil cutbacks were spread to all industrial states as the result of deliberate decisions by the international oil companies. Although the companies observed the Arab embargo on the United States and the other targeted countries, they used their non-Arab oil supplies to make up the deficit. Thus, American imports from Saudi Arabia fell by 80 per cent, but her Iranian imports increased by 40 per cent, her Nigerian imports by 70 per cent, and so forth.

On the other hand, Britain, which was not embargoed by the Arab states, lost 75 per cent of her Iranian imports.[45] The IEP allocation formula follows the same principle: no matter what the particular trade pattern might be, a loss of oil will be spread among the member states. And even if the IEP is not implemented in a future reduction of supplies, the companies are still likely to try to prevent particular markets from suffering shortages alone.

The geographic pattern of oil trade is an important variable in two respects: first, it shows the market strength of the various OPEC countries, and therefore helps to explain how their supply reductions can affect the world market. Second, it *influences* (but does not determine) the ability of the oil suppliers to target reductions on particular countries.

The Arab countries provided 58 per cent of world (excluding Communist bloc) imports in 1975 and 52 per cent of IEA imports. To cause an IEA supply loss of 25 per cent (equivalent to an IEA import loss of 36 per cent), they would have had to curtail their own production by 67 per cent. If Algeria and Iraq had not participated, the remaining Arab producers – Saudi Arabia, Kuwait, the UAE and Libya – would have had to curtail production by 80 per cent. If Saudi Arabia had not participated, all the other Arab countries combined could not have deprived the IEA of 25 per cent of its supplies. But market shares, and thus the severity of Arab oil disruptions, are likely to change in the coming years. A recent projection of OPEC exports by a leading consulting firm shows the Arab share increasing from 58 per cent in 1975 to 61 per cent in 1977 and decreasing to 58 per cent in 1980, as the OECD's own production from the North Sea and Alaska

becomes available.[46] In 1977, therefore, the Arab cutback needed to produce a 25 per cent IEA supply shortfall will decrease from the 1975 figure of 67 per cent to 57 per cent. These rough estimates, however, are intended only to give scale to the magnitude of the cutbacks needed by a particular group of exporters. They do not take account of intra-OPEC competition for market shares, or of the effect bilateral deals may have in increasing a particular country's exports.

The second respect in which the geographic oil pattern is important is that it affects countries which can be selected initially by producing states and influences the perception of what the *management* of the problem entails. For example, if a supply disruption took the form of an embargo against particular countries – e.g. the United States – the IEA and/or the oil companies would divert to the United States a certain amount of oil which would otherwise have gone to the other IEA members. But if the disruption included a general curtailment, the question of 'who helps whom' is more intricate and fundamentally dependent on the diversity of supplies available at the time.

The hypothetical disruption in Appendix 2 (p. 71 helps to show the effect of geographic oil patterns on crisis management; it assumes that a 9 million b/d reduction in Arab exports to the IEA occurred in 1975 and was managed according to the IEA formula. The United States would have lost about 3,200,000 b/d. During 1975, however, US average daily imports from Arab sources were only 1,770,000 b/d. Therefore, more than 1,430,000 b/d which the United States would have received from non-Arab sources would have been diverted to Europe and Japan, so the United States would be shifting non-Arab oil-flows to Europe and Japan. Thus, the geographic pattern establishes that the Arab states could have deprived the United States of only 30 per cent of her oil imports, and 10 per cent of her oil supplies, if a disruption had occurred in 1975. To impose a larger loss on the United States, the Arab states would have had to curtail supplies to Europe and Japan as well. This was in fact the tactic used by the Arab exporters in 1973. As President Gaddafi said, 'We are determined to affect America by striking at Europe'.[47]

[45] Percentages measure flows from December 1973 to March 1974 against flows from December 1972 to March 1973 (source: *op. cit.* in note 2, p. 20).

[46] Walter J. Levy's projection, see *The Economist*, 31 July 1976.

[47] *Der Spiegel*, 5 November 1973.

Political Patterns

Up to 1973, the geographic oil patterns were largely determined by commercial practices. After the Arab oil disruption governments began to consider ways to gain access to oil supplies directly. For instance, in 1974 the British and French governments pursued special supply arrangements with Saudi Arabia and Iran, and Britain concluded a one-year barter deal with Iran which involved a limited amount of oil. France was more ambitious. She concluded a contract with Saudi Arabia to buy 200 million barrels over three years and then sought, unsuccessfully, to make a much larger arrangement involving 6,000 million barrels over twenty years. This was an unprecedented incursion into the domain of Aramco, the producing company owned by Exxon, Socal, Mobil and Texaco. According to one account, this deal was jettisoned because Saudi Arabia would not give France access to oil on the same terms as Aramco enjoyed, and France was unwilling to build an export refinery in Saudi Arabia and agree in advance to import its products.[48]

Since 1974, bilateral negotiations have emphasized general rather than petroleum trade. The agreements usually involve industrial development projects in the OPEC states, credits and cultural exchanges, and leave oil trade to the established companies. Closer relations with oil exporters are desirable for several reasons. Increased trade obviously eases the payment problems of the importing country and in the process may give the oil producer a greater awareness of, and stake in, the importer's welfare. This is, in effect, a kind of economic deterrence against oil disruptions: it is intended to make the oil country more sensitive to economic changes in its customer. It is doubtful, however, that the increase in import purchases by the Arab states creates significant economic vulnerability to disruptions in those imports. Many of the industrial goods imported by OPEC states are components of construction projects that will take years to complete, and it currently takes months for ships to be able to unload cargoes in many of their ports. Thus, a trade counter-embargo by the OECD is unlikely to have as dramatic and sudden an effect on OPEC as an oil supply loss has on the OECD. Moreover, increased exports to OPEC make a rupture in relations all the more costly for the oil-importing state by giving the producer another option for influencing the importer: the threat to suspend purchases of its exports. Though such a threat may never be made, the possibility must be included in assessing the vulnerability of oil-importing states. As with oil supply curtailments, the general trade 'lever' is most potent in the hands of Saudi Arabia, which has the most revenues to dispose of.

Taking into account energy supplies, and now the overall economic importance of good relations with OPEC, an oil importing government's desire to respect the wishes of its oil suppliers seems more in the national interest than ever before. Among the industrial countries, France seems to have been the first to allow apprehension about oil supply security to influence her relations with Arab states and to back away from close identification with Israel.[49] The difference in European reactions to the oil disruptions of 1956 and 1973 illustrates this shift starkly. In 1956 Britain and France joined Israel to launch an attack on the Suez Canal, at that time the main passageway for Persian Gulf oil bound for Europe; in 1973 they endorsed the political demands of the Arab states and actively sought 'most friendly' nation status to avoid losing oil supplies. As it turned out, however, the latter actions did not protect Britain and France from oil losses, because oil distribution was still under the control of the oil companies, who refused to favour Britain and France over their other customers.[50]

Although all the OECD countries are trying to increase their contacts with oil producers, the most important relationship is between Saudi Arabia and the United States. Saudi Arabia dominates OPEC. She demonstrated her influence in the OPEC meeting of June 1976, when she blocked a price increase desired by nearly every other exporter. Sheikh Yamani, the Saudi

---

[48] For a detailed discussion of French government activities during the oil crisis see Horst Mendershausen, *Coping with the Oil Crisis* (Baltimore, Md: Johns Hopkins UP, 1976).

[49] For a more detailed analysis of the effect of oil dependence on French behaviour, see Henri Madelin, *Oil and Politics*, (Farnborough, Hants.: Saxon House, 1975).
[50] See *International Herald Tribune*, 23 November 1973, and Robert Stobaugh 'The Oil Companies in the Crisis', *Daedalus*, Fall 1975. Stobaugh (p. 189) claims that BP told the Heath government that their contractual obligations to their customers took priority over instructions from their shareholders, i.e. the government.

petroleum Minister, has rightly said that 'nobody can increase prices without Saudi Arabia'.[51] Her influence results from an immense production capacity (11 million b/d), and a willingness to let her actual production levels fluctuate with demand to a greater extent than any other exporter: from 5·8 million to 8·5 million b/d in the winter of 1975–6 alone, and Yamani has said that production could be reduced to 3·5 million b/d without affecting the country's immediate revenue needs.[52] This flexibility also makes Saudi Arabia the key country in the Arab states' hopes of using oil as a political instrument.

But Saudi Arabia's one weakness is military insecurity: there are dozens of nations, including several Middle East neighbours, with sufficient military power to invade, conquer and hold her oil-producing provinces. This peculiar combination of great specific power in petroleum affairs and great vulnerability to military attack explains why the Saudi government has been receptive to, and in the past has actively pursued, a special relationship with the United States. The relationship rests upon three components: (1) an implicit security guarantee, evidenced by contingents of American military personnel and equipment;[53] (2) a close economic relationship – the United States exports more by value to Saudi Arabia than any other country, and imports more of her surplus revenues than any other country; and (3) a close commercial relationship between the Saudi government and American multi-national companies – not only Aramco but also the great engineering, chemical and banking firms. All the same, her apparent dependence on the United States did not prevent Saudi Arabia from launching the embargo of 1973–4. While it is reasonable to suppose that she was not anxious to disrupt the American connections, she nonetheless implemented the embargo, did not block the price increases of September and December 1973, and was instrumental in creating the 'energy crisis'. And, after all that, American companies and military advisers were still there, in even greater numbers.

Saudi Arabia is protected from retaliation by her control over a vast amount of oil. In 1973, when she reduced production from 8·5 to 5·4 million b/d, she could still respond to threats from the importers with counter-threats of further reductions; and in 1978, when she is likely to produce 10 million b/d,[54] that threat will still be salient. The sheer volume of her production enables her to adopt a flexible plan, deterring counter-measures with threats of more severe disruptions. Thus the 1973 disruption cost Saudi Arabia very little in the short term, and if the pessimistic forecasters are right, even in the long term. The OECD continues to demand far more of her oil than she needs to sell.

The Oil Companies

Commercially, the world can be divided into sectors where the major companies – Exxon, Shell, British Petroleum, Socal, Texaco, Gulf and Mobil – still dominate distribution, and those where they do not. A glance at individual companies' supply sources is sufficient to indicate that the Persian Gulf is the most important source of supply for the majors: British Petroleum receives 85 per cent of its total supplies from the Gulf, Socal 77 per cent, Texaco 71 per cent and Mobil 70 per cent.[55] Moreover, the majors still control the Persian Gulf oil trade to the virtual exclusion of the smaller independent and national oil companies. The latter play a more significant part in the oil trade of the other oil-producing areas – North Africa and the Far East.

The majors are thus the most important commercial link between OPEC and the market. But this commercially enviable position put them in a

---

[51] *Sunday Times*, 31 May 1976. Many observers believe that the complication in the price structure resulting from the OPEC meeting in Qatar in December 1976 – at which Saudi Arabia opted for a 5 per cent increase rather than the 10 per cent adopted by the other members – will be resolved in Saudi Arabia's favour. For a general explanation of Saudi influence within OPEC, see Robert Mabro, 'OPEC after the Oil Revolution', *Millennium*, Winter 1975.
[52] *Middle East Economic Digest*, 5 March 1976.
[53] According to press reports, there are 66 American 'technicians' and 142 'military advisers' in Saudi Arabia. See *Middle East Economic Digest*, 23 February 1975. In addition, the Saudi Arabian government used the US Defense Department as agent to procure the services of the Vinnell Corp. to train the Saudi National Guard. The contract calls for 1,000 advisers, many of them former US military personnel, for three years at a cost of $77 million. See *International Herald Tribune*, 10 February 1975.

[54] Walter J. Levy, cited in *The Economist*, 31 July 1976.
[55] Excluding supplies from the United States. Source: Commission of the European Communities, '*Report by the Commission on the Behaviour of the Oil Companies in the Community During the Period from October 1973 to March 1974* (draft manuscript dated 10 December 1975).

difficult situation in 1973. They were instructed by the Arab states to embargo the United States and the Netherlands, and, as they attempted to shift oil flows around to spread the loss, they were ordered by some governments to deliver the full supplies to which they considered they were entitled. In future disruptions the companies will again have to try to serve two masters, both of them trying to determine the direction of oil supplies. For example, the US Congress, in the 1975 Energy Bill, provided that 'the President may, by rule, require that persons producing, refining, distributing, or storing petroleum products take such actions as he determines to be necessary for implementation of the obligations of the United States under Chapters III and IV of the international energy program'. Since five of the seven major companies are American, it seems that the President has the necessary authority to ensure that the oil companies will serve the consumers.

However, one cannot ignore the preferences of the exporting states. In 1973, according to an Exxon official, his company complied with the Arab insistence that the United States should not receive any Arab oil, because 'otherwise the consequences would have been much more severe, and that was made clear to us by the officials of these countries.'[56] It is clear from this remark that Exxon, the largest oil company, is also vulnerable to the supply decisions of the producing governments – especially its major source of crude, Saudi Arabia. How could it be otherwise? Exxon wants to lose access to Saudi oil no more than France or Japan do; it is vital to its corporate well-being. Nonetheless, in 1973 Exxon and the other majors were able to abide by the desires of the Saudi government to embargo Saudi (and other Arab) oil to certain countries, while at the same time shuffling enough non-Arab oil to those countries to spread the loss relatively equally. And they did this in spite of pressure put on them by the French and British governments.[57]

The technical ability and political strength to shuffle oil around in this fashion cannot be taken for granted. If the international oil business had not been conducted by multi-nationals it is doubtful if the loss would have been spread as evenly, yet it is clear that many governments were dissatisfied with the performance of the majors. They have been under constant scrutiny and legislative attack. In the United States some Senators, as well as the Federal Trade Commission, seek to break them up. In Britain the Labour government has created the British National Oil Corporation to monitor activities in the North Sea, while Canada, Norway, Germany and Denmark have also created state-owned companies to monitor, and perhaps ultimately replace, the private firms.[58] It is not yet possible to determine how successful these ventures will be. At present, the majors still control most of the oil traffic between OPEC and the market, and for the rest of this decade they would still have to ship oil during a supply crisis, balancing the potentially conflicting demands of producers and consumers as they did in 1973. As with other elements in the oil security puzzle, one cannot be sure that the majors will be able to act as programmed by either side, but it is evident from their past performance that they will make considerable efforts to meet their international obligations.

We must consider whether the new national companies would follow this tendency to internationalize oil crises. It is obvious that a government can more easily require its own oil company to acquire oil solely for the national market, assuming it has the facilities to do so. However, it is important to note that BP and the Compagnie Française des Petroles (CFP), part-owned by the British and French governments respectively, were not prepared to give such preference to their home countries in 1973, because they had diversified their markets and felt obliged not to exempt their home markets at the expense of other customers. To increase unilateral security, therefore, the state-owned company should have its home market as its only market. But, even if it does so, there are several reasons to question its ability to safeguard the continuity of imports. First, it is possible that when a disruption occurs,

[56] Senate Committee on Foreign Relations (*op. cit.* in note 38), part 9, testimony of Emilio G. Collado.
[57] See EEC Commission (*op. cit.* in note 55), note 52; Stobaugh (*op. cit.* in note 52) note 47; Senate Committee on Foreign Relations (*op. cit.* in note 2).

[58] The oil companies owned or controlled by OECD states are: PetroCan in Canada, Dansk Ollie in Denmark, ELF-ERAP in France, Veba-Gelsenberg in Germany (43·7 per cent state-owned), ENI in Italy (established in 1953), Statoil in Norway, CAMPSA (established 1927) and HISPANOIL (established 1965) in Spain.

some of the available oil will be sold to the highest bidder, rather than to the historic customer. This occurred in 1973, when Iran and Nigeria received up to $20 per barrel for oil sold on the spot market. Second, a state-owned company may not be able to diversify its sources of supply and develop excess production capacity, as the majors have done. As a result it will be particularly vulnerable to its major suppliers. The history of the relationship between Occidental Petroleum Company and the Libyan government[59] shows how helpless a poorly diversified company can be – yet Occidental is as large as most of the new European state-owned companies are ever likely to become.

The new state companies can improve unilateral security only in a limited set of circumstances. If they can hold their share of world oil against competitive bidding, and if they have a well diversified supply base, they can increase the likelihood that their home market will not suffer unduly in a crisis. But in a global shortage of oil the welfare of one country can only be enhanced at the expense of others, and the rich countries are more likely to do better than the poor. The national companies will therefore not reduce the power of the producers, but they will reduce that of the major companies, limiting 'automatic' diffusion of a shortage the majors aim to achieve as a matter of corporate self-interest.

V. OIL STRATEGIES

In spite of the experience gained in the 1973–4 oil crisis, most industrial states are still vulnerable to disruptions of oil imports. Many are becoming even more dependent on imports from the Arab states that have used their control over oil supplies for political reasons in the past. If they chose, the Arab states, or the other exporters, could again use oil to put economic pressure on their customers. Furthermore, the potential cost of bad relations with oil producers has gone up another notch as a result of the new importance of their purchase of goods from the industrial states. In short, the oil producers are very important countries, and the industrial countries cannot regard disruptions in relations with them lightly.

Yet it is not very enlightening to say that the oil producers have more political influence and power: power can be adeptly or clumsily applied. Also, the economic power of the oil producers must be considered in the context of their military weakness. Their economic power and their political objectives exist in a wider context: their long-term economic health depends on the health of their market, the OECD; and their national security is affected by that of other countries. The use of the oil weapon for particular political objectives will therefore have to be integrated with the oil producers' other objectives. In considering various strategies for the application of economic pressure for political ends this section makes no attempt to define the producer's specific objectives. Rather, it seeks to arrive at some general propositions regarding the effective use of the oil weapon, and tries to describe the security problems these pose for the industrial states.

The geographic, political and commercial patterns discussed in the previous section influence the manner in which the oil weapon can be used for political purposes. Vulnerability, specific patterns of dependence, political relationships and commercial controls combine to determine who will be most and least affected, and the manner in which governments will react to oil disruptions.

Past Conflicts

The key factor in the management of oil crises is the difference in vulnerability among the importing states. A related factor is the tendency of some countries, especially the United States, to give energy security a lower priority in formulating their foreign policy than others. This tendency was an important factor creating divisions among ostensible allies in the 1973–4 crisis.

To explore these political problems further we must look back into the history of oil. In the

[59] Libya was able to force Occidental to agree to a unilateral price rise because the company had no alternative to Libyan oil. Once Occidental came to terms, many other companies followed to protect their access to Libyan oil. There are many accounts of the crucial Libyan negotiations, the latest being Anthony Sampson, *The Seven Sisters* (London: Hodder & Stoughton, 1975).

1950s and 1960s, the 'Middle Ages' of the oil era, producing governments had little power over the oil market because the companies could offset supply losses in one place with increases in another. Furthermore, the producing governments were divided in their approach to the market and, more importantly, were even in awe of the companies and their home governments. When the government of Iran, under Mossadeq, tried to nationalize the assets of BP in 1951 the companies responded in unison to close the market to Iranian oil. The modern era of oil politics was ushered in when the demand for oil supplies had reached such levels that there was no more shut-in capacity under company control, when the OPEC countries realized they could advance their individual interests by working together, and when they learned to separate their adversaries. The Libyan price ultimatum of 1971 and the Arab embargo of 1973 were successful because the strategy of the producers was to divide the most vulnerable producers from the rest. Attempts by oil companies and governments to create a 'united front' in these conflicts failed because the losses could not be spread evenly. In 1971 the 'independent' oil companies, which had not diversified their sources of supply, had far more to lose by opposing Libya than the majors, even though a united front on the part of the oil companies might have forced the Libyans to scale down their demands or suffer the kind of embargo Iran suffered in 1951. In 1973 the attempt to create a united OECD front also failed because Europe and Japan had far more to lose than the United States.

This recurring 'downstream' disunity is a key characteristic of the oil world in the 1970s and its political implications are profound. When the companies controlled the level of supply, rather than OPEC, the production of oil in Arab lands gave Egypt, Syria and Jordan no assistance in their conflict with Israel. With no means of exerting pressure on the West – and particularly the United States – and with little financial assistance from the Gulf, Egypt and Syria could only turn to the Soviet Union, and this in turn contributed to the antagonism between these countries and the staunchly anti-Communist King Faisal of Saudi Arabia. In 1971 control over oil began to shift to the producers and brought in its wake a fundamental political realignment within the Middle East. For the first time ever, the lost

Arab oil could not be replaced, and the Arab oil weapon became a credible threat. With Nasser's death relations between Egypt and Saudi Arabia improved dramatically, and a new political alignment took shape; Israel's occupation of Arab land was its cement, and oil and oil money its sources of international power.

This remarkable political change, facilitated by the change in the oil market, confronted the United States with a dilemma. For the first time her support of Israel presented a clear threat to the economic security of American allies. Europe and Japan, in turn, also faced a new situation: their energy security was no longer exclusively in the hands of multi-national companies but also in those of governments which had a political objective.

The US State Department had previously reacted to oil crises (Iran, Suez, the Six-Day War, and the Libyan negotiations) by allowing, and even encouraging, the oil companies to act together – several times at the expense of anti-trust initiatives then in progress in other parts of the government. In 1973 the Department tried to get the importing governments together. But this no longer addressed the real problem; 'getting together' did not loosen the grip of the producers on the level of oil supply, nor could it any longer prevent damage. At best, it could only spread the damage to countries which did not want to get involved in the dispute to begin with.

In any case, although the oil shortage could be spread evenly, the *economic* damage varied. In 1973, the United States could still be compared with Exxon in the 1950s – a well-diversified energy concern not vulnerable to any individual country – whereas Italy could be compared to its own company, ENI – much smaller, less diversified, and terribly vulnerable to its primary suppliers. Exxon had been able to afford to take the 'hard line' against the producers; ENI never could, and could only secure oil by granting more generous terms than its competitors. Similarly, the United States could take a 'hard line' against the producers in 1973 while Italy could not.

Future Strategies

The Arab oil producers – Saudi Arabia, Kuwait, Libya, Iraq, Algeria and the UAE – can still use the differences in the vulnerability of importing countries to enhance the effectiveness of the oil weapon. They have analysed the oil world and devised a set of strategies to fit various conflicts and objectives, and can continue to do so. This does not mean that we must assume that these countries are looking for ways to damage the industrial world; nonetheless, we are interested in discovering what their planning options may be, should conflicts occur.

A disruption of oil supplies can be described in terms of three variables: level, duration and target. The oil exporters have the greatest control over duration, although the importers' oil stockpiles enable them to replace lost supplies for a limited period of time. The importers, along with the oil companies, hope to determine the level of oil loss any particular country experiences, and hence the extent to which any country can be targeted. This is the purpose of the IEP.

Of the three variables, the choice of targets is the most visible sign of specific conflict the exporters can give. When they singled out the United States in 1973 they made it clear that their primary objective was a change in American policy, and by curtailing production beyond the level required to implement the embargo on the United States they effectively made Europe and Japan hostages in the conflict. (Insofar as the curtailments affected the developing countries, they became innocent victims of the allocation decisions of the oil companies.) The intention of the IEP is to deny the producers the ability to choose a target. If it works, the agreement requires the producers to increase the level of their production cuts if they want to deprive the target states of politically significant quantities of oil. But if the producers do this the IEP can do little about the fact that the individual importers will feel differing degrees of anxiety, since some are substantially more vulnerable than others. For that reason, some importers have intensified their economic and political relations with their oil suppliers to a greater extent than others.

With this in mind, we can examine ways in which the oil countries can counter the IEP. We will consider two strategies. The first challenges the industrial countries to implement the IEP in the face of a deliberate attempt to discriminate against particular importers; the second is an indiscriminate curtailment of OECD imports.

In discussing the first strategy, let us assume that a group of exporters singles out the United States and a few others as targets of an oil import curtailment, and that they decide to spare the remaining importers (chosen by their apparent willingness to accept the exporters' demands, which is likely to be a function of their vulnerability). They will therefore reduce their production by an amount equivalent to the normal level of exports to the embargoed countries. Let us also assume that the exporters instruct the oil companies to abide by the embargo, threatening that production will be cut further if the companies do not obey. Perhaps the most important factor determining the success of this strategy is the extent to which the producers' choice of targets matches the importers' political positions. A 'good match' would be one in which the oil cutbacks are aimed at countries whose policies impede the producers' objective. A 'bad match' would be one in which the cutbacks are aimed at countries which are either already on the producers' side or are insignificant in determining the outcome of the political issue.

If the match is bad, there is greater likelihood that the cutbacks will be seen as 'unfair' or as exploiting the weak, and will enhance the prospect of the importers feeling they are confronted by irresponsible and dangerous adversaries. In this atmosphere, the tendency will be greater to resist the demands and to create a united front against the producers. If the match is good, a substantially different mood is likely to prevail. The cutbacks against specific countries will confront each of the IEA members with the difficult decision of whether to implement the emergency programme. A decision against activation may seem to run counter to the principle of 'consumer solidarity' but may indeed be the more appropriate response to the political forces created by a targeted embargo.

Starting with the presumption that the match is good, a decision to activate the IEP is likely to produce the following sequence of reactions (assuming that the disrupters are the Arab states):
1. The embargo on the targets would be spread among the IEA members. For instance, if the United States, Holland and Germany were initially embargoed by the Arab states, the IEA would lose 11 per cent of its aggregate supplies and 17 per cent of its aggregate imports (using 1975 data as in Appendix 3). Thus, an oil loss that would create a serious problem for Holland and Germany would be turned into a manageable problem for all the IEA members.

2. But one cannot assume the contest will end there; the disrupters may choose to react to this neutralization of their offensive. Having already embargoed their primary targets, their only available response is to reduce supplies to other IEA members as well. They could justify this as 'retaliation' against an unfriendly act: participation in the IEP.

3. By curtailing their exports to the IEA by 50 per cent, the Arab states would have deprived the group of a little over 20 per cent, of its supply. At this level of loss the IEA stipulates that members should draw 10 per cent of their supply from stocks. At this rate of stock withdrawal, many members, including the United States, would begin to dip into their working stocks within six months.

In this scenario, the exercise of the Arab oil weapon would confront the importers with a very serious oil shortage within six months. What would follow this sequence of events, or at what stage the sequence would be interrupted by other actions not mentioned in the scenario, depends on the attitude of the importing governments.

Throughout the sequence of events, the producers can maintain the promise that any country that drops out of the IEP would be assured of its desired oil supplies. Although this means that the producers are asking an IEP member to go back on a ratified agreement, there are grounds for suspecting that the pressure on some countries would be very considerable, and a decision to do so, compelled by 'unforeseen circumstances', should not be surprising.

In the first place, it seems very likely that the producers would try to woo the most vulnerable and the most friendly to their cause from the IEP. In 1973 they warned European countries not to 'break' the embargo on the Netherlands, at the risk of being targeted themselves if they disregarded the warning,[60] and the other European governments did little to help the Dutch: that was left to the international oil companies. The French and British governments, as mentioned before, tried to make the companies' IEP-like allocation more difficult by demanding, unsuccessfully, to receive their supplies as entitled by being on the Arabs' 'most friendly' list. Secondly, there may be genuine disagreement among the OECD countries about the proper response to the

producers' demands. This again was the case in 1973: most European governments disapproved of Israel's occupation of the Arab land gained in 1967 and expressed their disapproval in support for UN Resolution 242, amplified in the EEC Foreign Ministers' communiqué in early November.[61] The United States had also supported the resolution, but her idea of the proper timing and circumstances surrounding an Israeli withdrawal was necessarily more specific than that of the European governments. However, the United States' unwillingness or inability (it is not clear which) to force the Israelis to withdraw caused the Arabs to extend the duration of the supply curtailments until March 1974, when Saudi Arabia, the lynch-pin of Arab oil power, agreed to give Kissinger's step-by-step approach a chance.

But in January 1974, the Arabs had eased the pressure on Europe by restoring some of their production. As it turned out, little damage was done by the supply losses, but the lesson of the experience is clear. Europe and Japan were clearly more anxious about oil losses than the United States. If the pressure had not eased in January 1974 economic damage would have resulted, and it seems likely that several European governments would have further disassociated themselves from American policy in the Middle East. They may even have used their leverage on the United States to urge a change in policy and accelerated their efforts to secure their oil imports unilaterally. The involvement of Europe and Japan in the oil crisis thus complicated American diplomatic efforts in the Middle East, since the United States could not be indifferent to the economic problems of her allies. In fact, Kissinger's war mutterings in late November 1973 seem likely to have been intended to reassure Japan and Europe, as well as to intimidate Arab leaders with a reminder that the United States would take effective action if the Arabs pushed their weapon 'to the brink'.

Given that the United States is in general much less vulnerable to energy losses than some other countries, and that she has a much lower dependence on imported and Arab oil supplies, one can question why the State Department chose to create an international agreement that automatically pulls the more vulnerable allies into future

---

[60] See *International Herald Tribune*, 28 November 1973.

[61] *Guardian*, 7 November 1973.

disruptions. The IEP 'burden sharing' could give the exporters a justification for spreading the embargo to countries they might otherwise have exempted. It is worthwhile to explore an alternative case in which the IEP is deliberately not activated in response to a targeted embargo. In this case, the following sequence of events seems likely:

1. The oil companies, following their natural commercial inclinations, would abide by the embargo demands of the disrupters, but they would also try to increase their liftings from non-disrupting producers to make up the deficit. The degree to which the lost supplies could be recouped in this manner would depend upon the reserve production capacity available at the time and the willingness of the owners of that oil to allow increases in production. In 1973 there was little shut-in production available, though Iran, Nigeria and Venezuela all showed slight increases in production through the embargo. In the future, the disrupters may call for 'producer solidarity', demanding that production not be increased. It is hard to say whether the other producers will heed this call.

2. In abiding by the targeting demands of the disrupters, the oil companies and the OECD governments could reduce the chance that the level of oil cutbacks would be increased, or that the cutbacks would be extended to other importers.

3. Although the resulting reduction would be successfully targeted, the shortage might not be beyond the abilities of the affected countries to manage. Since the most vulnerable states will have sided with the producers from the start, and been exempted from the curtailments as a reward, only the less vulnerable states would have to pay the price of their opposition to the producers' demands.

4. As a result, the crisis would be contained and limited to those countries willing and able to bear the loss. It would be smaller, involving a smaller amount of oil and fewer governments.

Besides probably limiting the size of the overall oil loss, this response has several obvious benefits. The most important is that it protects the most vulnerable from serious energy losses. In 1973 the oil market conducted the shock of the Arab–Israeli–American conflict throughout the world.

In part this may have occurred as a deliberate component of both Arab and American strategies – the Arabs wanting to affect the United States by striking at Europe and Japan, the United States wanting her allies to help meet the problem – but, either way, Europe and Japan became hostages to both sides.

The management of an oil crisis depends ultimately on the degree of political solidarity among the importers. That, in turn, depends upon the political issue. In 1973, as the *Strategic Survey* commented, 'energy interests and dependence provided the most concrete area of divergence' in outlook and policy among the allies. 'American manoeuvrability in the Middle East . . . need not be seriously restricted, whereas European manoeuvrability will; unless overriding security interests dictate otherwise, West European states would refuse to be drawn into taking a strong line against the Arab oil producers. . . . Close ties with the United States would be a *temporary* impediment for energy-dependent Europe for as long as the Arab–Israeli antagonism existed and the United States was seen to take a pro-Israeli line; for the United States, on the other hand, close ties with Europe could be a continuing impediment, since Europe's energy dependency on the Middle East could reduce American options there'.[62] In short, the need for oil makes it more difficult for Europe and Japan to view the Arab countries as adversaries or the United States as their ally on an issue, such as the Arab–Israeli dispute, that does not have 'overriding strategic significance'. If Europe and Japan are put in a position where they must weigh the importance to themselves of secure oil supplies against the case for Israel continuing to occupy Arab land, they may well decide that the former is more important and that the agreement to share oil losses is not in their interests.

But what if Europe and Japan decided that they did not want to be involved in the IEP? As currently drawn up, the agreement stipulates that its implementation is automatic unless a 'special majority' of members vote not to activate the programme. The United States commands such a large share of the combined voting weights (see Appendix 5 on p. 34) that she would only need three members' support to prevent a special majority from blocking IEP implementation.

---

[62] *Strategic Survey 1973* (London: IISS, 1974), p. 62.

The United States thus has an important voice in determining how an export reduction is managed. She could elect to 'go it alone' if she were embargoed by the Arab countries again, while her lower vulnerability would be a handicap to her allies if she insisted that they share the risks of her foreign policy. Since she is now the world's leading oil importer and can no longer act as the supplier of last resort for the other importers, it may be necessary that she should accept that the OECD's energy needs must at times supersede the desire for a united approach and that, if the political demand is acceptable, the other importers will follow their natural tendency to accommodate the interests of their oil suppliers.

We must also consider the consequences if the oil importers were not in disagreement but all opposed the demands of the producers – who had seriously miscalculated the political mood of the importers, or might have overestimated the potency of the oil weapon. This is a case where the OECD, and not only the United States, is the target of the producer's actions.

The first thing to consider is what the OECD could do to counter the economic pressure which the producers might bring to bear. In 1974 the American government considered a trade counter-embargo against the Arab states, but, in the words of a State Department official, 'that approach would not work unless it included all the consuming countries of the world against all of the producing countries of the world. Even then, it probably would not work because of the producers' indigenous resources, their ability to tighten their belts, or because of leakages in the system.'[63] Even the grain trade, over which the United States has a commanding influence, does not promise to give the OECD a potent counter-weapon, since the food import demand of the leading Arab oil producers (Saudi Arabia, Kuwait, Abu Dhabi and Libya) is but 2 per cent of the world food trade. And even if all OECD countries, including Canada and Australia, did agree to observe a counter-embargo, the Soviet Union and even China could provide the necessary supplies, getting much political benefit at very little economic cost.[64] The OECD countries,

therefore, would not be able to muster effective economic counter-measures against those oil exporters most likely to participate in deliberate supply reductions; and those OPEC members vulnerable to disruption of their imports from industrial countries – Iran, Venezuela, Indonesia and Nigeria – have never participated in such efforts. Among the Arab states only Algeria and Iraq are vulnerable, having large populations, modest oil production levels and the ability to put imports to immediate use. Their contribution to a disruption, however, is not significant, and successful application of economic pressure on them would be a meaningless victory.

Having no effective economic response to an oil supply disruption, a united OECD therefore faces the choice of either enduring losses while efforts are made to produce a resolution, until the point is reached when it is necessary to capitulate to the demands of the oil producers, or else taking military action.

There have been numerous studies on the feasibility of a military campaign to take over the major oil-producing areas.[65] It is clear that the OECD countries could invade and occupy the Arab side of the Persian Gulf, though there do exist possibilities that the other producers would launch a sympathy embargo, and that the Soviet Union would become involved in the conflict. In spite of these complications, vulnerability to oil supply losses is such that at some point the OECD would have to consider, threaten, and finally take, military action against the disrupting oil producers. According to this assessment that point may be as low as a 20 per cent loss in supply which lasted long enough to run down emergency stocks (six months or so).

The ability of the oil producers, particularly the Arab countries, to use the full strength of the oil weapon is limited by their relative military weakness. That weakness becomes politically relevant when the industrial states are sufficiently united – if only in their anxiety about oil shortages – to reach collective approval for armed attack. Only a severe miscalculation by the pro-

[63] *Op. cit.* in note 38, p. 157.
[64] US Congress, Joint Economic Committee, *A Reappraisal of US Energy Policy* (Washington DC: USGPO, March 1974).

[65] Among these are: Peter Mangold, 'Force and Middle East Oil', *The Round Table*, January 1976; Miles Ignatus, 'Seizing Arab Oil', *Harpers Magazine*, March 1975; Congressional Research Service, *Oil Fields as a Military Objective* (Washington DC: USGPO, March 1975); Robert W. Tucker, 'Oil, The Issue of American Intervention', *Commentary*, January 1975; *Strategic Survey 1974* (London: IISS, 1975).

ducers of the degree to which the industrial states would tolerate a particular political demand could create this kind of situation, but the assumption that the producers are conscious of where the limits of tolerance lie, and are sensible enough not to trespass beyond them, rests on their recognition of the limits to the political power of the oil weapon.

To summarize, the use of oil supplies as a political weapon is a complex, strategic problem. To be effective, a deliberate reduction in oil supplies must surpass, or threaten to surpass, the 'built-in' conservation potential of oil-dependent economies. The existence of stockpiles, the actions of the oil companies, general market conditions, and the potential application of the IEP must be taken into account. The strategy which seems most likely to overcome these defences is one which has proved effective in the past: that is, exploiting the desire of the more vulnerable states to avoid oil losses. This approach is promising because vulnerability varies significantly among the importing states and – equally important – the strength of the political commitment to whatever issue is at stake is also likely to vary. Finally, the very need for security of oil imports is affecting the foreign policy preferences of many importers, and they are more likely than before to 'tilt' towards the policies of their oil suppliers.

VI. CONCLUSIONS

Energy import dependence will confront countries with many additional economic challenges, but only severe, sudden and long-lasting reductions in oil supplies can be considered immediate threats to national security. The various energy security measures adopted since 1973 have not removed the threat. Rather, they have modified the way the oil weapon will have to be used.

The most important observations concerning the three groups of importers which have been considered can be summarized as follows. The oil import dependence of most non-OECD states is so small that it is difficult for the oil producers effectively to target oil reductions against them. Indeed, for many of the developing countries, particularly those with no access to the sea, the more serious threat is that their neighbours might disrupt their oil supply.

The Communist oil importers also are not vulnerable to OPEC supply reductions. Their vulnerability is to Soviet energy moves, and those moves are a part of an economic and political relationship that differs fundamentally from that between OPEC and the OECD. Over the next decade, however, the Communist bloc may become dependent on OPEC for a vital portion of oil supplies. This would bring it into the competition for secure access and require a closer involvement in world trade and its politics than has been necessary in the past.

The most profound consequences of dependence on energy imports are in OPEC–OECD and intra-OECD relations. The vulnerability of industrial states to OPEC and Arab supply reductions is a fact. The military superiority of the industrial states makes it unlikely that a reduction of supply will ever be pushed to the point where it could destroy an economy, but it must be noted that even the military counter-threat will be less effective if the Soviet Union develops an important oil stake in the Middle East. There are, however, more certain, though more subtle, implications that demand our attention.

Students of the Middle East and the oil industry know that access to adequate and continuous supplies of oil has been a concern of Europe, Japan and the United States for decades. Developments in the Middle East have been dominated by the search for oil, mixed with colonization and (more recently) decolonization and the establishment of Israel, though the resulting conflicts did not threaten the economic welfare of the industrial world until 1973. By then the OECD nations' need for imported oil had become so vast and vital that even a 15 per cent reduction in Arab supplies could not be replaced. Even if, as in this Paper, generous allowance is made for the ability of economies to reduce the demand for oil quickly and for willingness among states to share the loss, neither the IEP, nor oil stocks, nor current domestic energy programmes could long delay significant losses in employment and production if OPEC or the Arab states were determined to cause them.

Given their relatively weak military strength, the oil producers have acquired an extraordinary degree of political influence – and none more so than Saudi Arabia. She has embargoed the United States; she has raised the price of oil to over one hundred times the cost of production; and yet American diplomats, soldiers and businessmen are still there. This is simply because access to Saudi oil cannot be lost. Saudi Arabia can demand and get many economic and political concessions out of the reach of other countries.

Where is the limit? One critical factor, as in the past, is the point at which the oil producers' adversaries are united. In 1973 the Arab states would have faced grave risks if their political demand had been considered unreasonable by all the importers. But it was not, and some countries were willing to secure their oil with political concessions. Another critical factor is the producers' own national interests. In a rational calculation of their long-term welfare, they must figure that they cannot benefit from economic reverses in the industrial world. In addition, Saudi Arabia, which still maintains a firm anti-Communist foreign policy, cannot disregard the condition of the United States and her military alliances, which directly and indirectly safeguard the Gulf.

Consequently Saudi Arabia – and to a lesser extent the other producers – must frame her political objectives to take account of these factors. The limits can be breached (momentary irrationality cannot be discounted), but in the most realistic projection of the political future, the producers are likely to realize that their oil weapon is most effective in those conflicts where their interests are clearly involved, where their objectives are considered reasonable and where their exercise of influence is predictable – a logical extension of their control over a vital resource. It is probable, therefore, that the most significant effect of energy dependence in the 1970s and 1980s is that oil producers will be able to create alliances that further their national interests.

These energy-based relationships will confront existing alliances with an adjustment problem. Among the industrial countries, this will require an understanding, if not an expectation, that some governments would rather accommodate their oil suppliers than a traditional ally. This will be most significant for the United States. In 1973, when the United States did not get the co-operation from Europe she wanted, Secretary of State Kissinger was quoted as saying, 'I don't care what becomes of NATO, I am disgusted', and Secretary of Defense Schlesinger said, 'We had not expected much, but they should not have given in at the first small difficulty'.[66] But for Europe the threat to oil supplies was not a small difficulty.

The 1973–4 crisis illustrates the impact of energy dependence and the use of the oil weapon. It complicates foreign policy decisions by changing the costs: it is now expensive to oppose the interests of the oil producers. The political costs an importer has to pay for energy security is dependent upon its own expectations: if the United States wants to oppose the producers when many of the other industrial nations do not, she might have to pay a higher price than in 1973. In that case, the costs might be reduced if she opposed the producers alone.

---

[66] *Der Spiegel*, 5 November 1973.

Appendix 1: French and West German Inland Oil Use (1974), assigning hypothetical sector priorities

	France		West Germany	
	Volume (000 tonnes)	%	Volume (000 tonnes)	%
Highest priority				
Agriculture	3,212	2·9	1,280	1·1
Armed forces	n.a.		n.a.	
	3,212	2·9	1,280	1·1
Second priority (heavy industry)				
Chemicals	7,932	7·2	10,918	9·1
Mining	722	0·6	4,585	3·8
Textiles	1,195	1·1	1,178	1·0
Primary metals manufacture	2,638	2·4	4,407	3·7
Fabricated metal products	1,317	1·2	1,222	1·0
Rail transport	553	0·5	671	0·6
Air transport	1,863	1·7	2,527	2·1
Inland shipping	n.a.	—	875	0·7
	16,220	14·7	26,383	2·12
Third priority				
Power plants	13,679	12·4	6,885	5·7
Fourth priority (light industry)				
Food manufacture	2,450	2·2	2,816	2·3
Paper and printing	1,430	1·3	1,603	1·3
Building materials	1,844	1·7	4,585	3·8
Other	19,489	17·7	9,823	8·2
	25,213	23·0	18,827	15·7
Fifth priority				
Residential and commercial heating	26,019	23·7	40,939	34·2
Lowest priority				
Private transport	25,569[a]	23·3	25,305[a]	21·1
Total inland oil consumption	109,912	100·0	119,619	100·0

n.a. = not available.

[a] Roughly one-third of this volume was used by the industrial motor freight sector, which would probably be given a higher priority by the government.

SOURCES: *Energy Statistics Yearbook 1970–1974* (Luxembourg: Statistical Office of the European Communities, January 1976); *Pétrole 74* (Paris: Comité Professionnel du Pétrole, 1976); *Tätigbeitbericht 1973–74* (Essen: Vereinigung Industrielle Kraftwirtschaft, 1975).

Appendix 2: Calculations Illustrating the Effect of the IEP (1975 data)[a]

Member	Consumption (000 b/d)	Production (000 b/d)	Imports (000 b/d)	Imports as % of group total	Supply right (000 b/d)	Required stock drawdown (000 b/d)	Supply right as % of consumption	Drawdown as % of consumption	Average stock level (000 b)	Days' imports in stock	Drawdown maintainable (days)[b]
Austria	215	40	175	0·8	147	46	68	21	8,729	50	189
Belgium/Luxembourg	545	—	545	2·6	343	148	63	27	39,907	73	270
Canada[c]	1,735	1,735	850	4·0	1,333	228	76	14	135,133	159	592
Denmark	310	—	310	1·5	193	86	63	27	35,831	115	416
Ireland	105	—	105	0·5	66	29	63	27	7,494	71	258
Italy	1,925	20	1,905	9·2	1,209	524	63	27	162,263	84	309
Japan	4,905	10	4,895	23·6	3,070	1,345	63	27	324,000	66	240
Netherlands	710	—	710	3·4	445	194	63	27	18,729	26	96
Spain	880	—	880	4·2	553	239	63	27	50,584	57	211
Sweden	530	—	530	2·6	329	148	63	27	39,362	74	265
Switzerland	260	—	260	1·3	160	74	63	27	28,509	110	385
Turkey	275	60	215	1·0	190	57	69	21	n.a.	n.a.	n.a.
Britain	1,875	25	1,850	8·9	1,180	507	63	27	149,462	80	295
USA[c]	15,845	9,995	5,850	28·2	12,654	1,607	80	10	922,366	158	574
W. Germany	2,665	115	2,550	12·3	1,698	701	64	26	168,990	62	241

[a] The IEP allocation formula can be expressed as follows:

$$\text{Supply right} = cC_x - P_x - \frac{I_x}{\Sigma I}(c\Sigma C - \Sigma P - \Sigma I),$$

where c is the level of oil consumption allowable under the IEP agreement (the value will be 0·93 or 0·9, depending upon the severity of the oil supply reduction); C is consumption of oil; x refers to an individual member's consumption, production or imports; ΣC, ΣP and ΣI refer to the total consumption production and imports of the IEA as a group; P is production of oil; I is imports of oil; and ΣI_r is imports remaining to the group during the crisis. Required drawdown is established by the expression $(I_x/\Sigma I)(c\Sigma C - \Sigma P - \Sigma I_r)$.

The hypothetical import reduction is nine million b/d. The values of the Σ variables are:

$$\Sigma I = 21,000,000 \text{ b/d}$$
$$\Sigma I_r = 12,000,000 \text{ b/d}$$
$$\Sigma P = 12,000,000 \text{ b/d}$$
$$\Sigma C = 33,000,000 \text{ b/d}$$

[b] This calculation is based on the assumption that all the stocks could be used in an emergency. This is not in fact the case, as the IEP agreement itself implies. Article 15 stipulates that when 50 per cent of the emergency reserve is exhausted, the Governing Board must meet to consider whether additional actions are required, including further decreases in permissible consumption.

[c] Canada and the United States are special cases: their oil markets are 'incompletely integrated', in the parlance of the IEP agreement (i.e., oil is produced in a distinct region of the country). Article 17 of the agreement stipulates that the allocation programme can be activated if a major region in such a market suffers a loss of oil imports exceeding 7 per cent of consumption in the previous four quarters.

SOURCE OF CONSUMPTION AND PRODUCTION DATA: *BP Statistical Review of the World Oil Industry – 1975.*

Appendix 3: Average Month-end Stock Levels for Selected OECD Countries (1975)

Country	Stock level (million barrels)	Days' consumption
United States	922	57
Canada	133	83
Japan	324	66
Britain	140	88
France	214	113
West Germany	169	73
Italy	157	83
Netherlands	22	55
Belgium	40	96

SOURCE: Office of Economic Research, Central Intelligence Agency, *International Oil Developments: Statistical Survey* (Washington DC: CIA, 6 May 1976).

These data should be interpreted as only very rough approximations, since stock levels fluctuate to a considerable extent during the year. In addition, certain estimates, such as the figures for the Netherlands, probably do not take into account stocks held by export refineries.

These estimates should not be interpreted as providing a realistic assessment of the number of days each country could do without imported supplies. As a rule of thumb, about half of the stocks held should be considered the working inventory of the oil industry. This varies from country to country, however, and the United States has probably the largest working inventory level requirement.

Appendix 4: Oil Production, Consumption and Trade in the Communist Countries (000 b/d)

	USSR	Eastern Europe	China
Production			
1973	8,420	409	1,090
1974	9,020	417	1,310
1975	9,630	421	1,620
Consumption			
1973	6,330	1,797	920
1974	6,790	1,822	1,030
1975	7,180	1,977	n.a.
Imports			
1973	290	1,576	—
(intra-COMECON)	—	1,044	—
1974	110	1,621	—
(intra-COMECON)	—	1,118	—
1975	150	n.a.	—
(intra-COMECON)	—	n.a.	—
Exports			
1973	2,380	182	20
(intra-COMECON)	1,350	—	—
1974	2,340	216	85
(intra-COMECON)	1,440	—	—
1975	2,600	n.a.	174
(intra-COMECON)	1,550	n.a.	—

n.a. = not available.   SOURCE: *Op. cit.* in Appendix 3.

Appendix 5: Voting Weights of Members of the IEA (1975)

Country	General voting weights	Oil consumption voting weights	Combined voting weights
Austria	3	1	4
Belgium	3	2	5
Canada	3	5	8
Denmark	3	1	4
Germany	3	8	11
Ireland	3	0	3
Italy	3	6	9
Japan	3	15	18
Luxembourg	3	0	3
The Netherlands	3	2	5
Spain	3	2	5
Sweden	3	2	5
Switzerland	3	1	4
Turkey	3	1	4
United Kingdom	3	6	9
United States	3	48	51
Totals	48	100	148

NOTE: The 'special majority' requires 60 per cent of the total combined voting weights and 36 general voting weights.

SOURCE: Article 62 of the Agreement on an International Energy Programme, Brussels, 27 September 1974, reprinted in US Senate, Committee on Interior and Insular Affairs, *International Energy Programme: Hearing before the Committee on Interior and Insular Affairs* (Washington DC: USGPO, 26 November 1974).

3 Prospects for Nuclear Proliferation

JOHN MADDOX

INTRODUCTION

The proliferation of nuclear weapons is now a more urgent issue than at any time in the past decade, and for several reasons. First, there is now in prospect a rapid growth of the nuclear generation industry, with the result that fissile material, the raw material of nuclear explosives, will be produced in very large quantities in the 1980s. Secondly, the technology of producing fissile material has become more widely familiar. Thirdly, the explosion of a nuclear device beneath the Rajasthan Desert in India on 18 May 1974 has been a pointed reminder to many other states that the circumstances of the 1960s have changed.

This is the background against which the Review Conference of the Non-Proliferation Treaty will be convened in Geneva in May 1975. Inevitably, that conference will revive some of the arguments which made the original negotiation of the treaty in the period 1966–68 contentious. Amendments will not be possible[1] but far-reaching questions are certain to be raised. Some parties to the treaty will have doubts about its fitness for its stated purpose of inhibiting the spread of nuclear weapons. Others will ask whether the nuclear powers, and especially the Soviet Union and the United States, have fulfilled their obligations under the treaty. Some reluctant parties may ask whether the goal of non-proliferation is still worthwhile.

What follows is an analysis of current pressures and restraints on proliferation. The chief objective is to identify the weak points – political as well as technical – of the Non-Proliferation Treaty (NPT) and to suggest how

the treaty, or the goal of non-proliferation of which it is the most tangible expression, can be strengthened. There is much that can be done. The safeguards system which is an essential feature of the treaty could be simplified and, in the process, made more credibly a means of accommodating the rapid growth of nuclear power in the years ahead. The asymmetry of the treaty, much resented by non-nuclear powers, could be softened. The benefits of signature could be made more real. All these are worthwhile short-term goals.

None of this, however, implies that the NPT is an end in itself. Even if it were suitably strengthened and extended by the accession of states not now party to it, the NPT would not be a perpetual assurance that nuclear wars had been prevented. Indeed, the treaty itself requires continued agreement among the parties. The first review conference in May 1975 is intended 'to review the operation of this Treaty with a view to assuring that the purpose of the preamble and the provisions of the Treaty are being realised'. It also provides for further review conferences at intervals of five years, at the request of a majority of the parties, and for a conference 25 years after the entry of the treaty into force (that is, in June 1995) to decide whether it should survive beyond that. Moreover, any government may withdraw on three months' notice if it considers that 'extraordinary events related to the subject matter of this Treaty have jeopardized the supreme interests of its country' (Article X(I)).

These provisions reflect the hesitations of non-nuclear powers expressed during the long process of negotiation of the NPT. The treaty requires non-nuclear signatories not to use nuclear materials for military purposes nor to carry out peaceful nuclear explosions independently, and to allow their own account of how

---

[1] The procedure of the review conference was provisionally defined at the third meeting of the Preparatory Committee on 3–14 February 1975. Full parties to the treaty will be voting members of the conference, signatories will have observer status and non-signatories may also attend but not vote. The provisions of the treaty make amendments at the conference impracticable.

their nuclear installations function to be verified by international inspection. These restrictions do not apply to the nuclear powers (defined as those which had carried out nuclear explosions before 1 January 1967), whence the charge by non-signatories such as India that the treaty is discriminatory. In reality, however, the treaty is a compact between the non-nuclear and nuclear signatories in which the latter undertook to negotiate a comprehensive and permanent ban on nuclear tests (Preamble) and to 'pursue negotiations in good faith on effective measures relating to the cessation of the nuclear arms race at an early date and to nuclear disarmament' (Preamble and Article VI). To meet the fears of non-nuclear powers that the treaty would impede the free development of nuclear energy for peaceful purposes, the nuclear powers undertook to foster peaceful nuclear energy 'especially in the territories of non-nuclear weapon states party to the treaty' (Article IV) and to make arrangements for providing peaceful nuclear explosions (Article V).

In the years ahead, much will depend on how successfully the nuclear parties to the treaty (the Soviet Union, Britain and the United States) can demonstrate that they have discharged their obligations. Further ahead, there are more serious obstacles. Will the non-nuclear parties to the treaty remain content if the Chinese People's Republic (not to mention France or even India) remains outside its framework? Will they be satisfied with the steps so far taken by the nuclear powers to provide security guarantees against nuclear attack or the threat of it? Will the Indian devotion to the importance of peaceful nuclear explosions, typified by the explosion of 18 May 1974, goad some non-nuclear states already parties to the treaty to resign so as to carry out nuclear explosions of their own?

It is therefore important that the NPT should be recognized as merely a part, even if a central part, of a more extensive strategy aimed at inhibiting proliferation. Thus decisions taken outside the scope of the NPT itself may either strengthen the treaty or otherwise inhibit the development of independent nuclear forces. Conspicuous among these are the arrangements, among the suppliers of commercial nuclear equipment to non-nuclear states, for the co-ordination of contractual conditions and the terms in which nuclear powers, collectively or singly, are prepared to guarantee non-nuclear states against nuclear attack or the threat of it.

The NPT system is an evolving system, dynamic and not fixed. Although the NPT itself is aimed explicitly at preventing the emergence of nuclear weapon capability among non-nuclear states, experience may well demonstrate that this objective is in the most literal sense unattainable. Indeed, it will be surprising if, in the decades ahead, the company of nuclear states remains exactly what it is now, in 1975. It follows that a successful strategy on nuclear proliferation must be robust enough to survive developments like these, a proposition which entails something of a contradiction. The difficulty is that of seeking, on the one hand, to strengthen the NPT and the arrangements that support it, and, on the other, to arrange that explicit 'failures' of the NPT system are of no account. To the extent that the hypothesis on which the NPT is founded is that 'the proliferation of nuclear weapons would seriously enhance the danger of nuclear war' (Preamble), the parties to the NPT will need continual evidence that their continuing obligations are indeed worthwhile.

At the same time is required of them a recognition that the risks that nuclear weapons will spread are at all times specific, involving particular states and not states in general; that the NPT and the arrangements that support it must continually be adapted to changing circumstances; and that, in the last resort, the NPT system is a means to an end and not an end in itself. What follows is coloured by these pragmatic considerations.

I. THE NPT SYSTEM NOW

Of the existing instruments for arms control, the NPT is in many ways the most significant – unlike arms-control agreements, such as the Antarctic and Outer Space Treaties for example, it circumscribes the freedom of both nuclear and non-nuclear powers to pursue policies that are practicable and even, from many points of view, desirable. Moreover, if adherence to the treaty were universal, it would indeed prevent the spread of nuclear weapons. But the treaty is now complemented by the Treaty of Tlatelolco (Treaty for the Prohibition of Nuclear Weapons in Latin America, 1967), establishing a nuclear-free zone in Latin America by formal undertakings by some of the parties to the treaty on the security of non-nuclear states and the commercial supply of nuclear materials and equipment, as well as by unilateral declarations of various kinds. Undoubtedly the months ahead will see further additions to this untidy apparatus of formal and informal self-restraint.

Historically, the NPT is the most tangible so far of several international exercises for regulating the spread of nuclear weapons, including the Baruch Plan (1946) for the international custody of nuclear materials, and the advocacy in the mid-1950s of a comprehensive test-ban by governments such as that of India. Its direct antecedent is the Irish Resolution adopted by the United Nations General Assembly in 1961. Negotiation of the treaty that now exists began in earnest in the Eighteen Nation Disarmament Committee at Geneva on the basis of draft treaties submitted by the Soviet Union and the United States in August 1965. The process was completed three years later, when a final text of the treaty was commended to member states by the UN General Assembly. The treaty entered into force on 5 March 1970 with the deposition of instruments of ratification by the United States and the Soviet Union, and by 28 February 1975 had been ratified by 84 states altogether. (Appendix 1 on p. 34 shows the present position of the 137 members of the United Nations with respect to the NPT.)

As with most voluntary societies, the interest of the membership list lies largely in the names of those who have elected not to join. Thus the non-parties to the NPT include two nuclear powers (the Chinese People's Republic and France), two states which are almost explicitly near-nuclear powers (India and Israel), several states which could in the near future be in a position to make nuclear explosions (Argentina, Brazil and South Africa) and several open critics of the treaty during the process of negotiation (Algeria for example). Other states have for various reasons chosen the path of quasi-membership of the club – signature but not ratification – and among these Egypt, Japan and Italy are conspicuous.

Why should there be states unwilling to become parties to a treaty which, on the face of things, is as innocent as motherhood used to be considered? Although it would be ingenuous always to suppose that explanations and reasons are identical, the arguments of the past decade do accurately point to some of the defects of the NPT as they are perceived by some non-parties to the treaty – and even by some who have duly ratified it.

The essence of the NPT is that nuclear states undertake not to provide non-nuclear powers (whether or not they have signed the treaty) with 'nuclear weapons or other nuclear explosive devices' and not to help ('assist, encourage or induce') in their acquisition (Article I) and that non-nuclear states undertake not to receive nuclear explosive devices or help in their acquisition from any source 'whatsoever' (Article II). These reciprocal proscriptions are simple and (for parties) uncontentious, even if they do not formally prevent non-nuclear parties to the treaty from helping with the development of nuclear explosive devices elsewhere by means other than the supply of fissile material or equipment for the processing of fissile material.[2]

Dissatisfaction

Discontent with the NPT has centred on other issues – the obligation of non-nuclear states to accept international inspection (Article III), and

---

[2] So far as the treaty is concerned, there is nothing to prevent a non-nuclear party to the treaty, such as Iran, from helping financially and even technically to support the development of nuclear weapons by non-parties to the treaty, Pakistan for example, provided that in the process they do not acquire control over nuclear explosives.

the obligations of nuclear states to contribute to the development of civil nuclear energy (Article IV); to make the 'potential benefits from any peaceful applications of nuclear explosives' available on a non-discriminatory basis through an international organization (Article V); and to 'pursue negotiations in good faith on effective measures relating to the cessation of the nuclear arms race at an early stage' (Article VI). Precisely what is meant by effective measures of nuclear arms control is defined by the preamble to the NPT, which singles out a comprehensive test-ban and repeats a well-worn objective, 'the cessation of the manufacture of nuclear weapons, the liquidation of all existing stockpiles, and the elimination from national arsenals of nuclear weapons and their means of delivery pursuant to a treaty on general and complete disarmament under strict and effective international control'.

Broadly speaking, there are four foci of dissatisfaction among non-parties to the NPT, shared to some extent by the reluctant and potentially recalcitrant parties to the treaty. First, there are protests that the treaty is politically inequitable as between nuclear and non-nuclear parties, imposing obligations (inspection under a safeguards system) on the latter but not the former and, more generally, sanctifying the status of the nuclear powers. Secondly, more particularly, there have been and remain complaints that the treaty perpetuates the commercial advantages of nuclear powers, especially by reserving to them the right to develop peaceful nuclear explosions. Thirdly, non-nuclear states have argued that the general obligations imposed on nuclear powers to work towards measures of nuclear arms control are an insufficient *quid pro quo* for the obligations non-nuclear states are required to accept. Finally, there are fears about the security of non-nuclear states, an issue dealt with by the treaty only by its provision for resignation on three months' notice but exacerbated by the absence from the list of signatories of the Chinese People's Republic (China) and, to a lesser extent, of France.[3]

---

[3] China has repeatedly declared that she will not be the first to use nuclear weapons in a conflict, an undertaking that does not bear directly on the question of how the Security Council would deal with other conflicts.

The asymmetry of the treaty has been a bone of contention from the beginning. The Chinese complaint that the treaty is a plot by the superpowers to perpetuate their dominance of international relations has been echoed by other governments, some of them parties to the treaty, but usually on more restricted and more specific grounds. That the treaty is indeed asymmetrical is self-evident, although the Soviet Union and the United States can claim that this merely reflects the balance of power in the world, and their own dominance in nuclear weapons, together with means of delivery. For at least some decades to come, it is inconceivable that this strength could be matched by other nuclear powers (China, France and Britain) or by near-nuclear powers of any kind. So far as the treaty itself is concerned, the most explicit political asymmetry is that, under the terms of the safeguards provisions, the uses made of nuclear materials by non-nuclear powers are verified by international inspection, but there is no means by which non-nuclear powers can verify that the nuclear powers are carrying out their obligations not to help with the proliferation of nuclear weapons.

The complaint that the NPT entails commercial discrimination against the non-nuclear powers has historically taken several forms. South Africa has stated that inspection by an international authority would jeopardize the secrets, whatever they may be, of the South African process for producing enriched uranium. Similar fears were voiced by the governments of West Germany and Japan. Although these fears persist, peaceful nuclear explosions have become a sharper issue. States such as Argentina, Brazil, India and Nigeria (which is nevertheless a party to the treaty) have repeatedly emphasized their commercial interest in peaceful nuclear explosions. One question still undecided is how far the Indian explosion of 18 May 1974 will reinforce these arguments.

Article V of the NPT, elevated during the negotiation from a part of the Preamble, does indeed require that the nuclear powers should make peaceful nuclear explosives available to non-nuclear weapon states, either through an international organization or bilaterally. In 1969, however, the board of the International Atomic Energy Agency (IAEA) decided that the agency itself was competent to arrange for and to supervise peaceful nuclear explosions; this view was endorsed by the UN General Assembly in December, and guidelines on the procedures suggested were circulated to member states in June 1972. So far (February 1975), there has been no official request from a member government to provide such a service, although there have been preliminary enquiries to the agency from Czechoslovakia, Rumania and Madagascar, none of which has yet led to a feasibility study. Formally, however, the requirements of Article V of the treaty have been met. Whether the parties to the NPT will consider them satisfactory is another matter.

What makes the issue of peaceful nuclear explosions contentious is, first, the consideration that there is no reason why the first Indian explosion should not be a cloak for a programme of military development, and, second, the difference of opinion between the Soviet Union and the United States about the utility of peaceful nuclear explosions. American enthusiasm has waned steadily since the mid-1960s, but Soviet interest in peaceful nuclear explosions persists.

A third series of complaints is that the NPT requires too little of the nuclear powers in nuclear disarmament. So much is clear from the arguments during the negotiation of the treaty.[4] Mr V. C. Trivedi, the Indian representative at the Geneva disarmament committee, was one of several who protested on the presentation of the first drafts of the treaty that 'by vivisecting the corporate body of non-proliferation', the nuclear powers had 'confused the issue'. The nuclear powers, Britain included (France has never taken her seat at the Geneva committee and was thus not involved in the discussions), held that the NPT should be considered on its own, and not as a part of a package deal on nuclear arms control, for fear that no agreement of any kind would be reached, and because 'the best may be the enemy of the good'. Nevertheless, the objectives included in the Preamble to the treaty and in Article VI make reasonably explicit the obligations undertaken by the nuclear powers. The immediate objective was a comprehensive test-ban, but there were also to be negotiations on nuclear arms control.

[4] Elizabeth Young, *The Control of Proliferation: The 1958 Treaty in Hindsight and Forecast*, Adelphi Paper No. 56 (London: IISS, April 1969).

Obligations of nuclear powers

The non-nuclear powers spelled out their expectations at the conference in August–September 1968, which among other things asked for a comprehensive test-ban as a matter of 'high priority', a halt to the development of nuclear weapons and delivery systems, as well as to the production of fissile material for weapon purposes, and 'the reduction and subsequent elimination' of nuclear stockpiles. (The Conference of Non-Nuclear Weapons States had nothing new to contribute to the concern of the super-powers, and of the United States in particular, that an agreement of this kind should be verifiable.) This reciprocal obligation was acknowledged both by the draft agenda for the Conference of the Committee on Disarmament, which replaced the Eighteen Nation Disarmament Committee in 1968, and by statements such as that by Mr Harold Wilson, at the time the British Prime Minister, who said on 5 March 1970, 'We know that there are two forms of proliferation, vertical as well as horizontal. The countries which do not possess nuclear weapons and which are now undertaking an obligation never to possess them have the right to expect that the nuclear weapon states will fulfil their part of the bargain.'

How adequately have the nuclear powers carried out their obligations? The comprehensive test-ban has not come about, but the Soviet Union and the United States agreed in Moscow on 3 July 1974 that there should be an upper limit to the explosive power of underground tests (equivalent to 150,000 tons of TNT) from 31 March 1976. The announcement by the Soviet Union and the United States, at the signing of the NPT in 1968, that they would hold bilateral talks on 'the limitation and reduction of both offensive and strategic nuclear weapon delivery systems' led, in May 1972, to the first Strategic Arms Limitation Talks (SALT I) agreement limiting the deployment of anti-ballistic missile systems and specifying upper limits for the numbers of offensive long-range missile systems to come into force in 1977. At Vladivostok in November 1974, the two super-powers agreed on guidelines for a second SALT agreement, due to be negotiated in detail by 1977. They also reached agreement on instruments 'reducing the risk of nuclear war', signed in Moscow on 30 September 1971; the four-power agreement on Berlin signed earlier that month; the sea-bed treaty which prohibits the placing of nuclear weapons on the sea-bed, which came into force in 1973; the Convention on Biological Warfare (not yet in force for lack of British and Soviet ratification); and, indeed, the whole apparatus of *détente*, which has been a conspicuous part of Soviet–American relations for the past three years.

Long though the list may be, it has some noticeable defects. So far as the nuclear powers are concerned, SALT I is a substantial step forward, for it has avoided the development of a range of weapons systems not vividly foreseen when the NPT was signed, but the full implications of SALT II are still imponderable. It is also beyond dispute that the process of negotiation has provided the super-powers with a more realistic appreciation of the difficulties the NPT obligations entail. Opinions differ,[5] but non-nuclear powers may fairly hold that the threshold test-ban agreement and the two instalments of SALT are insubstantial steps towards nuclear disarmament, the consequences of which may even be to permit an actual increase of nuclear warheads in the control of the United States and the Soviet Union. That is one complaint of the non-nuclear parties to the NPT. A second is that the bilateral character of the negotiations of these agreements is anomalous; even Britain, one of the sponsoring nuclear powers, has not been engaged in them. There is little reason to expect that those states that have declined to join the NPT on the grounds that the obligations of the nuclear powers are too vaguely defined will be persuaded to change their minds by what has been accomplished, at least so long as the non-nuclear powers are excluded from negotiations on nuclear arms control.

Security guarantees

The problem of the security of non-nuclear weapons states within the NPT has played an unexpectedly inexplicit part in public discussions of the past five years. The problem is obvious. If non-nuclear powers are required by the NPT not to manufacture or acquire nuclear weapons,

who is to safeguard their interests against the threat of nuclear attack? The NPT itself has nothing to say about security guarantees, although it does acknowledge that parties to the treaty may opt out in circumstances where they consider their security to be threatened,

The nuclear sponsors of the NPT responded with a set of identical declarations that they would 'provide or support immediate assistance' to non-nuclear weapon states subject to attack or the threat of attack with nuclear weapons, declarations given formal backing by a resolution of the UN Security Council on 19 June 1968. This device has been widely criticized as being meaningless, partly because each of the overt nuclear powers is now a permanent member of the Security Council, and has veto power there. Moreover, there is no prospect that the nuclear signatories of the NPT would commit themselves unilaterally or multilaterally to the assistance of non-nuclear powers in general; even within alliances, the credibility of nuclear guarantees is perpetually in doubt. In reality, critics of the Security Council resolution probably underestimate the degree to which the threat of a nuclear attack would necessarily become a *cause célèbre*, with consequent military intervention (conventional as well as nuclear). A more cogent criticism of the Security Council resolution is that it foresees a more explicit use of military nuclear power by emerging nuclear states than is likely to occur in practice. The cases of India and Israel show that unspoken threats may often have the effect of deterring conventional conflicts.

One of the most significant setbacks for the cause of non-proliferation in the recent past has, indeed, been the impression that even a modest nuclear striking force may enhance a nation's security, even if only temporarily, and that there may be circumstances in which the strategic interests of the super-powers will not inevitably be engaged. Thus India may calculate that Pakistan is less likely to go to war over, say, the Kashmir dispute if she considers that India could retaliate with nuclear weapons, but there is no reason why the established nuclear powers should consider themselves bound to redress the balance and no obvious way in which they could do so. This hypothetical situation points to a dilemma for the nuclear sponsors of the NPT: formal security guarantees for the non-

---

[5] William Epstein, 'NPT Article VI: How have the parties met their obligations' in *NPT: Paradoxes and Problems* (Washington DC: Arms Control Association/Carnegie Endowment for International Peace, 1975).

nuclear signatories of the NPT may be impracticable, but, in the absence of security guarantees by the nuclear powers, there is likely to be a steady erosion of the non-proliferation front.

Although the question of security guarantees has played a relatively inconspicuous part in public discussion during the past few years, there is good reason to suppose that in the long run, as in the past, it is considerations of national security that will persuade potential nuclear powers to calculate, perhaps wrongly, that nuclear weapons are desirable. The French Gallois doctrine is not, after all, forgotten, but has been taken up by China,[6] which argues that the NPT is a device for preventing non-nuclear powers from acquiring weapons needed for their self-defence. One of the chief arguments that follow is that proliferation will have to be contained, not exclusively within the framework of the NPT, but rather on a regional basis, which directs attention to the Treaty of Tlatelolco (the Treaty for the Prohibition of Nuclear Weapons in Latin America).

The Treaty of Tlatelolco

This treaty has its origins in 1963, and was signed in February 1967, before negotiation of the NPT was complete. The treaty is a model of how to set up a nuclear-free zone. It requires parties not merely to refrain from the development or acquisition of nuclear weapons but also provides for a permanent control system, and includes among its provisions for verification the novel principle of 'verification by challenge' – the permanent council (OPANAL) may ask for special explanations of suspicious happenings, while parties to the treaty may ask for special inspections to be carried out (at their own expense) on grounds certified as reasonable by the council. States external to Latin America are joined in the treaty by means of protocols dealing separately with states having jurisdiction over territory in Latin America (Protocol I) and with pre-existing nuclear powers – who are invited to respect the restrictions imposed on parties to the treaty (which does not prevent a state in Latin America from allowing the transit of nuclear weapons through its territory), and also to refrain from the use or the threat of use

of nuclear weapons against parties to the treaty (Protocol II). The potential benefits of such an agreement are several, but two have, as will be seen, an important bearing on the NPT – the safeguards procedures are simplified, and the security of the states concerned is enhanced not merely by the assurance that their neighbours will not become nuclear powers but also by the provisions of the two protocols.

The potential value of the Treaty of Tlatelolco does not, unfortunately, imply that its full benefits have already been won. Thus Latin American states differ in their understanding of what the treaty does and does not allow under the heading of peaceful nuclear explosions. Brazil is one of several states (Argentina is another) which hold that the treaty allows peaceful nuclear explosions (which have to be notified in advance and which are open to inspection); Mexico, like others, holds that peaceful nuclear explosions would be possible under the terms of the treaty only when the peaceful nuclear devices concerned are technologically distinguishable from nuclear weapons – an unattainable goal. A second difficulty is that the provisions of the treaty may be binding on some of those that have signed and ratified it only when all Latin American states are party to the treaty and all states that might be concerned have acceded to the two protocols. Formally, the treaty allows Latin American states to waive this restriction as it applies to them, a course which has been followed by only some. Others, Brazil for example, have not done so, with the result that the treaty is, for the time being, inapplicable. Argentina and Chile have signed but not ratified, while the Soviet Union has declined to sign Protocol II on the grounds that the transit of nuclear weapons and the conduct of peaceful nuclear explosions should also be prohibited. (One obvious bone of contention is the use of the Panama Canal by American naval vessels.) Thus, for the moment, the Treaty of Tlatelolco is not so much an assurance that Latin America is already a nuclear-free zone as a model of how such a zone may ultimately be established. One is bound to ask whether it does not deserve more attention from those concerned to foster the NPT system, both for its own sake and as a model of what might be accomplished in other regions (where, admittedly, circumstances are more complicated).

---

[6] Harry Gelber, *Nuclear Weapons and Chinese Policy*, Adelphi Paper No. 99 (London: IISS, 1973).

The future of the NPT

What else can be done, if necessary outside the framework of the NPT? The past few years have seen a number of unilateral declarations which bolster the NPT system. China's no-first-use declaration is one, but of limited credibility. France has also repeatedly declared that she would behave in her dealings with non-nuclear states as if she was a party to the NPT, which is better than nothing but not nearly as good as signature (see Chapter IV). Then several suppliers of nuclear equipment, all of them signatories of the NPT, have made concerted undertakings to the IAEA not to supply certain items of equipment to states in which safeguards agreements are not functioning. As will be seen, there are several ways in which the commercial benefits of accession can be made substantial, but, for the rest, the acid test of whether the NPT will be strengthened rests chiefly on increasing the membership list. Much will depend on whether Italy and Japan ratify the treaty. The developing attitude of France could have a powerful influence.

In the long run, however, nothing can permanently conceal the fact that the NPT unites three of the nuclear powers with a diverse group of non-nuclear powers, and that the two groups have often radically different perceptions of their common problem. The nuclear powers are most of all concerned to prevent the emergence of further independent nuclear powers. Non-nuclear parties to the treaty, even if they regard as desirable the prevention of what is awkwardly called horizontal proliferation, are also concerned that the nuclear powers should implement their explicit undertaking on nuclear arms control, an argument also advanced (not usually in isolation) by non-signatories. The tension between the two groups is reinforced by fear, or resentment, of big-power dominance and, indeed, by the kinds of tensions that have led in the past two years to the rapid increase in the price of oil and the demand, at the Special General Assembly of the UN in April 1974, for 'a new economic order'. It is probable that both the industrialized West and the Soviet Union have underestimated the strength of these arguments.

II. NEW WAYS WITH WEAPONS

In the twelve years since the Partial Test-Ban Treaty was signed and the negotiation of the NPT began, the technical task of developing nuclear weapons independently has become less formidable for many states. The same, of course, is true of the development of other technical innovations, radio receivers for example. But nothing that has happened implies that the manufacture of nuclear weapons is now child's play, or that it will become so in the immediate future. Technical innovations may have an important bearing on the spread of nuclear weapons in the years ahead, but the most striking innovation is the now widespread familiarity with technology.

Of the conceptual changes that have occurred, by far the most significant is the recognition that a state embarking on the acquisition of nuclear weapons does not necessarily commit itself to the technically difficult and financially burdensome course of what may be described as the classical evolution of nuclear power, the development of a range of weapons (including thermonuclear weapons) and of sophisticated delivery systems (including ballistic missiles). There are circumstances in which a relatively unsophisticated nuclear device and conventional aircraft may be sufficient to provide some assurance that narrow strategic objectives may be assured.

The case of Israel's nuclear reputation is a vivid illustration. Technically, it is entirely possible that Israel could have accumulated enough plutonium for a small number of fission

81

bombs by the careful operation of the Dimona reactor in the past fifteen years, and some earlier suspicions[7] were confirmed in December 1974 by the statement of the Israeli President that Israel 'is in a position to make atomic bombs'.[8] Although there has been no test, countries such as Egypt and Syria would plainly now be unwise to suppose that Israel could not mount a nuclear attack on a small number of targets. The political risks for Israel of using nuclear weapons in some future conflict over the territories captured in 1967 would be enormous, but, by the same test, the use or the threat of the use of nuclear weapons in the case of an Arab invasion of Palestine itself might be reckoned (at least in Israel) to be relatively free from the risk of losing American support and could also be an effective deterrent. It goes without saying that even an unspoken threat may profoundly influence the long-term calculations of Egypt and Syria, and conceivably even of the Palestine Liberation Organization.

A more subtle case is that of India, which is in her nuclear posture a mirror image of Israel. Israel has held no tests but suggests that she could be a nuclear power; India has exploded a nuclear device but says she has no military intentions. To the extent that potential adversaries may be sceptical of declaratory policies in this field – and there is plenty of room for doubt about India's objectives – there will be some strategic benefits, at least in the short run. Pakistan, for example, will be more circumspect about military excursions along the border with India or Kashmir, at least until her own air defences can assure a much higher attrition rate against Indian aircraft. Although the advantage of a temporary stabilization of the border with Pakistan may be small, given Indian superiority in conventional arms, and although it may eventually be cancelled out, it is a tangible gain for India. Other states, in the years ahead, may consider that they have similar gains to make from an independent nuclear striking force. Inherently, there is nothing intrinsically novel in this concept, which is indeed a close echo of General de Gaulle's early concept of the utility of French nuclear weapons. To be able to 'tear off

an arm' from a potential adversary might constitute a sufficient deterrent for a smaller power. The novelty consists in the demonstration by both Israel and India that it is possible to make ventures into the nuclear field, however ambiguous they may be, which secure limited strategic gains.

In some circumstances, even a threat, or an implicit suggestion, that a non-nuclear power might exercise a nuclear option may be a source of tangible advantages. Thus there is a chance that both Israel and Pakistan have been able to strengthen their claims on the United States for supplies of conventional military equipment by suggesting that the alternative may be the emergence of another nuclear power.[9]

Another innovation of the past few years is the argument, dramatized by Willrich and Taylor in a recent book,[10] that nuclear weapons can be made from forms of fissile material intrinsically more rudimentary than those on which the established nuclear powers have traditionally relied. The newly recognized possibilities concern fission bombs and, in particular, those based on plutonium. First, the argument goes, it may be possible to construct nuclear weapons from plutonium of the kind extracted from commercial nuclear power stations, containing substantial amounts (say 10 per cent or more) of plutonium-240, a material which differs from the nuclear explosive plutonium-239 in not being fissile under the circumstances encountered in fission bombs. Secondly, Willrich and Taylor have drawn attention to the possible use of plutonium and other radiological weapons by using conventional explosives to disperse quantities of damaging radioactivity among a population. (This is an alternative to the 'cobalt bomb' of the late 1950s.)

These technical possibilities have an obvious bearing on the ways in which national or international safeguards systems might be subverted by, say, groups of terrorists. Legitimate governments bent on the development of nuclear weapons will not, however, find it advantageous to follow routes like these. Radiological weapons may suit terrorists but are not military weapons.

---

[7] Leonard Beaton and John Maddox, *The Spread of Nuclear Weapons* (London: Chatto & Windus, 1962).
[8] *The Times*, 3 December 1974, p. 1.

[9] *Aviation Week*, 17 February 1975, p. 47.
[10] Mason Willrich and Theodore B. Taylor, *Nuclear Theft: Risks and Safeguards* (Cambridge, Mass.: Ballinger Publishing Co., 1973).

They constitute credible threats only against centres of population, while the damage that they might do is at once uncertain and, in any case, would be delayed not merely by days but by years.

Fission bombs based on commercial plutonium are unlikely to be used by legitimate governments, but for different reasons. For smaller powers, one of the serious bottlenecks in the development of fission bombs is the availability of plutonium, which is in turn dependent on the amount of time for which a reactor free from safeguards may be used for military purposes. But the rate at which plutonium of all kinds is produced in a reactor (kilograms per year, for example) is less if the reactor is operated commercially than if the fuel is withdrawn at frequent intervals. Then commercial plutonium containing large proportions of plutonium-240 is less efficient as an explosive than plutonium-239. The amount needed to construct a fission bomb is greater than with plutonium-239, while the explosive power of the device is less. What this implies is that governments embarking on self-contained programmes of nuclear weapons development will have powerful incentives to follow the traditional route to military plutonium. The use of plutonium from commercial nuclear reactors is relevant only to situations in which governments seek to avoid the full rigours of the safeguards system, or when parties to the NPT abrogate the treaty.

Taken together, these considerations imply that the smaller nuclear powers of the future will equip themselves with well engineered nuclear weapons, whose explosive power will be in the range of those dropped on Hiroshima and Nagasaki in 1945.[11] Quite apart from the need to economize in plutonium, putative nuclear powers will be aware that inefficient nuclear weapons may not constitute a decisive improvement on conventional explosives. Weapons yielding the equivalent of, say, 100 tons of TNT would probably not allow the nation deploying them to establish an unquestioned strategic advantage over its potential adversaries. It is significant that the performance of weapons based on commercial plutonium is inherently difficult to predict and that the range of their explosive power may extend as low as the equivalent of 100 tons of TNT.

Taken together, these considerations imply that putative nuclear powers will ordinarily have a powerful incentive to develop efficient weapons. On the other hand, in present and foreseeable circumstances, many near-nuclear powers will be aware that modern conventional aircraft constitute delivery systems which are entirely satisfactory, given that the nature of their current strategic goals is limited. This is the assumption underlying the discussion that follows.

For practical purposes, there are at present two nuclear explosives – plutonium-239 and uranium-235.[12] The first must be made in nuclear reactors – for the time being, reactors using natural or slightly enriched uranium as fuel – the second by means of some physical device for separating the isotopes of uranium from each other. The task of fashioning explosive devices from these materials involves two steps – the theoretical design of an explosive device, and the advance testing of the components necessary to make it function. These steps will be dealt with separately.

Making plutonium

Any nuclear reactor using uranium fuel will produce plutonium as a by-product, but the quantity obtained will depend on the design of the reactor, its power output, and the way in which it is operated. Would-be nuclear powers will ordinarily choose reactors that can use natural uranium as a fuel. For practical purposes, they have three choices of design – heavy water reactors built along the lines of the Canadian CANDU reactor; gas-cooled reactors using

---

[11] The equivalent of 16,000 tons and 8,000 tons of conventional explosive respectively. The first Indian nuclear explosion is estimated by Indian sources to have been the equivalent of 11,000 tons of TNT, but this may be an overestimate. See R. Chidambaram and R. Ramanna, *Some Studies on India's Peaceful Nuclear Explosion Experiment* (Bhabha Atomic Research Centre, Bombay).

[12] In due course, thorium will be used as a fuel for nuclear reactors, and will yield the nuclear explosive uranium-233 as a by-product. Such a fuel cycle is indeed at present under development in the United States for the Shell-Gulf Atomic High Temperature Reactor. But the extraction of uranium-233 raises formidable problems in chemical engineering, and even in India, well supplied with thorium ore deposits, plans for manufacturing uranium-233 in large quantities are unlikely to be fulfilled until the 1990s.

graphite for decelerating fission neutrons; and special-purpose air-cooled reactors, again dependent on graphite for moderating the speed of the neutrons. The first two types of design entail larger capital costs for a given output of plutonium, but can be made to produce electricity as a by-product. Heavy water reactors are best suited for small-scale production, and many potential nuclear powers will no doubt have taken to heart the recent revelation that the first air-cooled reactors built in Britain for the manufacture of plutonium were only barely able to function as sources of plutonium because of a miscalculation of the effects of impurities in the graphite on the efficiency of the nuclear reaction.[13]

Although the past two decades have seen a rapid spread of familiarity with the technology of nuclear reactors, it would be wrong to underestimate the complexity of the task facing a state embarking on the independent construction of reactors for manufacturing nuclear explosives. The manufacture of pure uranium metal is a piece of chemical engineering comparable in difficulty with the operation of a small-scale nickel extraction plant. Manipulating the gaseous compound uranium hexafluoride, a necessary step in the purification process, is a serious technical problem. The production of moderating material, either graphite or heavy water, is a task of comparable difficulty, while heavy water reactors require that the fuel should be clad in alloy cans made largely of zirconium, an unfamiliar technology with few applications in industries of other kinds. Although each of these steps is in principle straightforward, each of them requires a substantial effort on technological development in the absence of external assistance.

This is why, even with the spread of reactor technology which the past few years have seen, the manufacture of plutonium is bound to separate the industrially advanced powers from the less advanced. It is a task well within the competence of non-nuclear powers such as Australia, Canada and Sweden, as the events of the past two decades have plainly demonstrated. States such as Pakistan, by contrast, would find the development of a self-sufficient reactor

industry a formidable undertaking. India is a borderline case, now self-sufficient in reactor technology after a train of technical developments begun more than fifteen years ago which has benefited substantially from external technical assistance, principally from Canada.

The degree to which non-nuclear powers are provided with technical assistance from established nuclear reactors is certain, in the years ahead, powerfully to determine the potential for the spread of nuclear weapons. There is a world of difference between knowing what should be done to manufacture the components for a reactor system and being able to carry out these tasks with confidence. But reactor suppliers embarked on the construction of a nuclear reactor customarily acknowledge the need that the industrial resources of the recipient state should be as fully used as possible. In the process, the technologists of the recipient state inevitably acquire at first hand some of the skills required for the operation of an independent reactor system for manufacturing military plutonium. If the recipient state is not a party to the NPT, the particular reactor concerned will ordinarily be subject to safeguards, either bilaterally with the commercial supplier or internationally through the IAEA. The course of events in India has, however, shown that there is no technical or legal impediment to the use of the same techniques in the construction of reactors which are, in a common Indian phrase, 'safeguards-free'.

To the extent that the value of technical assistance to a non-nuclear state may often consist in the acquisition of novel skills, the transfer of nuclear technology (as distinct from the supply of self-contained equipment) to non-parties to the NPT is bound to facilitate the recipient's task of making nuclear weapons. The steps taken by the major suppliers of nuclear equipment (see Chapter IV) to ensure that reactor fuels and certain reactor components should not be supplied, except under safeguards, do not, and cannot, meet the objection that, simply by learning new techniques, reactor recipients will become more able to mount their own programmes of explosives manufacture independently. In retrospect (see Chapter III), Canada's major contribution to India's potential nuclear capability rests not so much in the provision of the 40 megawatt (MW) reactor at Trombay, with its ambiguous safeguards provisions, but

---

[13] Margaret Gowing, *Independence and Deterrence*, Volume 2, *Policy Execution* (London: Macmillan, 1974).

in the foundation of the Indian reactor industry now being developed. It is, however, only proper to acknowledge that, with the passage of time, all states become technologically more skilled; this stable door cannot permanently be shut.

Once equipped with a reactor, a potential nuclear power can easily estimate the rate at which fissile material accumulates. A reactor producing I MW of thermal power (equivalent to between a quarter and a third as much in terms of electricity) operating day and night will yield between 0·17 and 0·25 kg of plutonium-239 a year. This fissile material is increasingly converted into the contaminant plutonium-240 as more energy is extracted from the fuel, while some of the plutonium-239 itself becomes a source of energy and is lost to explosives manufacture. The result is that the efficient production of fissile material requires that uranium should be withdrawn from reactors sooner than if the prime objective is to produce electricity. A 100 MW reactor might in these circumstances produce between 25 and 35 kg of plutonium a year, but would require an input of more than 35 tons of natural uranium fuel, some of which might be reused in later years. It goes without saying that the supply of uranium is likely always to be a difficult problem for states without ore deposits of their own.

The extraction of plutonium from uranium fuel is in principle well and widely understood, and small-scale plants of this kind have been in operation for several years, not merely in India but in countries such as Argentina. Technologically, the problems of operating such a plant on a scale sufficient to produce usable amounts of fissile material are chiefly those of manufacturing in bulk (quantities running into tens of tons) certain simple chemicals such as nitric acid and of fabricating certain chemical reaction vessels from stainless steel. Large-scale separation plants raise problems that are qualitatively more difficult. (Appendix 2 on p.108 attempts to illustrate the degree of advancement in reactor technology of several non-nuclear weapon states.)

Enriching uranium

The second practicable route to fissile material is the separation of the fissile isotope uranium-235 (in its nuclear properties very similar to plutonium-239) from the natural uranium of which it constitutes 0·71 per cent. Fissile uranium for the first American bombs was produced by two distinct devices: electromagnetic machines in which atoms of uranium-235 are distinguished from the other isotopes of uranium by their different mass, and diffusion plants in which the separation depends on the different speeds with which the isotopes diffuse through the pores in specially sintered membranes. For would-be nuclear powers with non-independent economic motives for manufacturing enriched uranium (cf. South Africa and Australia), each of these techniques is likely to be less attractive than the plutonium route to nuclear explosives.

May other methods of isotope enrichment simplify the process of obtaining uranium-235? One significant development is that of the centrifuge technique of separation by the Anglo–Dutch–German consortium known as Eurenco. Compared with the diffusion plants now operated by the five nuclear powers, centrifuge separation can be made to function economically on a smaller scale, and the existence of centrifuge plants could be concealed. Moreover, the essential design parameters of the centrifuge process are now widely known.[14] The development of such machines is largely a problem in precision engineering and materials development with some awkward electro-mechanical accompaniments. Non-nuclear powers embarking on the development of a centrifuge separation plant would be unable, without outside assistance, to estimate the chances that their programme would succeed. Again, without outside assistance, the development of efficient centrifuge machines would necessarily be time-consuming, occupying perhaps a decade, but thereafter the manufacture and assembly into an isotope separation plant of the 300 or so machines would be merely a substantial drain on highly skilled labour. For the time being, in other words, centrifuge enrichment is such a speculative and difficult route to uranium-235 that, in spite of its long-term interest, would-be nuclear powers of modest technological means are likely to find plutonium manufacture simpler.

There are several still hypothetical alternatives, perhaps the best-known of which is a scheme for separating the isotopes of uranium by forcing a

---

[14] P. Boskma, 'Uranium enrichment technologies and the demand for enriched uranium' in *Nuclear Proliferation Problems* (Stockholm: SIPRI, 1974).

mixture of uranium hexafluoride and helium gas to flow through a curved expanding nozzle. Theoretically, the system should be effective in bringing about a high degree of separation, but it is also a profligate consumer of electric power. German interest in the system continues, but Indian interest in nozzle separation has, according to officials of the Indian Atomic Energy Commission, been abandoned. Japan is supporting research along these lines, but without much enthusiasm.

Three other principles by means of which isotopes such as those of uranium may be separated from each other have greater potential promise, even if they are, for the time being, merely pointers to the future. Variously, they depend on the differing degrees to which atoms of uranium isotopes in chemical compounds can be absorbed by certain material, on their capacity to absorb light from lasers and their slightly different speed in a mixture of uranium hexafluoride and helium. Theoretically again, the third of these systems is reckoned to have potentially great advantages in that it should be possible to produce a much greater degree of separation in each single unit of a separation plant. But theory is no substitute for practice, and each of these principles is as yet untested (unless it is that the South African process depends on a variation of the first).

By the 1980s, however, circumstances could well have changed. One of these processes, or some other, could well turn out to have important advantages for would-be small-scale separators of uranium-235, while research may show that the technical development of such a process is not nearly as formidable as that of, say, a centrifuge separation process. What all this implies is that there is a high chance, but no certainty, that the technology of uranium enrichment may be substantially simplified, and the impediments to nuclear proliferation correspondingly diminished, in the foreseeable future.

Techniques for the enrichment of uranium bear on the issue of nuclear proliferation in another sense – the major suppliers of uranium ore have a powerful economic incentive to sell not ore as such but the enriched uranium suitable for making into reactor fuel elements. The logic is precisely that by which members of the Organization of Petroleum Exporting Countries have in the past few years moved 'downstream' in the petroleum business, manufacturing petrochemicals on their territory, in an attempt to secure as large a share as possible of the economic rent to be won from the exploitation of crude oil. This is the chief motive for the South African development of an enrichment process, but in the past few years countries as different as Australia, Canada, Zaire and Gabon have discussed the building of enrichment plants with potential partners overseas. With the exception of South Africa, the principal uranium suppliers are at present parties to the NPT, but Brazil and India have potentially large supplies to offer. In due course, much will depend on the terms on which they are prepared to supply enriched uranium.

Designing nuclear explosions

The principles on which nuclear explosions are arranged have been publicly well understood since the publication of the Smyth Report in 1946, but the numerical data on the nuclear properties of uranium and plutonium isotopes are also now available in the open literature. There is no reason why a small group of competent physicists should not be able to devise the principles on which nuclear weapons might be constructed in a matter of weeks. Few of the non-signatories of the NPT do not have access to the necessary skills, for example among their university teachers.

As always, the difficulties are practical, not conceptual. First, laboratory work is needed to verify that the nuclear explosives which have been produced do indeed have the properties predicted for them. Secondly, whether or not the device is based on uranium-235 or plutonium-239, experimental work with conventional explosives is unavoidable. This part of the task of devising an explosion is especially important for plutonium explosions, where efficiency requires that a sufficient quantity of plutonium is rapidly compressed by means of a carefully controlled explosion in a surrounding mass of conventional explosive. So as to economize in fissile material, it is also necessary to investigate experimentally the effects of surrounding fissile material with shields of materials which reflect neutrons back into the explosion – natural uranium is one of the most suitable materials. Efficiency may also require the provision of an extra source of neutrons, usually made from small quantities of beryllium and polonium, the latter a radioactive material made by exposing quantities of bismuth in a nuclear reactor.

An indication of the effort involved in the practical development of nuclear weapons can be inferred from a recently published account[15] of the British nuclear weapons project, which was admittedly aimed at the development of highly engineered devices suitable for use as weapons. Although several members of the British bomb team were aware of several of the technical details of the research and development carried out at Los Alamos during World War II, the technical effort was provided by more than a hundred scientists and engineers, while important parts of the research (in electronics and polonium manufacture) were contracted out to other research establishments and commercial organizations. From start to the first test explosion, the project lasted for five years. The implications are plain – making plutonium weapons, as distinct from conceiving of them, was in the 1950s a formidable undertaking, chiefly because of the need to bring to fruition several parallel development programmes.

Although many would-be nuclear powers might be satisfied with less ambitious goals (200 fission bombs at the end of eight years), and although intermediate test explosions would provide considerable simplifications, the development of nuclear weapons based on plutonium probably remains as complicated a task as, for example, would be the development and construction of a 1940s aircraft, say a DC-3.

Weapons based on uranium-235 are intrinsically simpler, but, for the time being, the supply of the fissile material is a more serious bottleneck.

[15] Margaret Gowing, *Independence and Deterrence*, Volume I, *Policy Making* (London: Macmillan, 1974).

Producing the materials
However successfully an intending nuclear power may carry through a development programme along these lines, the rate at which weapons can be produced will depend on the availability of fissile material and on the amount of material needed for the manufacture of a single weapon. Precisely what quantities of plutonium or uranium are needed for a nuclear explosion depends sensitively on the purity of the materials as well as on the design of the neutron reflector. In ideal circumstances, as little as 4 or 5 kg of plutonium might be made to cause a nuclear explosion, but it would be necessary to use roughly twice as much plutonium if it were contaminated with plutonium-240 to the extent of 10 per cent. Uranium enriched to the extent of 90 per cent in uranium-235 would explode if some 10 kg were brought together in a spherical arrangement within a good reflector (the weight of which might be in excess of 50 kg). Less pure material would require disproportionately larger amounts of uranium-235.

These numbers are of critical importance for nations intending to acquire a substantial stock of nuclear weapons, and in particular imply that would-be nuclear powers fully in charge of modest production facilities will have powerful economic incentives to aim at the development of the most efficient weapons. With the passage of time, however, circumstances will change. By the early 1980s, for example, India (see Chapter III) will have a plutonium production capacity free from safeguards of roughly 600 kg a year. Several other medium powers will have comparable nuclear generating capacity, which is why much interest centres on the integrity of the safeguards systems to which these growing nuclear industries will be subjected (see Chapter IV).

III. INDIA – A CASE STUDY

The Indian nuclear explosion of 18 May 1974 has been described by the government of India as part of a programme for the development of peaceful nuclear explosions, but, both technically and politically, its significance is much wider. For one thing, it has raised in some quarters – in Pakistan for example – the possibility that India may in the near future be able to exercise modest military nuclear power. Certainly the explosion has demonstrated that India is embarked on a course of development that will provide a military nuclear option in the near future, by the 1980s for example. Then the explosion has called in question the arrangements which exist for the supply of nuclear equipment to non-signatories of the NPT, as well as the place of nuclear explosions in the peaceful applications of nuclear energy. What follows is an analysis of these issues based on conversations with officials in India and Pakistan in the early weeks of 1975.

Technically, Indian interests in nuclear energy go back to the closing months of World War II. The competence and technical originality of the Indian Atomic Energy Commission (AEC) has been widely recognized since the mid-1950s (when India made several significant contributions to the first UN conference on the peaceful uses of atomic energy). Now the organization stands out among other public corporations in India for its western style of management, its technical leadership (in fields such as electronics and mechanical engineering), its achievement in building up the ingredients of a virtually self-sufficient nuclear industry, and the size of its budget, which has risen steadily over the years to more than $125 million a year. It has rightly been called 'a state within a state'.

The notion that India might become a military nuclear power has been widely canvassed since the early 1960s. The late Homi J. Bhabha, then chairman of the AEC, was in the period 1959–62 a tireless advocate of nuclear weapons for India, partly on the grounds that such a development was indispensable to the assurance of India's non-aligned policy, but also because it would be a necessary means of keeping the strategic balance with China. Publicly, the Indian position on nuclear proliferation has the merit of consistency, which can be traced back to 1954, when the Prime Minister, Mr Jawaharlal Nehru, urged on the UN Disarmament Commission a standstill on nuclear tests and an agreement on the cessation of production of fissile material for military purposes. From the beginning of the negotiation of the NPT, India asked that safeguards should be applied equally to the production of fissile material by nuclear and non-nuclear states (which does not imply the destruction of existing nuclear weapons) but also claimed that a non-proliferation treaty 'should not prohibit any peaceful uses of nuclear energy or technology'. The peaceful nuclear explosion has been a persistent theme in the public statements of Indian prime ministers since the mid-1960s. Declarations that India has no

intention of developing nuclear weapons have, however, been intercalated by statements that circumstances could change in such a way as to 'force' India to become a nuclear power.[16]

Even if policy declarations are accurate representations of what governments at present intend, they have no permanent validity. Governments can change their minds, or even be replaced by governments with different policies. The Indian response to external criticism of the explosion in May 1974 has frequently been to reiterate that India has no military ambitions in the nuclear field.[17] What the Indian government unreasonably discounts is that external perceptions of its intentions are more significant than its own policy declarations.

Technically, the explosion of May 1974 was no great surprise. The device itself used plutonium as an explosive, and the nuclear reaction was initiated by means of conventional explosives, as in the Nagasaki bomb. The plutonium was extracted from fuel from the Cirus heavy water reactor, built at Trombay (a few miles north of Bombay) with the assistance of Atomic Energy of Canada Limited during the early 1960s. The reactor has been operating since 1964, and can produce up to 40 MW of heat. Plutonium has been separated from the reactor fuel at a small-scale separation plant at Trombay, and indeed both plants are within the boundary fence of what is now the Bhabha Atomic Research Centre, the chief research and development laboratory of the Indian AEC.

The efficiency with which the reactor functioned over the decade 1964–74 is not known, and it is not known whether fuel has been loaded and discharged from the reactor on a pattern that would make the fullest use of its plutonium-generating capacity. In the best case, India may have accumulated 10 kg of plutonium a year for the best part of a decade. It is probably reasonable to suppose that the reactor has been made to yield at least 50 kg of the material during that period, and that plutonium is now accumulating at roughly 10 kg a year. Allowing for the uncertainty that persists about the quality of the plutonium used, and about the

[16] Mrs I. Gandhi, interview published in *Al Ahram* (Cairo), March 1973.
[17] V. C. Trivedi, 'India's approach towards nuclear energy and non-proliferation of nuclear weapons', in *NPT: Paradoxes and Problems, op. cit.*

sophistication of the device exploded in May last year, the chances are that India now has enough unused nuclear explosives to carry out between four and eight further explosions. And for the next three years, until other reactors free from the safeguards come into service, plutonium enough for one or two explosions will be added to the inventory each year.

Nuclear self-sufficiency

The use of plutonium from the Cirus reactor for the first Indian nuclear explosion is itself significant. As long ago as 1962, before the reactor came into service, it was plain that the agreement between Canada and India on the use to which the plutonium might legitimately be put was likely to be contentious. It made no provision for objective safeguards or inspections, but merely required an undertaking from the government of India that the plutonium would not be used for military purposes. By 1970, when Indian interest in peaceful nuclear explosions was apparent, the Canadian government sought assurances from India that the plutonium would not be used for making explosive devices of any kind, but without success. Since Mrs Indira Gandhi's negative response to a letter from the Canadian Prime Minister in 1971, it has been plain that India would not provide these assurances. India's justification of this position is at least self-consistent. The original agreement with Canada, the argument goes, does not prohibit peaceful nuclear explosions, which are in any case of potential economic benefit to India, while it would be discriminatory to accept more stringent conditions on the allowed uses of the reactor than were originally foreseen. In the event, Canada was not given advance warning of the explosion on 18 May 1974.

In passing, it is important that India appears grossly to underestimate the way in which her handling of this matter has given offence to Canada. The Cirus reactor was the first of substantial size to function in India (an indigenous research reactor with small capacity went into operation roughly a decade earlier) and has become the pattern on which the Indian AEC now plans to develop much larger civil nuclear power stations. Reactors already in operation include two boiling water reactors of American design at Tarapur (100 kilometres north of Bombay), which between them produce 400 MW of electricity but which are fully covered by safeguards, and the first of two reactors of the Canadian heavy water type at Rana Pratap Sagar in Rajasthan. Ultimately, the two reactors will produce 400 MW of electricity (and could yield perhaps 240 kg of plutonium a year), but the completion of the second is now held up by the Canadian decision not to supply further nuclear assistance to India without an assurance that plutonium will not be used for nuclear explosions, even for supposedly peaceful purposes. In February the negotiation of a new treaty was deadlocked, and Indian officials were speculating on the possibility that, if they were required to complete the reactor without further assistance, both of the Rajasthan units might be held to be free from safeguards on the grounds that Canada had broken the original agreement.

The use of the Cirus reactor for making the first charge of nuclear explosives is, in reality, less significant than the way in which Canadian technical assistance during the 1960s helped to create India's self-sufficiency in reactor technology. Canada has helped with the development of the Indian heavy water plants, four of which (with a total output of 300 tons a year) are now planned to supplement that already in operation (and producing 14 tons of heavy water a year), and the Indian nuclear fuel complex at Hyderabad, chiefly distinguished by its capacity to refine zirconium and fabricate zirconium alloys into fuel cans for uranium fuel. These facilities are the industrial base on which India has embarked on two further nuclear power stations at Narora (Uttar Pradesh) and Madras, originally intended as replicas of the Rajasthan power stations but with more than 80 per cent of the construction undertaken indigenously. The Narora reactors, originally due to come into service in 1981 and 1982 respectively, may be delayed if the dispute with Canada is not quickly settled, but India will be able to follow through the programme on which she has embarked by the mid-1980s even without further assistance from outside. The design is also complete of a 100 MW (thermal) reactor on the same pattern to be built on the site of the Bhabha Atomic Research Centre at Trombay, and this, if built, should augment the supply of plutonium in the early 1980s.

What the collaboration between India and

Canada has demonstrated most vividly of all is the ease with which a country such as India, well endowed with technical skill of her own, rich in natural resources and with economic resources large enough (in aggregate) to be deployed on a single technological development, can become self-sufficient in nuclear technology. The total cost of the Indian development during the past two decades does not amount to much more than $1,000 million, although the years ahead are likely to require steadily increasing expenditures.

Military applications

So is India already a nuclear power in the military sense? For the time being, the answer is probably negative. First, the explosion in May 1974 is probably not a sufficient basis for the deployment of nuclear weapons. Even if the nuclear parts of the device were suitable for use in a nuclear bomb, the British experience in the 1950s shows that technical problems such as the techniques for arming (priming) a nuclear weapon and for suspending the nuclear explosive within an aerodynamically stable shell are not trivial, even though their solution need not require the testing of a weapon in the atmosphere. (India is in any case a party to the Partial Nuclear Test-Ban Treaty.) Secondly, the supply of plutonium is at present, even on the most optimistic assumptions, not enough to sustain a military programme. For, so long as the only means of delivery are conventional aircraft, military planners will have to take into their calculations a potentially high attrition rate. To threaten the use of nuclear weapons but to be unable to implement it would be to run a serious risk.

What of the future? The supply of plutonium will become more nearly sufficient to support a credible weapons programme by 1981, when the first of the Narora reactors is due to come into service, and possibly a year or so earlier if the 100 MW reactor at Trombay is built quickly. Even if the outcome of the renegotiation of the Canadian agreement on the Rajasthan reactors is negative, and if India afterwards feels free to use plutonium from these reactors for any purpose she chooses, it would be necessary to build a separation plant other than that at Tarapur for extracting the plutonium, which implies that substantial supplies of plutonium

would not be available much before the end of the 1970s.

The prospect that more sophisticated delivery systems than conventional aircraft will be available is more distant. Although India supports a steadily growing Space Research Organization (and has arranged with the Soviet Union that a satellite for scientific purposes should be launched from the Soviet Union in April this year – nearly six months behind schedule), the indigenous rocket programme is for the time being aimed at the development of a four-stage solid-fuelled rocket (somewhat similar to the American *Scout*) capable of putting a payload of 45 kg into a circular orbit about the earth. This programme, four years old, is already three years behind schedule, but should reach fruition before the end of this decade. The specification and conceptual design of a much larger rocket, capable of launching telecommunications satellites, is complete, but the date at which such a programme (which would have obvious military implications) would be complete must at this stage be problematical. What does seem plain is that the cost of developing a long-range solid fuel rocket for military applications would require expenditures much greater than those now available to the Space Research Organization, and greater even than have been devoted to the nuclear energy programme. Expenditure by the organization in 1973–74 amounted to $25 million, but would probably have to be increased considerably (approximately ten-fold) if it were to include the development of a strategic rocket system. Such a system, in other words, is unlikely to be a reality during the 1980s.

For the present, then, both the shortage of plutonium and the need to rely on conventional aircraft for delivering nuclear warheads suggests that the Indian government's public declarations are also a prudent acknowledgement of reality now and for the next year or two. India is not now a nuclear power, but may choose to become one in the next year or so, at least if conventional aircraft are considered suitable as delivery systems. But India cannot hope to be a strategic nuclear power for a decade.

Nuclear intentions

One of the reasons why Indian nuclear intentions are so frequently regarded sceptically elsewhere is that the goal of self-sufficiency, in rocket as well as nuclear technology, has been followed with a zeal that makes very little economic sense. India, for example, has an economic need for communications satellites, and is indeed engaged in an imaginative experiment to make use of a United States satellite for educational television broadcasting beginning in August 1975. What sceptics ask is why, if the need is so great, India should not follow Brazil and Indonesia in purchasing from the United States communications satellites which could provide the desired service now, not ten years from now, and much more cheaply than will be the cost of an indigenous programme of rocket development. In the circumstances, India has only herself to blame if outside observers, especially those whose self-interest is directly engaged, interpret the developments of the past few years as a sign that India, although not now capable of exercising military nuclear power, has secured an option to deploy nuclear weapons in conventional aircraft at the end of the decade or thereabouts, which may in due course yield a still more sophisticated nuclear capability. It is proper to add that at no time in the foreseeable future, say the next fifteen years, will India be in a position to match the nuclear strength of the established nuclear powers, not merely the super-powers but also China, France and Britain.

What purpose would be served by such a nuclear capability? Indian officials are quick to argue that there are no obvious military uses for indigenous nuclear weapons, and go on to cite this as yet another reason why India's pacific intentions should be taken at their face value. The argument is that India's conventional superiority over Pakistan is sufficient to assure supremacy in some future conflict within the sub-continent, while the inferiority of Indian delivery systems is a proof that India will not in the foreseeable future be able to engage in a dialogue about mutual deterrence with China. To the extent that Pakistan considers her to be a nuclear power already, however, India has already derived those military advantages that flow from knowing that the chances of a conventional attack by Pakistan have been substantially reduced. And, although the border dispute with China is for the time being quiescent, the possible use of nuclear weapons in a tactical role in some future conflict cannot be ruled out,

even though such a development would probably be counter-productive.

Outside the government, the view that nuclear weapons would indeed have military value is held by a small but influential section of opinion. The notion that India should become an independent nuclear power is not, after all, novel, and did not disappear with the death of Dr H. J. Bhabha. The most moderate version of the argument for an Indian nuclear option, typified by publications[18] of Dr K. Subrahmanyam, Director of the Indian Institute of Defence Analysis, is based on uncertainty about the future relationship of India and China. Nobody in India can be sure, the argument goes, that China and the Soviet Union will always be at daggers drawn, nor about the extension of Chinese influence in south-east Asia if or when the United States withdraws from the area. But, if Soviet and Chinese differences should be patched up, the now valid calculations that a Chinese attack on India would be inhibited by the Soviet Union would become invalid. And if China should seek to extend her influence in south-east Asia there is no means of telling how Indian interests would be affected. Finally, if India's future security should come to depend on a *rapprochement* with China, the possession of nuclear weapons will make it possible to secure better terms. Thus it is sufficient that India should be able to exercise an option to become a nuclear power in the next few years – in other words, present policies are entirely satisfactory.

A less moderate version of the argument for an independent nuclear capability, held by a small but isolated section of the Congress Party, would foreshorten the timescale. Thus it is held that there are already several circumstances in which Indian strategic interests may be threatened and in which nuclear weapons could play a useful countervailing part. The intervention of a power from outside the sub-continent in Pakistan or Bangladesh may be a remote possibility, but subversion of the parts of north-east India which adjoin Burma and China is more real. So, too, is the build-up of American and Soviet nuclear power in the Indian Ocean, while India – the

---

[18] K. Subrahmanyam, 'Indian nuclear force in the eighties?' in *The Institute for Defence Studies and Analyses Journal*, New Delhi, April 1973.

argument goes – should be capable of intervening militarily in conflicts throughout the region (from Indonesia to Israel) of Indian strategic interests. For the time being, at least, there is nothing to suggest that the government of India regards its strategic interests as being as widely spread, and indeed the views of both the 'moderate' and the extreme pro-bomb schools are frequently described as 'mad' (which is not to deny India's intense interest in and resentment of the presence of the nuclear powers in the Indian Ocean).

The Indian government does, however, appear to share with the pro-bomb schools the belief that nuclear explosions bring not merely prestige but influence. Soon after the first explosion in May last year, Indian officials spoke of the possibility of being able 'to talk to China on equal terms'. In the past six months this ambition appears to have faded, or at least to have receded, but India is much concerned with the effect of her first explosion on non-nuclear powers. Delhi has seen more visits by non-aligned heads of state in the past six months than in most comparable periods in the past few years, as if to suggest that India has been seeking to regain some of the influence among countries of the Third World that she enjoyed during the heyday of the non-alignment policy. There are some signs, as at the visit of President Kenneth Kaunda of Zambia to Delhi in January 1975, that east African states are more impressed by what India has accomplished than are those of west Africa, where there is some anxiety that the Indian explosion may in the long run endanger the flow of Western aid to all developing countries. The most tangible signs of achievement in this field are the agreement reached at the end of 1974 with Argentina and Brazil on scientific and technical collaboration, the former of which at least refers specifically to collaboration in nuclear energy and to the exchange of material and equipment. For the time being, it is not clear what significance must be attached to the agreement on economic and technical collaboration with Iran, which was signed in October 1974.

Consequences of the explosion

What, then, will be the consequences of the Indian explosion? And how should the supporters of the NPT system in particular respond?

The classical danger, that the first Indian explosion and the perception elsewhere in Asia of the emergence of a putative nuclear power will stimulate other states to follow suit, is not an immediate danger. Pakistan is the obvious case in point, especially because the Pakistani government appears to be ambivalent in its appreciation of what is happening in India – some officials take the view that India is already technically capable of mounting a nuclear attack towards the West, others take the more realistic view that what India has done is to announce that she has an option on military nuclear power.

Technically, however, Pakistan is a long way from being able to follow India in the manufacture of nuclear explosives. Although Pakistan has flirted with the peaceful applications of nuclear energy for fifteen years, for practical purposes there is only one substantial reactor in the country, the 125 MW (electrical) heavy water reactor at Karachi, supplied by Canada and safeguarded by means of a bilateral agreement through the IAEA. Plans for building a second larger nuclear power station are drawn up, but construction has been delayed both by the wish of potential suppliers, Canada in particular, to reassess the safeguards provision in the light of the Indian explosion and by simple lack of funds. Pakistan differs from India in being short of skilled manpower, especially in engineering, while the thoroughly competent research organization that has grown up over the years, although technically capable of designing nuclear weapons and then of organizing their production, appears not to have taken the steps along this road that India had already taken in the early 1960s.

Pakistan's capacity to develop nuclear weapons will be largely constrained by financial considerations. The country is, after all, merely an eighth the size of India, but it could not carry through a programme of nuclear development on its own without spending sums of money comparable with those devoted to the Indian project. (The possibility that such a development might be financed by Iran, widely discussed in India and Pakistan, is not to be considered seriously.) Pakistan is also, for the time being at least, painfully aware of her military weakness after the 1971 conflict with India.

To the extent that the objectives that underlie non-proliferation will be more easily attained if, for the present, Pakistan is dissuaded from following India in the development of a nuclear option, there are plainly several steps that might be taken to hold the present position. Perhaps the chief of these is to help strengthen Pakistan's defences against conventional aircraft, on the calculation that, for the next decade, India cannot have more sophisticated means of delivery. The lifting of the arms embargo by the United States will in principle allow Pakistan to acquire modern surface-to-air missiles. In the nature of things, formal security guarantees for Pakistan by China or by the United States, politically unlikely, would not be effective (in the sense of being credible).

So far, the perception elsewhere in southern Asia of India as an emergent nuclear power has been less immediate. The Japanese debate on the ratification of the NPT (not yet complete) has been little influenced by considerations of what has happened in India. Much will depend, in the years ahead, on the way in which India's view of her role in south-east Asia develops, but there is a possibility that at some stage India's exercise of her option to manufacture nuclear weapons could carry weight in Indonesia, in which case it is unlikely that Australia would continue to refrain from making nuclear weapons. The truth is that, for the time being, India's military interests (as distinct from her public declarations) are confined to the sub-continent, and that the prospect of her emergence as a nuclear power will provoke emulation only in two groups of states – those directly concerned (Pakistan alone at the present time) and those geographically unrelated which are persuaded by the events of the years ahead that India's non-military gains are substantial.

What are the non-military benefits of the explosion? Even if it were the case that the first Indian explosion had no military significance, there is very little doubt that India would set great store by being recognized as a source of nuclear technology. Even if India is unlikely, in the foreseeable future, to be able to supply complete nuclear reactors on a substantial scale, with the non-nuclear non-signatories of the NPT increasingly constrained by the restrictions of the major suppliers of nuclear equipment, the opportunities for earning foreign exchange by the supply of nuclear skill are plainly attractive to her.

Indian policy on overseas deals of this kind, obviously crucial for the future of the NPT, is characteristically ambiguous. Privately, both government officials and officers of the Indian Atomic Energy Commission say that it is India's policy not to supply equipment or technical assistance that would help in the emergence of further nuclear powers. One government official said earlier this year that even requests for assistance with peaceful nuclear explosions would be referred to the IAEA, which 'could do the work more cheaply'. On the face of things, then, India's policy coincides with that of France, which has repeatedly stated since the signing of the NPT that France would behave in her commercial dealings as if she were a party to the treaty.

The inconsistency in the Indian position is that the government will not make its policy public. 'To do that would conflict with our principles', said one official. 'If you quoted me on this', said another, 'I would deny that I'd said it.' In reality, however, India's unwillingness to make her professed policy public is not merely internally inconsistent but is also in conflict with her assertions that the explosion in May 1974 was not only the first step in a programme to develop nuclear weapons. The principles which supposedly inhibit a public declaration along these lines are simply those underlying the Indian justification of her independent development of nuclear explosive devices – that the NPT is discriminatory in favour of the nuclear weapon states, and that non-nuclear weapon states must be expected, independently and severally, to take whatever steps seem appropriate to redress the balance. In this sense India and China are at one.

It is hard to think that India can persist for very long with such a policy. Canada and the United States, both of them important suppliers of nuclear equipment for India, are in a position to force a clarification of this policy. Other signatories of the NPT similarly have a vested interest in helping to force such a clarification, while it is clear that the members of the Indian Aid Consortium can exercise a powerful influence.

Another and equally vulnerable inconsistency in Indian policy is the secrecy surrounding the programme of nuclear tests, of which the explosion of May 1974 was the first tangible expression. The factual account of the explosion so far published says that the objective of the explosion was to demonstrate that radioactivity could be contained. It is also clear that the test was not directly a test of the feasibility of using peaceful nuclear explosions to extract metal ores or petroleum – the strata in which the explosion took place contained neither. A realistic assessment cannot be begun until there has been at least a second explosion, but information on where or when this will take place is for the moment kept secret. If, however, the programme's objectives are strictly peaceful, there is plainly no reason why India should not follow the United States in making public her plans well in advance. (For that matter, the same demand might be made of the Soviet Union.) Nothing could be lost, while the adverse reaction overseas to a second explosion would be softened. The Indian assertion that there is, against the odds, a possibility that the Indian Atomic Energy Commission will be able to discover economic uses for nuclear explosions that have so far eluded the much larger 'Plowshare' programme in the United States, would be strengthened if Indian scientists had contributed something significant to the technical literature. Sceptics of India's policy declarations, therefore, have grounds for asking that India (and the Soviet Union) should make public, in advance of the next explosion, the technical basis on which the experiment is devised.

What this implies is that there are ways in which India, without becoming a party to the NPT, could powerfully help to allay the widespread scepticism of her intentions which has built up since May 1974. There are signs that, in the past six months, India has indeed been impressed by the volume of overseas criticism, as well as by the difficulties of renegotiating the agreement with Canada on the supply of equipment for the heavy water reactors, and by the recalcitrance of some (but not all) European members of the Aid Consortium. In the years immediately ahead, attitudes towards the nuclear programme may also be determined, in part at least, by faltering enthusiasm for nuclear power as a source of electricity. Although the Atomic Energy Commission has been technically successful, the major reactor programmes are several years behind schedule. Given the chronic shortage of electricity in India, as well as the growing claims on resources of other novel

technical enterprises, and the recognition that India could earn substantial amounts of foreign exchange by the export of conventional engineering and electrical equipment if only the technical skill were made available, it is not surprising that there is now a powerful voice within the government urging the development of conventional power sources, especially hydroelectricity and coal-burning power stations. In short, India's nuclear programme may falter for purely domestic reasons.

What remains unchanged is India's attitude towards arms control, especially in the nuclear field. As recently as February 1975, the Indian government seemed not to have changed its view, first expressed in the 1960s, that a sufficient condition for India becoming a party to the NPT would be an undertaking by the nuclear parties to the treaty to stop producing fissile material for military purposes, and their acceptance of safeguards in principle the same as those now imposed on non-nuclear parties to the treaty. Paradoxically, the accession of France and even of China is not considered at this stage to be essential, on the grounds that nuclear strength is at present 'irrelevant'. It is perhaps worth recalling that this position is unlikely to be tested in the near future.

Nuclear-free zone
A more immediate issue is the notion that India's strategic interests might be secured outside the framework of the NPT by means of a nuclear-free zone covering some part of southern Asia and the Indian Ocean. This issue was raised at the 1974 meeting of the UN General Assembly and now seems likely further to exacerbate relations between India and Pakistan. The concept of a nuclear-free zone in south Asia is not new, but in November 1974 Pakistan introduced a resolution asking the Assembly to endorse the good sense of a nuclear-free zone in the region and requesting that the Secretary-General should call a conference on the subject. An alternative resolution by India asked the assembly to acknowledge that the initiative for a nuclear-free zone should come from the states directly concerned. Both resolutions were carried, but the established nuclear powers abstained (except that China voted for Pakistan's resolution and the Soviet Union for India's).

One curious consequence of the informal

discussions in the United Nations is that Pakistan has been left with the impression that India is prepared to begin informal discussions about a nuclear-free zone for the sub-continent early in 1975, but that the Indian government thinks it has offered an opportunity to discuss Pakistan's fears about Indian nuclear intentions. The truth is that India has no stomach for a nuclear-free zone confined to the sub-continent, and in particular for any arrangement that fails to regulate the nuclear presence of the super-powers in the Indian Ocean. Indeed, the pro-bomb school takes the view that the only acceptable nuclear-free zone would stretch from Indonesia to Israel and would in any case depend on even more explicit assurances of restraint from China than have accompanied her accession to Protocol II of the Treaty of Tlatelolco. Nevertheless, there are grounds for supposing that the issue of a nuclear-free zone in the sub-continent is not entirely academic. Indeed, to the extent that the sub-continent engages the strategic interests of China, the issue offers the nuclear powers of the West an opportunity not merely of testing Indian intentions but also of bringing China into meaningful discussions of measures of arms control which need not founder before they begin on the repeated Chinese opposition to the NPT. Curiously enough, the state best placed to take the initiative in organizing the necessary discussions is Iran, which co-sponsored with Egypt at the 1974 UN Assembly a proposal for a nuclear-free zone in the Middle East, is in any case strategically concerned with the future of Pakistan and would no doubt value an opportunity to exercise her new-found power on an international stage.

The importance of the role Iran may choose to play in Asian affairs is a good illustration of the paradox of the Indian technical success in carrying out the first nuclear explosion by a developing country. In relation to her immediate neighbours, India is militarily strong, but economically not so well provided as Iran, only one-twentieth the size. India is alone among developing countries (with China possibly excepted) in having a self-sufficient nuclear industry, but being unable to keep her industries – and her hotel elevators – supplied with electricity.

Technically, the Indian nuclear programme has been a great success, but it is also an economic strain that will become more and not less onerous as the economy of India as a whole develops. Domestically, the Congress Party is increasingly under pressure from the newly prosperous, if numerically small, sections of the rural population, while its external economic failures are increasingly galling. There is of course no reason why logic should prevail, and India abandon a programme of no immediate civil or military utility, but there is at least a chance that India might settle for less than she is now asking for in return for a more explicit policy on non-proliferation and even on the Asian nuclear-free zone. The explosion of 18 May 1974 was not in any sense a damp squib; it may yet backfire.

IV. SAFEGUARDS AND THEIR ADEQUACY

The NPT requires of non-nuclear powers that their nuclear activities shall be subject to safe-guards administered by the IAEA but negotiated separately with the agency (Article III). The same article requires all parties not to provide nuclear materials or equipment designed to process or produce nuclear materials unless the 'source or special fissionable materials shall be subject to the safeguards required by this article' (Article III.2). The safeguards article clearly displays the different treatment of non-nuclear and nuclear states – the latter are not required to accept safeguards. It also gives the IAEA a judicial role in the working of the treaty, which is a sufficiently large extension of its previous responsibilities as to constitute an innovation in international relations whose importance has so far been unremarked.

Thus the safeguards system is an essential part of the NPT. Are the principles on which it is designed likely to survive the growth of commercial nuclear power? Is the IAEA, a largely technical organization, able to play the role defined for it, at least implicitly, as the ultimate arbiter of what is permissible within the terms of the NPT? What in any case is to be made of declarations such as that of the French government that France will behave in her commercial dealings with non-nuclear powers as if she had signed the NPT? And how can the safeguards be improved?

The role of the IAEA

The involvement of the IAEA in safeguards goes back to its early days and to the late 1950s. Its charter requires that nuclear material or equipment supplied to member nations shall not be used for military purposes. But, since the early 1960s, the agency has also become the custodian of a number of bilateral agreements between pairs of member countries – broadly speaking, most British, Canadian and American safeguards agreements on the uses made of reactors elsewhere in the world are now supervised by the IAEA. These earlier agreements,[19] however, refer only to specific supplies of either nuclear material or equipment. If, for example, a member state is supplied with enriched uranium for a reactor, the agency is required to safeguard the uses made of that material, both in the reactor and in any subsequent chemical separation plant in which it may be reprocessed, but only for as long as the material originally supplied is there. These safeguards arrangements also apply to fissile material produced by means of safeguarded material – plutonium produced in a fast reactor, for example. If, on the other hand, what has been supplied is a reactor, the safeguards agreement usually extends to whatever plants into which the products of that material may find its way – reprocessing plants and storage facilities, for example.

The NPT safeguards,[20] as they apply to non-nuclear parties to the treaty, are in principle more comprehensive. They apply to all nuclear facilities, research establishments and research reactors, just as much as to nuclear power stations and commercial separation plants. The IAEA is required to verify that 'material is not diverted to nuclear weapons or other nuclear explosive devices'. The technical basis on which such a comprehensive system should be agreed between the agency and each non-nuclear party to the treaty was worked out by a committee of the agency, in which 47 members participated, between June 1970 and March 1971. The recommendations of this agency committee were approved by the board of governors of the IAEA in April 1971 and have become the basis on which the IAEA had negotiated 46 agreements on safeguards with non-nuclear parties to the NPT by the end of 1974. One ironical feature of this procedure is that the 1970 safeguards committee included a number of conspicuous non-parties to the NPT, such as Argentina; Brazil, Chile, India, Pakistan, South Africa and Spain.

Among other things, the committee's recommendations gave the agency wide powers of supervision and inspection. NPT states are required to provide information about the design of nuclear facilities and also to maintain a system of accounting for nuclear material, furnishing regular reports to the agency, which then has the right to verify that no material has been diverted for carrying out explosions. In the specification of an inspection routine, the agency is allowed to take 'due account of the technical effectiveness' of a state's national system of accounting. In practice, the agency concentrates attention on strategic points in the nuclear fuel cycle chosen in such a way that entire plants, or parts of entire plants, can be considered separately as self-contained units.

Inspection

How accurate can a system like this be? In turning uranium ore into uranium fuel for reactors, there is in principle no substantial source of inaccuracy. Even if some uranium fails to finish up as fuel, prudent managers or half-awake inspectors should be able to tell how much has finished up as scrap. The conversion of uranium to plutonium in nuclear reactors is a greater source of uncertainty. There may be errors in calculating how much plutonium is produced from each kilogram of uranium, although prudent operators will usually check their theoretical calculations by measurement,

---

[19] IAEA, *The Agency's Safeguards System, 1965*, INFCIRC/66 (Vienna).
[20] IAEA, *The structure and content of agreements between the agency and states required in connexion with the treaty on the non-proliferation of nuclear weapons*, INFCIRC/153 (Vienna, 1972).

96

and, under the terms of safeguards agreements, IAEA inspectors are in any case empowered to do so. The operation of chemical reprocessing plants for the extraction of plutonium from irradiated uranium fuel involves other kinds of problems. The IAEA itself says that, with a new chemical separation plant, there may be a discrepancy of as much as 5 per cent between the quantities of plutonium thought to be entering the plant and the quantities collected at the output end, but that, for well-established plants, the 'material unaccounted for' should ordinarily be less than 2 per cent and ideally less than 1 per cent. Apart from uncertainty about the input, some plutonium may be carried away on the metal fuel cans and other scrap material, but cannot easily be measured, and some may accumulate within the plant.

These errors, whatever their cause, are potentially a cloak for cheating. The large commercial separation plants now coming into operation typically process a thousand tons of uranium fuel a year and would in many cases aim to separate more than ten tons of plutonium. Even a 1 per cent shortfall of plutonium production would amount to 100 kg a year, enough for several nuclear explosions. So far as the safeguards inspectors are concerned, the consistency with which a plant operates is an important but technically complicated question. But the inspectors have on their side the knowledge that, in the operation of chemical separation plants, the managers are likely to be as concerned as they are to know that the material lost from the fuel cycle is accounted for as accurately as possible.

What this implies is that the most vulnerable parts of the safeguards system are those in which plutonium or enriched uranium is stored or fabricated into fuel elements for reactors. One independent study[21] of a plutonium fuel manufacturing plant suggests that it should, by the proper design of inspection procedures, be possible to detect a diversion of 1 per cent of the throughput of a plant with a certainty of 95 per cent – a 1 in 20 chance of failure. But practice may fall short of the ideal. Plutonium stores are

[21] E. Drosselmeyer, D. Gupta, A. Hagen and P. Kurz, *Development of safeguards procedures and simulation of fissile material flow for an ALKEM type plant fabricating plutonium fuel elements for fast breeder reactors*, KFK 1110 (Karlsruhe: Kernforschungszentrum, August 1971).

inherently a greater source of difficulty, chiefly because of the physical difficulty of checking stated accounts of what the store contains.

In principle then, given the manpower and the money, there is no reason why the NPT safeguards system should not efficiently serve the purpose for which it has been designed. There are, however, two sensitive points. First, the suspicion that material has been diverted from peaceful uses will always be couched in terms of probability – the inspectors will find themselves saying that there is a certain chance that there has been an illicit diversion. Secondly, lacking operational control of stores of fissile material, plutonium and uranium-235, inspectors will always be uneasy about their safeguards at this point of the fuel cycle at which the diversion of nuclear materials is simplest.

Practical problems

The practical problems of implementing the NPT safeguards raise more serious problems. One difficulty is the availability of inspectors, who must in the nature of things be experienced scientists and who should ideally be permanent employees of the IAEA, if only so as to help satisfy the agency's undertaking to 'take every precaution to protect commercial and industrial secrets and other confidential information coming to its knowledge'.

The safeguards division of the IAEA is at present growing moderately quickly with a staff of 136 (compared with 120 in 1973). In 1976 the staff will increase by 9. At present, just over a half of the manpower consists of professional people, and the agency reckons that present needs can be adequately met. It also expects, with some justification, that the increasing size of individual nuclear installations in the coming decade may to some extent mitigate the rate at which the inspectorate will have to grow. Research directed towards more efficient safeguarding techniques may also yield improvements in the efficiency of inspection.

Broadly speaking, however, the implementation of the NPT safeguards will in principle require a staff that grows not much less quickly than the nuclear industry, which may be doubling every four years in the early 1980s. Moreover, it seems at present to be acknowledged that, for sheer lack of manpower, the agency would not be able to take up the United States' offer to

put her civil nuclear plants under NPT safeguards – that exercise, some knowledgeable officials estimate, would require an immediate
ten-fold increase of the inspectorate. (A similar
offer from Britain has in part been accepted.)
What this amounts to is that the agency's confidence that the NPT safeguards system can be
maintained for the indefinite future is rightly a
powerful stimulus of disbelief. Attempts to
recruit people on permanent contracts, not on
secondment from national atomic energy agen-
cies, have been unsuccessful. Safeguards account
for only 13·5 per cent of the IAEA budget, and,
although the proportion is growing, not even the
optimists expect that the proportion can be
doubled. In all the circumstances, it is inevitable
that the agency, and the parties to the NPT, will
have urgently to seek a safeguards system which
is not merely technically more efficient but
which is structurally simpler than the comprehensive system now in force.

Alternatives and improvements

How might this be done? The ideal would be
that all plants at which fissile material arises,
uranium enrichment plants and plutonium
separation plants, should be subject not merely
to inspection but to operational control by the
IAEA – in that case it would be possible enormously to relax the intensity of inspection at
other parts of the nuclear fuel cycle. Manpower
and political questions make this unlikely.
A more practical alternative would be to make
the agency responsible for the custody of stocks
of fissile material, releasing them to their owners
for approved purposes and following up by
inspection wherever necessary. The benefit
would be that the safeguards system would be
simplified and thus, in the long run, made more
effective. Although such a scheme would offend
the suceptibilities even of many willing parties
to the NPT, it deserves further consideration as
one means of preventing the NPT system from
collapsing under its own weight.

Regional safeguards systems are another means
by which the system could be simplified. The
agreement between the IAEA and the European
Atomic Energy Community (Euratom), signed
in September 1973 as a treaty between the IAEA,
Euratom and the non-nuclear members of
Euratom, is a model of what might be done. The
Euratom agreement (not yet in force for lack of

Italian ratification of the NPT) has its origin in
Euratom's titular ownership of all fissile material
within the European Communities and the setting
up of an independent safeguards system. During
the negotiation of the NPT, states such as West
Germany also argued that Euratom safeguards
were sufficient, but eventually conceded that
there should be an agreement between the IAEA
and Euratom, which is in practice likely to
require less of the IAEA than would a series of
separate agreements with Euratom states. There
are now good reasons why regional safeguards
systems along the Euratom lines would offer
economies of manpower, more assurance that
nuclear secrets will indeed be kept and the added
security that comes from knowing that the most
vigilant overseers of one nation's nuclear
activities are likely to be its immediate neighbours.

The elevation of the IAEA to a novel kind of
judicial body, with responsibility for policing
the NPT, raises other issues for the safeguards
systems. As yet, nobody knows what procedures
the agency will follow if its inspectors decide that
there is a possibility of a breach of a non-nuclear
power's undertaking under the NPT. Formally,
the Secretary-General of the IAEA is required to
report his suspicion that there has been a
violation to the board of governors of the IAEA,
which may then ask the state concerned to take
urgent steps to ensure that nuclear material is
not being diverted to 'nuclear weapons and other
nuclear explosive devices'. A procedure is laid
down for arbitration of disputes arising in such
circumstances, between the agency and the state,
but the agency's ultimate sanctions are far from
fearsome. It can expel an offending state and ask
for the return of any nuclear material supplied.
The important question, not explicitly determined, is how the other parties to the NPT
would react.

Before violations become public knowledge,
there are serious questions of principle to be
determined. The safeguards agreement requires
that the agency shall not make public information
gathered in the course of its inspections, which
means in practice that the director-general of
the safeguards division is the sole repository of all
technical information on the working of the
safeguards agreements. The decision whether to
report the suspicion of a violation will rest
personally with him. In many ways, this is an

impossible position. At what stage, for example, would the director-general decide that persistent failure by one state to operate a chemical separation plant efficiently was to be explained by illicit diversion rather than by technical incompetence? And how would he ensure that the suspicion of a violation was not the consequence of his own inspector's incompetence?

These difficulties stem from the requirement of secrecy attaching to the reports of inspectors. Only those within the IAEA with a specific need to know the details of the operation of particular nuclear plants are entitled to receive that information. In reality, however, it would be much easier for the governors of the IAEA to make decisions, and for the rest of the world to judge their good sense, if basic information about the flow of nuclear material within the states covered by the safeguards agreement were made public. This could be done without compromising either the commercial secrets of nuclear installations or the strategic interests of the states concerned – it would be necessary simply to publish the state's own estimate of how much uranium has been fed into reactors, how much of it has been processed each year and how much plutonium has been put into stock, and to compare these estimates with those of the inspectors. Until the safeguards system can be modified along these lines, its credibility will remain in doubt.

The more widespread publication of information could also be a basis on which the asymmetry of the NPT might be softened. Although, in the years immediately ahead, nuclear powers such as the United States and the Soviet Union are unlikely to accept a cut-off of the production of fissile material for military purposes, an agreement to make public basic information about the flow of nuclear material within their systems would go a long way to meet, or at least disarm, complaints by the non-nuclear powers of the asymmetry of the NPT safeguards. Even if published information included figures showing how much fissile material is added to their stock each year, their strategic interests would not thereby be threatened, for, until fast reactors are commercially applicable, the quantities of plutonium added to the world's stockpiles will be much greater than could conceivably be used for making weapons. This, then, is a modification of the present safeguards system

that could help not merely to make it more credible but which could also strengthen the NPT itself.

In summary, the NPT safeguards system, as an indispensable part of the treaty, is for the time being largely an untested instrument.

What all this implies is that it is hard to foresee how the NPT safeguards system, an indispensable part of the treaty as at present conceived, can survive the strains that will follow the rapid growth of nuclear power in the next few years. Although the IAEA may be right in claiming that its inspectors are able to meet the demands now being made on them, it will be a great surprise – but a triumph for those who have designed this as yet largely untested system – if unforeseen difficulties do not complicate even their present task. And it is not easy to envisage the present system being extended to meet the needs of the near future. This is why, even before the safeguards system has come fully into operation, there is a need for seeking structural modifications whose effects would be to decentralize the routine operations of the safeguards system, making its operations simpler but at the same time more effective.

One question remains, the solution of which is at present by no means clear. Responsibility for preventing the diversion of fissile material to non-government groups lies plainly, at present, with national government, but other states have a right to ask that national systems for the physical protection of nuclear material are satisfactory. The NPT safeguards system does not bear directly on this point, although, for non-nuclear parties to the treaty, the supervision of the IAEA will be a useful check on national accounting systems. The IAEA has circulated draft regulations, which have the status of recommendations to governments, for the physical protection of fissile material, but the need would be better met by an international convention which would, among other things, provide international assurance of the adequacy of national protection systems. It goes without saying that such a system would be ineffectual if the nuclear powers, signatories of the NPT or otherwise, were excluded. Although the risks of diversion may not be as great as has recently been suggested, there is no doubt that a problem of some degree exists. It argues for a system of supervised national accounting for fissile materials which would by definition have to be more comprehensive than the NPT safeguards system.

V. COMMERCIAL PRESSURES AND INDUCEMENTS

That there will be a rapid growth, in the years ahead, of the use of nuclear technology throughout the world is now plain. One of the questions that bear closely on the integrity of the NPT system is the degree to which the commercial interests of the nuclear industry will erode the treaty. Given the overlap of civil and military nuclear technology, there is an obvious danger that the years ahead will see more non-nuclear powers able to set about the development of weapons. The case of India has shown that a determined non-nuclear power can establish a nuclear industry of its own with only a moderate amount of technical assistance from outside. But the IAEA safeguards that apply to non-parties to the NPT concern only the specific materials and equipment supplied, not technical assistance and advice. Plainly there is a possibility that suppliers will compete for business by offering less restrictive terms than their competitors. Moreover, some suppliers (France, for example) and some potential suppliers (India and South Africa) are not parties to the NPT, and their trade with other non-signatories is formally unrestrained.

In this connection, the repeated declaration of the French government that it will behave, in its dealings with non-nuclear states, as if France were a party to the NPT, is not a sufficient assurance. In practice, France appears to interpret this undertaking, where non-parties to the NPT are involved, by requiring either that material or equipment supplied should be covered by the less restrictive 1965 IAEA safeguards or by equivalent bilateral safeguards (which is apparently the device intended for regulating the supply of the first charge of fissile material for a low-power fast reactor being designed in India, at Madras). Moreover, France has not joined with a number of other nuclear suppliers (see below) in undertaking publicly to keep the IAEA informed of its supplies of nuclear material, while there can be no assurance that France would fall in with such other restrictions on nuclear supply as the parties to the treaty may devise. For what it is worth, India and South Africa have not even followed France in making public declarations about their policy on supplies of nuclear materials.

In these circumstances, it is exceedingly improbable that in the near future an agreement not to supply nuclear materials to non-parties to the NPT could be negotiated between the principal suppliers. Two specific cases illustrate the difficulties likely to be encountered by nuclear suppliers. Since the Indian explosion last year, Atomic Energy of Canada Limited has tried to tighten an agreement to supply a heavy water reactor to Argentina by requiring that the plutonium extracted from it shall not be used for making nuclear devices of any kind, but (given Argentina's declaration about the importance of peaceful nuclear explosions attached to the Treaty of Tlatelolco) is unlikely to succeed and, at the same time, it is unlikely willingly to forgo the export business, estimated to be worth $250 million. Secondly, on the proposed supply of nuclear reactors by the United States to Egypt and Israel, Under-Secretary of State Joseph Sisco told a Subcommittee of the House Foreign Affairs Committee in September 1974 that it was not proposed to require the recipients to sign the NPT because

it is clear that neither Israel nor Egypt sees its national interests presently served by becoming a party to the NPT. Over the short run, virtually nothing is likely to alter these perceptions . . . It is our hope that provision of peaceful nuclear facilities under strict controls against military use can create in time a momentum toward climate consistent with the goal of non-proliferation within the region and between both nations and the United States.

In other words, if there are short-term advantages, in this case political, in supplying nuclear equipment (or offering to do so, for Israel has finally declined the American proposal), even the strongest supporters of the NPT may find it prudent not to require recipients to sign. (It is proper to add that the American proposals for supplying reactors to both countries would have required that the fuel should be sent abroad for processing.)

Strengthening the NPT
The arrangements reached by the major suppliers of nuclear material in the second half of 1974 may therefore be as much as can be done, in the near future, to bolster the NPT by creating

more explicit restrictions on the commercial supply of nuclear materials. The immediate objective of the states involved[22] was to clarify their obligation under the terms of the NPT that nuclear materials and equipment will be supplied to non-parties only if the recipient governments accept safeguards administered by the IAEA and undertake not to carry out peaceful nuclear explosions. The declaration of the potential suppliers, which took the form of letters[23] to the director-general of the IAEA, included specific lists (the 'trigger lists') of nuclear equipment such as reactors, reactor pressure vessels and control mechanisms, heavy water and graphite, as well as fissile material. Although, ostensibly, these undertakings do no more than clarify existing obligations under the NPT, they make it plain that the IAEA must be the supervisory agency for the safeguards required, even in a deal with a non-signatory, and that the restrictions required apply to the conduct of any nuclear explosions. For those who would modestly strengthen the NPT system, these undertakings could become the basis for a convention which might be acceptable even to those states that have declined to sign the NPT itself.

The supply of enriched uranium for nuclear reactors is another area of difficulty. The years ahead are almost certain to see a worldwide shortage of capacity for enriching uranium, which is why potentially large consumers of nuclear energy (Japan and, a little surprisingly, Iran), as well as potential suppliers (Canada, Australia and Zaire), have been for some years engaged in negotiations with the suppliers of enrichment technology. The objective is to provide consumers with a lien on future supplies of enriched material. Similar motives underlie the tripartite agreement between West Germany, the Netherlands and Britain on the development of centrifuge technology and the proposal, initiated by France, that a group of European states, together with Iran, should finance the construction of a gas diffusion plant in Europe.

There are powerful commercial incentives for the suppliers of enrichment technology to make favourable commercial deals with consumers of enriched uranium. In principle, a supplier of the technology can hope that his customer-partner will provide more than his fair share of the cost of building a separation plant. As things stand, the 1974 undertakings to the IAEA of the main suppliers would prevent collaboration on projects not subject to IAEA safeguards. But the absence of France and, ultimately, South Africa from the list of those that have given undertakings is a potential source of proliferation. So long as the policies of these countries are ambiguous, the dangers for the NPT are obvious.

The collaboration between states in the building of enrichment facilities as well as in the provision of facilities for separating fissile material from irradiated fuel is, however, a pointer to a more constructive way of strengthening the NPT system. Although the NPT requires (Article IV) that all parties should take steps to smoothe international collaboration in nuclear energy, the record of the past few years is not spectacular. The IAEA reports a modest growth of its technical assistance programme, but as an international agency it is prevented by the terms of its charter from discriminating between member states. In any case, however, the point has been reached in the development of nuclear energy where the most effective services that can be rendered by technically advanced states consist of the supply of reactors for making electricity and the fuel to keep them working. And, whatever the charter of the IAEA may say, there is no reason why supplier states which have acceded to the NPT should not decide among themselves to provide special forms of help to non-nuclear states which are also parties to the NPT.

There are three technical areas in which such assistance may be effective – uranium enrichment, plutonium separation and the supply of uranium fuel. In present circumstances, however, enrichment and reprocessing facilities are scarce, and few purchasers of reactors are able to negotiate contracts for fuel and reprocessing spanning more than a decade. Inevitably, the sense of insecurity engendered is likely to accentuate the tendency for national enrichment and separation plants to proliferate. One obvious solution would be to arrange to build and operate enrichment and reprocessing facilities

[22] The states concerned are Australia, Britain, Canada, Denmark, Finland, the Netherlands, Norway, the Soviet Union, the United States and West Germany.
[23] IAEA, INFCIRC/140 (Vienna, 1974).

101

on a collaborative basis between potential customers, and to build adequate safeguards into the design of the plants concerned. For some nuclear powers, the United States and Britain for example, such a development would entail that the promise of profitable business in the years ahead should in part be forgone. (To the extent that their expectations of future profit are based on the assumption that their technical superiority will persist, they may in any case be illusory.)

One important sign that the major suppliers are prepared to consider such devices was contained in the declaration by Dr Dixie Lee Ray, chairman of what was then the US Atomic Energy Commission, to the general conference of the IAEA in September 1974 that steps to establish collaborative enrichment and separation facilities under international supervision were regarded by the United States as an important practical objective.

The supply of uranium on favourable terms to parties to the NPT is another potential means of strengthening the system, but one which is inherently more difficult. The rapid growth of the nuclear industry is likely, by the end of the 1980s, to create a situation in which uranium demand will exceed supply and, in any case, major suppliers of uranium will, if they are prudent, seek to maximize their profit from selling nuclear fuels and their ores. The result is likely to be that in the 1980s the price of uranium will fluctuate widely, about a sharply rising trend. In the long run, uranium prices will be limited by technical considerations and in particular by the success with which the technically advanced countries are able to develop reactors that produce more fissile material than they consume, fast reactors in particular. But in the short run, and possibly for the distant future, all consumers of nuclear electricity would profit from mechanisms by which the price of uranium was stabilized, which suggests the creation of the an international system for the management of a buffer stock of uranium. The International Tin Council is a model.

The benefits of access to such a stable uranium market, if restricted to parties to the NPT, could be a powerful inducement to some that have not yet adhered to the treaty and could even, in the long run, benefit the major nuclear powers as well. There would be formidable obstacles to be surmounted, but the difficulties are not insuperable. Their solution would be a powerful reinforcement of the NPT system.

Threats to the NPT

What this implies is that the commercial pressures of the next few years are likely to be a serious threat to the integrity of the NPT system, at least for as long as important suppliers such as France and South Africa remain outside it. (It is also conceivable that China could become an important nuclear supplier in the near future.) The urgent need is that the policy of the non-signatories should be clarified in such a way, possibly by means of conventions outside the direct scope of the NPT, as to ensure that the NPT as such is not made unworkable by commercial competition. But, within the framework of the NPT, there are a number of important devices by means of which the benefits of membership could be made much more apparent, especially to those non-nuclear powers outside the treaty. The IAEA's technical assistance programme is likely to be much less influential than other steps that might be taken.

A much more contentious issue in the commercial exploitation of nuclear energy is that of peaceful nuclear explosions. The NPT requires non-nuclear parties not to carry out nuclear explosions and nuclear parties to be prepared to make the necessary facilities available through the IAEA (Article V) or by means of bilateral agreements. During the negotiation of the NPT, non-nuclear states were quick to argue that they should not be denied the benefits of peaceful nuclear explosions, taking as their text the frequent declarations of the United States and the Soviet Union that there are indeed important benefits to be derived in this way. Now, however, there is a conflict of opinion on the economic value of peaceful nuclear explosions. The United States 'Plowshare' programme has in 15 years produced only the most equivocal evidence of commercial benefit and, during the whole of that long period, has produced no significant innovations in plans for using these techniques. Schemes such as the plan for excavating a second canal across the isthmus of Panama have been abandoned. Schemes for increasing the flow of natural gas from impervious underground reservoirs have revealed both that the gas produced contains often unacceptably high amounts of radioactivity and that, in any case, substantially to increase American reserves of natural gas by these techniques would require perhaps several hundred underground nuclear explosions over the next one or two decades.[24] The position has now been reached where Congress in 1974 explicitly prohibited research and development funds set aside for energy research from being used for peaceful nuclear explosions.

The Soviet Union has reported some success with an earth-moving experiment (in 1965), which produced an artificial dam across a Siberian river but also scattered substantial amounts of radioactivity into the atmosphere. Although some Russians[25] consider that the problem of radioactivity release 'has not been solved', enthusiasm persists, and the most ambitious of the Soviet schemes now being canvassed is for the use of up to 200 nuclear explosions for diverting a north-flowing Siberian river into the Volga system. Schemes[26] for increasing the production of underground oil reservoirs, although apparently economic, are probably less so than would have been the application of a standard technique of petroleum engineering involving the reinjection of natural gas (associated gas) into the reservoir.

As long as this sharp disagreement between the Soviet Union and the United States persists, it is hard to see how the bearing on the NPT system of the issue of peaceful nuclear explosions can be understood, let alone regulated. For the integrity of the system, the danger is that other states not parties to the NPT will follow India in carrying out nuclear explosions under the guise of a peaceful programme. The case of India has shown that by this means it is possible to move some way towards securing an option on a weapons programme without openly incurring the full countervailing pressure to which emerging nuclear powers are likely to be exposed. This is the sense in which Article V of the NPT has been called 'an invitation to proliferation'.

[24] Herbert Scoville, Jr, 'Peaceful nuclear explosions – an invitation to proliferation', in NPT: Paradoxes and Problems, op. cit.
[25] V. Emilianov in Nuclear Proliferation Problems (Stockholm: SIPRI, 1974).
[26] Milo D. Nordyke, A Review of Soviet Data on the Peaceful Uses of Atomic Energy, UCRL 51414 (Livermore Laboratory, US AEC, 1973).

What can be done? First, the NPT signatories have fulfilled their obligations to specify a system by means of which peaceful nuclear explosions might be carried out in the territory of non-nuclear weapons states, and it is hard to think that these arrangements could be abandoned while the Soviet Union and the United States report such different experiences with the economic exploitation of peaceful nuclear explosions. There is however a case for making sure that any signatories of the NPT making use of the IAEA arrangements for peaceful nuclear explosions should pay the full cost, and thus contribute to the present meagre understanding of the economic value of these devices. Still more urgent is the need for an objective and independent appraisal of the experiments that have so far been carried out, not merely in the United States but also in the Soviet Union (where only the most sketchy accounts of past work have been made available). Although the IAEA has convened a series of panel meetings on the subject, the most recent in February 1975, it has not yet taken the initiative in helping the rest of the world to understand whether this is a technique of great economic potential or a pipe dream.

A further commercial consideration impinging on the NPT is that created by the development, in the past few years, of techniques for causing exceedingly small thermonuclear explosions by the use of energy from powerful lasers. In principle, the technique is one that might become the basis of a commercial method for the application of thermonuclear power, and is regarded with varying degrees of enthusiasm in this light in the United States as well as countries such as Japan and Switzerland. It is also clear that the same technique can be used as a means of perfecting the design of thermonuclear weapons (which suggests a means of avoiding the full consequences of a comprehensive test-ban agreement if one should ever emerge). What the emerging technique implies for the non-nuclear signatories of the NPT is that, formally at least, they would be prevented from following a potentially valuable line of commercial research. In reality, it is not clear that research programmes along these lines would be a formal breach of the NPT, although it is plain that an understanding to this effect would be in everybody's interest.

VI. SECURITY AND NUCLEAR-FREE ZONES

In the last resort, the reasons why states may seek to become nuclear powers will be determined by their perceptions of their strategic interests. The NPT system itself will, over the years, enhance the security of many non-nuclear weapons states if it can be seen to be a restraint on the spread of nuclear weapons. Other states will however remain discontented with the undertakings of the nuclear powers sponsoring the NPT that the use of or the threat to use nuclear weapons against a non-nuclear party to the treaty would be raised as an urgent issue within the Security Council. So what can be done to improve on these security assurances? And what, in any case, are the practical steps that might be taken by the nuclear powers to negotiate agreements among themselves that would disarm the complaints of non-nuclear states that too little has been done to control vertical proliferation?

In the long run the role of China is crucial. So long as the strategic intentions of China in regions such as south-east Asia remain unclear, while the dispute between China and the Soviet Union persists, and while China remains outside most recent arms-control agreements (with the exception of the Treaty of Tlatelolco), it is plainly impossible for the nuclear signatories of the NPT to provide convincing guarantees for other parties to the treaty and also to negotiate substantial reductions of their own nuclear weapon stocks. But few would consider that these obstacles can quickly be overcome.

For the present, the practical difficulty is that China, although now a member of the United Nations, does not participate in international discussions on arms control. For that reason, but for more general reasons as well, there is a case for asking that the Soviet Union and the United States should admit some part of the widely shared Chinese objection to the work of bodies such as the Committee of the Commission on Disarmament (CCD) that proceedings are unreasonably dominated by the interests of the major powers. The notion that the Soviet Union and the United States should be permanent joint chairmen of the CCD is a particular focus for discontent. A relaxation of this and other practices could dramatically widen the representation of bodies such as the CCD, and,

at the same time, provide the major powers with a more sympathetic appreciation of the difficulties there must be in negotiating the self-denying measures of arms control for which the non-nuclear powers are asking.

To the extent that the NPT is a compact between non-nuclear and nuclear states, under which the latter's obligation is to work towards a comprehensive test-ban and the reduction of stocks of nuclear weapons, it is also anomalous that the NPT provides for no regular opportunity by means of which performance can be verified and assessed. Although the political difficulties that underlie technical discussions, within the framework of SALT II for example, are now more widely appreciated than when the NPT was signed, it is not conceivable that the non-nuclear parties to the treaty will indefinitely be satisfied with a system in which the nuclear powers pursue negotiations bilaterally, without reference to the other parties to the treaty. In reality, however, the major powers could disarm much of the criticism of their tardy attainment of limited objectives in nuclear arms control if they would agree to render regular reports on progress to the other parties, possibly within the CCD, possibly through the intermediary of a secretariat which was a part of the NPT itself.

Although the creation of yet another international forum for the negotiation of nuclear arms control would be a potential source of confusion, and might even undermine the declared objective of the major powers that universal adherence to the NPT is the only acceptable long-term solution, it is also clear that the strength of the Treaty of Tlatelolco stems from its permanent control organization (which nevertheless, in practice, delegates routine safeguards procedures to the IAEA). Such an organization would in any case be needed within the framework of the NPT if effective steps were to be taken to implement some of the commercial inducements suggested in Chapter V.

What can reasonably be expected in the next few years from the major powers is inevitably a subject for debate. The Soviet Union and the United States still, however, have to provide a convincing explanation why the upper limit of nuclear explosions under the 1974 Threshold Test-Ban Agreement (which is in any case bilateral, excluding Britain) is as high as the equivalent of 150,000 tons of TNT. Moreover, suggestions that the test-ban agreements should be supplemented by an annual quota restriction are unlikely to satisfy the dissident non-nuclear parties to the NPT. In the same vein, it is incumbent on the major powers to explain why the SALT agreements, useful though they may be, have so far brought the opposite of progress towards the goal of reducing nuclear stockpiles, as specified by the NPT. It is also noteworthy that both France and India have declared that a cut-off of the military production of fissile material would persuade them to membership of the NPT. Distant though that objective may be, it is, at least in logic, the objective in arms control which, if attained, would make possible a much more durable NPT system.

The problem of security for non-nuclear weapon states cannot be settled within the NPT, at least so long as China and France are not parties to it. So what can be done? The most constructive possibility for the years immediately ahead is that suggested by the Treaty of Tlatelolco. Although not yet applicable in full to states such as Brazil and Argentina, that treaty does at least suggest that non-nuclear states reluctant to adhere to the NPT itself may more easily agree to the denuclearization of the regions to which they geographically belong, particularly if by that means they are assured of a measure of independence from the nuclear powers. (One of the minor absurdities to have come to light within the NPT system is that Panama, a party to the Treaty of Tlatelolco but not the NPT, has not been able to negotiate a safeguards agreement with the IAEA.[27]) For the

[27] *Report on the implementation of the Treaty of Tlatelolco and some comments and views of OPANAL with respect to Article VII and other related provisions of the Non-Proliferation Treaty*, prepared by the Agency for the Prohibition of Nuclear Weapons in Latin America (OPANAL) NPT/PC.III/9, January 1975.

rest of the world, a regional association such as that represented by the Treaty of Tlatelolco is in principle as satisfactory as the adherence of the member states to the NPT. Safeguards are still supervised by the IAEA, while parties to such regional treaties have the keenest interest in making sure that there are no violations by neighbouring states.

There is a strong case for thinking that the negotiation of further nuclear-free zones, however difficult, may be the most effective way of providing the non-nuclear parties with the security assurances for which they rightly ask. Not surprisingly, the geographical pattern of the distribution of non-parties to the NPT shows states that cluster into groups. In the Indian sub-continent, Pakistan and Sri Lanka have said explicitly that their reason for not adhering to the treaty is that India is not a party to the treaty. The positions of Egypt and other states in the Middle East are in part determined by Israel's policy on nuclear weapons. And the policies of many of the non-parties to the treaty in Africa south of the Sahara have in part been determined by the absence of South Africa from the membership list. So the negotiation of nuclear-free zones in each of these substantial regions of the world would serve both as a means of providing the states concerned with a measure of security – albeit of a negative kind which for practical purposes leaves them to their own (non-nuclear) devices – and, at the same time, broadening the scope of the NPT system as a whole. Each of these regions has indeed been suggested, in formal resolutions at the United Nations General Assembly, as potentially workable. What should now be recognized, by the sponsors of the NPT, is that further nuclear-free zones are not merely a useful adjunct to the treaty but possibly an effective way of strengthening its political base.

VII. CONCLUSIONS

All international treaties are to some extent empirical, concerned with the attainment of short-term objectives and also limited in their scope by the unwillingness of even the most ardent sponsors of a good cause to compromise what they consider to be their essential but conflicting interests. The NPT is no exception. Indeed, it is by its nature an attempt to reduce the risks of global nuclear war by concentrating on one aspect of the problem, the possession of independent nuclear forces by different countries. Moreover, as the text of the treaty makes plain, it is intended as an interim expedient, a temporary device for limiting the spread of the possession of nuclear weapons. The review conference in May 1975 and those that will no doubt follow are sufficient proofs of that.

To acknowledge this is not in any sense to discount the importance of the NPT. The major powers, whatever the discontents of the non-nuclear powers with the slow progress towards nuclear arms control, have invested heavily in the treaty as an assurance of future world stability. And many non-nuclear powers now parties to the treaty have in the process willingly forsaken some of the political leverage they might have kept for themselves. States such as Mexico, an early party to the treaty, have, for example, given up the opportunities now being savoured by Japan and Italy in seeking minor concessions from the major powers in return for ratification. It is also plain that if the NPT were to collapse, possibly by the mass defection of states now party to it, the world would quickly become a more dangerous place, because of the uncertainty and the suspicion the new situation would arouse, and hopes for nuclear or other arms control would be seriously set back. The NPT may not be the ideal treaty, but, now that it exists, the best hope is to keep it in being until it is superseded by something better.

This is the spirit in which the practical suggestions in the preceding chapters are offered. Like the NPT itself, they are mostly short-term expedients. There are circumstances, such as the emergence of India as a putative nuclear power, where diplomatic activity by the major powers could bring important benefits, if only by clarifying India's future course of action. There are important ways in which the safeguards system now operated by the IAEA could be strengthened, chiefly by making it much simpler and, at the same time but outside the formal framework of the NPT, there are ways in which the commercial trade in nuclear materials and equipment could be regulated, so as to reduce the risk of proliferation and to bring within the scope of the system states, such as France, which are not now parties to the treaty. Then there are devices for making the treaty less discriminatory against non-nuclear powers, notably devices for making more explicit the mechanism by which nuclear powers are required by the NPT to work toward nuclear arms control. Security for non-nuclear states is perhaps the most difficult problem of all, but here too the years immediately ahead could usefully see a wider application of the principle of nuclear-free zones. For many of these purposes a secretariat responsible for the administration of the treaty would powerfully reinforce the NPT system.

The NPT system is, however, intrinsically dynamic – like the spread of nuclear weapons it is intended to prevent. It cannot stand still, for then it will collapse, eroded by the emergence of further nuclear or quasi-nuclear powers. For the years immediately ahead, the most hopeful opportunities for substantial gains are in the development of regional arrangements, both for safeguards and security. Further ahead, it may come to seem that a cut-off of military production of fissile material, or some means by which nuclear materials are owned internationally (which would imply a revival of schemes like those discussed in the late 1940s), are the only expedients by which the NPT system can be preserved. Or it may turn out that the survival of the system depends critically on the accession of China. On all these issues, the nuclear powers sponsoring the treaty will find themselves increasingly obliged to compromise their national interests for the sake of keeping the treaty in being. That is one reason why the NPT is interesting and why, in the long run, it may accomplish more than the regulation of the spread of nuclear weapons.

APPENDIXES

Appendix 1: Parties and non-parties to the NPT, February 1975

Full parties			Signatories not ratified	Non-signatories
Afghanistan	Guatemala	Nepal	Barbados*	Albania
Australia	Haiti	New Zealand	Belgium	Algeria
Austria	Holy See	Nicaragua	Colombia*	Argentina
Bolivia	Honduras	Nigeria	Egypt	Bahamas
Botswana	Hungary	Norway	Gambia	Bahrain
Britain	Iceland	Paraguay	Germany (W.)	Bangladesh
Bulgaria	Iran	Peru	Indonesia	Brazil
Burundi	Iraq	Philippines	Italy	Burma
Cameroon	Ireland	Poland	Japan	Chile
Canada	Ivory Coast	Rumania	Korea (S.)	China
Central African	Jamaica	San Marino	Libya	Congo
Republic	Jordan	Senegal	Luxembourg	Cuba
Chad	Kenya	Somalia	Netherlands	France
Costa Rica	Khmer	Soviet Union	Panama*	Guinea
Cyprus	Republic	Sudan	Singapore	Guyana
Czechoslovakia	Kuwait	Swaziland	Sri Lanka	India
Dahomey	Laos	Sweden	Switzerland	Israel
Denmark	Lebanon	Syria	Trinidad	Korea (N.)
Dominican	Lesotho	Taiwan	and Tobago	Malawi
Republic	Liberia	Thailand	Turkey	Mauritania
Ecuador	Madagascar	Togo	Venezuela*	Nauru
El Salvador	Malaysia	Tonga	Yemen	Niger
Ethiopia	Maldives	Tunisia	(Arab Rep.)	Oman
Fiji	Mali	United States	Yemen	Pakistan
Finland	Malta	Upper Volta	(People's	Portugal
Gabon	Mauritius	Uruguay	Dem. Rep.)	Qatar
Germany (E.)	Mexico	Vietnam (S.)		Rwanda
Ghana	Mongolia	Yugoslavia		Saudi-Arabia
Greece	Morocco	Zaire		South Africa
				Spain
				Tanzania
				Uganda
				United Arab
				Emirates
				Vietnam (N.)
				W. Samoa
				Zambia

* Non-parties to the NPT for which the Treaty of Tlatelolco (see p. 7) is in force.

Appendix 2: Nuclear Threshold Powers

Country	Ore	Reactor power 1980 (megawatts, electrical)	Enrichment	Separation	NPT Ratified (R) Signed (S)	Timescale (years)
Argentina	Yes	1000*	n.a.	Yes	No	10
Brazil	Yes	1500	n.a.	No	No	8
Chile	Yes	500	No	n.a.	No	16
Egypt	No	600*	No	No	S	10
India	Yes	3000	No	Yes	No	—
Indonesia	No	500	No	No	S	16
Iran	Yes	2000*	No	n.a.	R	10
Israel	Yes	600	No	Yes	No	—
Japan	No	5000	No	Yes	S	3
Pakistan	Yes	1000	No	n.a.	No	8
South Africa	Yes	300	Yes	n.a.	No	3
South Korea	No	500	No	No	S	10
Spain	Yes	5000	No	No	No	10
Taiwan	No	1000	No	No	R	10

*Estimated.
n.a. = not available.

4 Nuclear Power and Weapons Proliferation

TED GREENWOOD, GEORGE W. RATJHENS AND JACK RUINA

INTRODUCTION

Once the United States demonstrated the technical feasibility of nuclear weapons, it was clear that any technically advanced state with substantial economic resources and the political will could, given time, also develop nuclear weapons. But in the early years of the nuclear age it was assumed that, by means of rigid controls on the disclosure of technical information, the process could be delayed, and perhaps even prevented in countries with low levels of technical and industrial capability. Despite efforts by the United States to maintain strict secrecy – even including discontinuing co-operation with Britain for a while – the Soviet Union, Britain and France succeeded with their nuclear weapons programmes. So too did China, a nation without a substantial industrial base – albeit with Soviet help initially. Such industrial countries as West Germany, Japan, Sweden and Switzerland have been restrained only by political considerations. Fortunately, the political situations of these and other advanced industrial states have now stabilized, so that whatever concerns there may have been about their nuclear ambitions have largely dissipated.

The secrecy policy was severely undercut with the inauguration in the mid-1950s of the American 'atoms for peace' programme. While this did not include explicit disclosure of bomb design information, it did result in the disclosure of much information relevant to weapons manufacture: e.g. details of processes for obtaining plutonium from spent reactor fuel. This American programme, technical assistance efforts by other countries and the efforts of the International Atomic Energy Agency (IAEA) also resulted in the training of many scientists, engineers and technicians and the wide dispersal of research reactors and other nuclear research facilities. Such diffusion of information and technology greatly accelerated India's ability to develop and test a nuclear explosive.

Throughout the 1960s attention shifted increasingly to less industrialized countries and to political and institutional devices for limiting proliferation. This resulted in the safeguard system of the IAEA, the Latin American Nuclear-Free Zone Treaty and the Non-Proliferation Treaty. While still regarded as useful anti-proliferation measures, these are increasingly perceived to be insufficient. Such critical countries as Argentina, Brazil, Egypt, Israel, Pakistan and South Africa are not even parties to the Non-Proliferation Treaty. But, over and above this, the current diffusion of nuclear *power* technology to many semi-industrial and non-industrial countries is accelerating their rate of acquisition of skills, facilities and material relevant to nuclear weapons development. With the decrease in technical obstacles, there is a widespread belief that political and institutional means alone may not be adequate to stem proliferation in a large number of less industrialized nations.

It is important to note that these countries need not copy the scale and sophistication of the nuclear weapons programmes of the first five nuclear states; a much more modest programme is sufficient to develop and produce a small number of simple, but militarily useful, nuclear explosives.

Most of the states now of concern have started down the nuclear electric power path, or at least are interested in doing so. But a nuclear weapons programme need not be based on facilities associated with the development of

109

nuclear power. A country could begin by building a small, simple reactor fuelled by natural uranium, together with a small reprocessing plant to extract plutonium from spent fuel; such facilities are much less difficult to construct and less costly (by at least a factor of 10) than a commercial power reactor together with even a small commercial type of reprocessing plant. A state that had no nuclear power industry would not be expected to acquire nuclear power-generation facilities for the sole purpose of obtaining weapons material, unless it wanted to conceal its intentions. But even if that were the object, it is by no means clear that concealment would be easier than constructing special facilities clandestinely, or than using existing research facilities for the purpose of producing weapons materials.

A state that has a commercial nuclear power reactor could divert materials from it, but such materials would not normally be well suited for weapons. Their use would add complexity and increase the risk of failure in the weapons design. Production of high-quality weapons materials requires operating the facilities in costly, non-optimum ways; furthermore, international safeguard arrangements and political commitments would inhibit most countries from diverting material from power reactors. Consequently, even states with existing nuclear power programmes would probably build special reactors if they wanted to produce plutonium for weapons.

Nevertheless a civilian nuclear industry could be helpful to a weapons programme. It would provide a base of relevant technology and trained scientists and technicians and, if it included facilities for reprocessing spent fuel and/or facilities for enriching uranium, these could be utilized for weapons purposes. (There are severe technical constraints on doing this with some types of enrichment plants built to produce reactor-grade uranium, but there are no difficulties with reprocessing facilities.) Also, if successful, new uranium enrichment techniques being developed for commercial use will reduce the cost and difficulty of producing weapons-grade uranium. Finally, new reactor types that use weapons-grade material as fuel might be introduced commercially. For these reasons the character of a country's nuclear power programme bears significantly on its nuclear weapons potential.

This paper examines the relationship between nuclear weapons development and nuclear electric power. It starts with a brief description of nuclear weapons design followed by a discussion of various aspects of nuclear power technology and how they bear on a nuclear weapons programme. It concludes with a discussion of possible political and institutional controls for limiting nuclear proliferation.

I. NUCLEAR WEAPONS TECHNOLOGY

The design of nuclear weapons is based on the following physical phenomena:

(1) NUCLEAR FISSION: Some heavy elements, particularly the isotopes of uranium and plutonium, when bombarded by neutrons will split into atoms of lighter elements and in the process emit more neutrons (two, three or more from each atom that splits) and release a great deal of energy – about ten million times as much, atom for atom, as is obtainable from ordinary chemical combustion. The total energy released from the complete fission of about 1 lb of fissionable material is about equal to that released from 8,000 tons (8 kilotons) of high explosive.

(2) NUCLEAR FUSION. At extremely high temperatures – in the range of tens of millions of degrees – the nuclei of certain light elements, particularly the hydrogen isotopes deuterium and tritium, can combine to form heavier elements and in the process release a great deal of energy and some fast neutrons. On an atom for atom basis the energy released in fusion is less than that released from nuclear fission, but the atoms involved are much lighter, so that the theoretical maximum energy obtainable from fusion is about three times as great per unit of weight as the theoretical maximum energy obtainable from nuclear fission (or about 25 kilotons per lb of thermonuclear fuel). Also, and perhaps more

110

important, the number of free neutrons available per unit of energy released from fusion reactions can be up to six times greater than the number available from fission reactions, and they are of much higher energy as well.

Pure fission weapons in the 10–20 kiloton (KT) range are the simplest practical nuclear weapons to design. Weapons of very low weight or very high yield are more complex and may use a combination of fission and fusion reactions. Although in principle possible, pure fusion weapons (that is where the high temperature necessary for fusion is not obtained from a fission explosion) have not as yet been developed in practical form and may never be.

Chain Reaction

Many heavy atomic nuclei are fissionable, but only a fraction of these are 'fissile': that is, fissionable by both fast and slow neutrons. Since the neutrons resulting from nuclear fission have a wide range of energies, nuclei which only fission from the capture of fast neutrons would generally not be able to sustain a chain reaction. From a practical point of view, fission weapons can only be made from fissile materials, particularly Uranium-233, U-235, Plutonium-239 or some combination of these. U-238 and Thorium-232, both abundant in nature, are also fissionable but only by high-energy neutrons, so that they cannot sustain a chain reaction by themselves. Nevertheless, these two materials can contribute to the yield in thermonuclear explosions where the many high-energy neutrons generated by fusion reactions can cause them to fission.

Small amounts of fissile material will not sustain a chain reaction, since too large a fraction of the neutrons escapes through the surface and is unavailable to cause fission in other nuclei. The minimum mass of material necessary to sustain a chain reaction is called the critical mass and is dependent on the geometry of the material. Because a sphere has the highest volume-to-surface ratio of any solid shape, and therefore has the least number of escaping neutrons per unit of material, it is the shape for which critical mass is smallest.

The critical mass for a bare sphere of U-235 is approximately 50 kg, that of U-233 about 12 kg, and that of certain dense metallurgical forms of Pu-239 as low as 10 kg. The critical mass

of Pu-239 is lower than that of U-235 because it has a higher fission cross-section (that is, each Pu-239 nucleus is more likely than a U-235 nucleus to capture a neutron and fission) and it produces on the average more neutrons per fission than U-235. However, the critical mass can be lowered in several ways. The fissile material may be surrounded by a shell of other material, to reflect some of the neutrons which would otherwise escape; practical reflectors can reduce the critical mass by a factor of two or three, so that about 5 kg (or 11 lb) of Pu-239 or U-233 and about 15 kg (33 lb) of U-235 at normal pressure can be made critical. The assembly of fissile material and reflector may also be surrounded by a tamper, to keep the bomb from exploding and becoming sub-critical before a reasonable fraction of its fissionable nuclei undergo a nuclear reaction. The critical mass is also lower if the material is compressed to increase its density. (Critical mass is approximately proportional to the reciprocal of the square of the density.) Consequently, an efficient practical bomb which depends on extremely high compression of the nuclear core might use significantly lesser amounts of fissile materials than mentioned above.

Fission Bomb Design

The two simplest designs for fission weapons involve use of either a gun or an implosion device. For a gun device two pieces of fissile material, each below critical mass, are forced together quickly by a chemical explosion in a gun-like assembly to form a single piece well above critical mass for its particular shape (perhaps by a factor of two). Gun devices are relatively simple and can be designed with high confidence of working without full-scale nuclear testing. Their design almost of necessity requires the use of U-235, rather than plutonium, for reasons discussed later.

The implosion device is somewhat more complex but can be made more efficient than a gun device. It involves a spherical assembly consisting of a core of fissile material below critical mass, surrounded by a material that acts as both a tamper and a reflector; the tamper is then surrounded by high explosive. When detonated, the explosive sets up an implosion, or ingoing shock wave, that can create overpressures of millions of pounds per square inch in the core,

111

increasing the density by a factor of two or so and thereby making the previously sub-critical assembly super-critical. The fraction of fissionable atoms that actually fission can be maximized by careful design of the bomb assembly in order to have maximum compression of the core and to achieve as symmetrical a compression as possible.

Weights and Yields of Fission Bombs

Pu-239 and the implosion principle were used for the first American nuclear test (*Trinity*) and also for the second American bomb dropped on Japan, at Nagasaki. The Hiroshima bomb, the first military use of a nuclear weapon, used U-235 in a gun assembly. Both weapon types weighed about 10,000 lb and yielded about 15–20 KT. The first implosion bomb (*Fat Man*) was just under 5ft in diameter but had a plutonium core which was probably smaller than a baseball. The rest of the assembly consisted mainly of tamper and high explosive, very carefully configured to create a uniform implosion at the nuclear core surface.

Many of the early explosions of every nuclear country seem to have been in the same range. This is not surprising since the first designs are undoubtedly conservative, using a sufficient amount of fissile material to assure a good yield without undue demands on the implosion or gun device used. (If substantially less than a critical mass of material at normal pressure is used, a much greater burden is placed on the performance of the chemical implosion device to achieve the compression needed for reasonable efficiency. In other words, the risk of a fizzle, or at least of a very inefficient explosion, is increased if there is an attempt to conserve fissile material in a first test.) A ten-kiloton yield corresponds to about 10 per cent efficiency for 10 lb of plutonium in an implosion device and 1–2 per cent efficiency for 100 lb of U-235 in a gun device. In order to get such efficiencies, a great deal of weight (at least for a first design) must be allocated to chemical explosive and tamper, although perhaps not as much as 10,000 lb. With currently available information and technology, a conservative first design by a technically rather advanced nation – e.g., Sweden, Canada, Switzerland or Japan – might weigh about 1,000 lb.

It is interesting, although not particularly significant, that the first nuclear test of five of the six countries that have developed nuclear weapons (the exception being China) used weapons made from plutonium.

For a very high yield, pure fission weapons must use other than a solid spherical core configuration, so that the assembly can contain a great deal of fissile material and yet remain below critical before chemical implosion. The largest pure fission device, tested by the United States in November 1952, yielded about 500 KT. Undoubtedly pure fission devices of higher yield can be designed, but they would be much heavier and a more costly way of getting the same yield as from a thermonuclear device which used nuclear fusion as well as nuclear fission in the explosive process.

Boosted Weapons

A fission bomb can be designed to include a small amount of light materials, typically isotopes of hydrogen, which will fuse at the high temperatures and pressures involved. This fusion adds slightly to the yield of the device, but far more important is the fact that an extra quantity of free neutrons is produced as a result of the fusion reaction. These in turn produce fissions in the plutonium or uranium in the weapon, resulting in an increase in the efficiency of the fission bomb. Thus, in boosted weapons, the thermonuclear fuel is used primarily as a source of neutrons to help the fission reactions, rather than as a direct source of yield. Boosted weapons are therefore basically fission weapons.

Thermonuclear Weapons

The extremely high temperature required for a fusion explosion is produced by a fission explosion. The thermonuclear 'fuel' is likely to be Lithium-6 deuteride, which is a convenient solid, rather than liquid deuterium or tritium. Li-6 is separated from natural lithium, which has about 7·5 per cent of Li-6 and the rest Li-7. The first full-scale American thermonuclear explosion (*Mike*, November 1952) used liquid deuterium and yielded about 10 megatons (MT), but this was a nuclear 'device' designed for experimental purposes, not as a prototype for an operational bomb.

There is no description in the open literature of how the energy from a fission explosion can be used to raise the temperature of a substantial amount of thermonuclear fuel to the level required for a fusion reaction. However, what is well known is that thermonuclear fuels are relatively inexpensive and can be assembled in large amounts and in any shape with no concern about going 'critical'; and that a fusion reaction can produce ten to twenty times as many free neutrons (all at very high energy) as fissile material of the same weight. The net effect is that at higher yields (over 50 KT) thermonuclear weapons can be produced at much lower cost and much less weight than pure fission weapons. For example, we can expect modern thermonuclear weapons to weigh about 1–2 lb per KT for weapons in the 100 KT to 1 MT range, and less than 1 lb per KT yield for weapons in the 5–10 MT range. (Compare this to the theoretical maximum yield-to-weight ratios of about 8 KT per pound for fission and 25 KT per pound for fusion.)

In addition, when thermonuclear fuels are used in nuclear weapons the abundance of high-energy neutrons can be used to cause fission in U-238, which is not fissionable by slow neutrons. By the expedient of surrounding a thermonuclear weapon with a natural uranium blanket, therefore, extra fission yield can be obtained very inexpensively.

In general, the energy released in the explosion of a large thermonuclear weapon stems from three sources – a fission chain reaction, 'burning' of thermonuclear fuel and the fission of the U-238 blanket (if one exists) – with, very roughly, half the total energy stemming from fission and the other half from fusion. However, to obtain special weapons effects or to meet certain weight or space constraints, different ratios of fission yield to fusion yield may be employed, ranging from pure fission weapons to a weapon where a very high proportion of the yield is from fusion.

Fissile Material
It is impossible to obtain U-233, U-235 or Pu-239 in pure form. U-235 in nature is mixed with U-238 in the proportion of roughly 7 parts per 1,000; U-233 and Pu-239 do not appear in nature but can be produced in nuclear reactors – U-233 from Th-232, and Pu-239 from U-238. In the production process other isotopes of these elements also appear, but for use in the core of fission weapons it is not necessary to have any of these fissile materials in pure form.

Theoretically, uranium weapons can be made from mixtures of U-235 and U-238 containing about 10 per cent U-235, but in practice enrichment to about 50 per cent or better would be needed, and even then the critical mass would be more than three times that of pure U-235. It is assumed that the level of enrichment used by the current nuclear powers for the core material in their uranium weapons is at a level of 90 per cent or more of U-235.

Production reactors – that is, reactors designed for producing plutonium for weapons – produce relatively pure Pu-239 with little Pu-240 or other plutonium isotopes, but power reactors (reactors designed for electric power generation) normally produce plutonium containing significant amounts of Pu-240 as well as some smaller amounts of other plutonium isotopes. In light-water reactors Pu-239 may constitute about 60 per cent of the total amount of plutonium produced, while Pu-240 constitutes about 21 per cent, the rest being heavier isotopes. There is no simple, feasible way of separating Pu-240 from Pu-239; the problem is much harder than that of separating U-235 from U-238, since these plutonium isotopes are closer to each other in weight and are much more hazardous to handle than uranium.

The most troublesome of plutonium isotopes for bomb design is Pu-240. When mixed with Pu-239 it would raise the critical mass of the mixture, and it also fissions spontaneously with a much shorter fission half life than Pu-239. This means that, for any given design, the likelihood increases of 'pre-initiation' (i.e., of a chain reaction starting before full compression of the core is reached), with a resulting loss in yield. Because of their particular sensitivity to pre-initiation, gun devices are never designed with plutonium of any quality. Moreover, Pu-240 and Pu-241 are more radioactive than Pu-239, and therefore generate more heat that must be dissipated if the integrity of the device is to be maintained for extended periods of time. Pu-240 is also more hazardous to handle than Pu-239, thus complicating further the design of weapons using 'reactor-grade' rather than 'weapons-grade' plutonium.

Despite these problems, the overall added complexity in bomb design and loss of efficiency resulting from use of 'reactor-grade' plutonium is not so great as to preclude its use. It is unlikely that any nation would forgo exercising its nuclear option solely because it did not have access to any plutonium other than plutonium of 'reactor grade'.

To date, only U-235 and Pu-239 seem to be used in stockpiled nuclear weapons, although U-233, too, is good fissile material. It is not clear whether any country has even tested a U-233 bomb, although surely experiments with this material have been made in order to understand its relevant properties for weapons. But with the abundance of Th-232 in nature (and in pure isotopic form) it is very possible that at some time U-233 bred from Th-232 in nuclear reactors would be an attractive material to use for a bomb core. When produced in a reactor, U-232 and U-234 also appear with U-233 and would increase the critical mass of the mixture. In small percentages they hardly affect the chain reaction, but U-232 decays naturally through several intermediate stages, and in the process it emits enough gamma rays to make it a significantly more hazardous material to handle than U-235.

Nuclear weapons are generally made from the metal form of U-235 or Pu-239, but they can also be made from some compounds of these materials, particularly their oxides. Weapons made from compounds would not perform as well, and we can assume that any organization that has the technical capability for designing and fabricating a bomb assembly would also be capable of separating the metal from its compound.

General Conclusions

The requirements for any organization to make a simple, practical, militarily useful fission bomb are:

(1) an understanding of the nuclear theory involved in fission;
(2) data on the physical and chemical properties of the basic materials in a nuclear weapon;
(3) technical facilities to fabricate a weapon and to test implosion or gun devices and other components;
(4) availability of fissile materials;
(5) the will to allocate the necessary resources to develop a weapon.

In the early 1950s each one of these steps represented a major hurdle for all but a few nations with a high level of technical sophistication. Now, however, the first three requirements are met in almost every country with a significant industrial capability, for the open technical literature, much of it stemming from nuclear reactor technology, contains a wealth of material which was very hard to come by twenty years ago. Most semi-industrial nations – including, for example, Korea and Taiwan – have the basic technological capability to fabricate reasonably efficient first-generation fission weapons, and could do so if weapons-grade bomb material were available to them. The problem of fabricating a nuclear device is even simpler if the purpose is only to demonstrate nuclear capability and no premium is placed on such military requirements as low weight and deliverability.

II. THE NUCLEAR FUEL CYCLE

Fissile materials that are usable for nuclear explosives are produced in the normal operation of the fuel cycle of nuclear power reactors. In order to see how these are produced, where they exist in the fuel cycle, and how to identify possible points of diversion, the structure of the fuel cycle itself must be understood. Figure 1 on p.115 gives a schematic diagram (though it is incomplete in that it does not include the flow of thorium through the high-temperature gas reactor fuel cycle or the possibility that thorium can be used in light and heavy water moderated reactors).

The major energy source for all commercial reactors and most research and development reactors is U-235, a fissile isotope that comprises about 0·71 per cent of natural uranium. The latest available data on the world's uranium is presented in Table 1 on p.116 though no information is available for the Soviet Union, Eastern Europe or China. The figures it gives are not estimates of the reserves that might ultimately be discovered and produced at the indicated prices. The state of knowledge about uranium reserves worldwide is rather incomplete, and although the recent rise in market prices has stimulated major

Figure 1: Simplified Flow Chart for Nuclear Power Generation and Weapons Manufacture

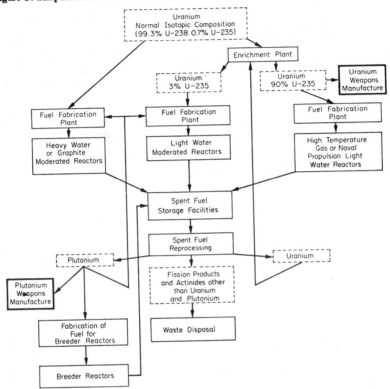

Starting with ordinary uranium, there are several routes to both power generation and weapons. Heavy water and graphite moderated reactors can operate using ordinary uranium; others require the uranium-235 content to be increased. If the proportion of uranium-235 is raised sufficiently, the material can be used directly for a nuclear weapon. In the reactors shown in the middle of the figure, plutonium is produced as a result of the capture of neutrons by the uranium-238 in the fuel (these are called 'converter' reactors). This plutonium can be chemically separated from the other elements in the fuel in a reprocessing plant and can then be used to make weapons. Alternatively (though this is not yet being done, except on an experimental scale) it can be used to generate power, either by feeding it back into a converter reactor or by using it in a 'breeder' reactor (in which the capture of neutrons by uranium-238 to produce plutonium is so efficient that more plutonium is produced than is consumed). When the spent fuel from a reactor is reprocessed, the unconsumed uranium is separated from the other elements and can be used again to manufacture new fuel.

exploration programmes in some countries (notably the United States and Canada), much of the world has yet to be explored. Because of lack of economic incentive, there has been little effort to date to delineate reserves in a cost range of $30–100 per lb but, since the cost of electricity is rather insensitive to the cost of uranium, such reserves are by no means irrelevant to the current generation of reactors. The major reserves are to be found in the United States, Australia, South Africa (including Namibia) and Canada. Except for Australia these are also the

115

Table 1: Uranium Resources and Production

Country	Resource Estimates (000 tonnes U recoverable at specific U_3O_8 cost per lb)[a]				Production (tonnes U per yr)			
	Reasonably Assured[b]		Estimated Additional[c]		Annual Production		Production Capacity (planned)	
	$15	$15–30	$15	$15–30	1974	1975 (est.)	1975	1978
United States[d]	430	210	655	405	8,800	9,000	12,000	19,000
Australia	243	—[e]	80	—[e]				760
South Africa[f]	186	90	6	68	2,711	2,600	2,700	9,200
Canada[g]	145	28[h]	303	302[h]	3,420	3,560	6,500	8,500
Algeria	28	—	—	—				
Argentina	9·3	11·3	15	24	50	60	60	120
Brazil	9·7	0·7	8·8	—				
Britain	—	1·8	—	4				
Central African Republic	8	—	8	—				
Denmark (Greenland)	—	6	—	10				
Finland	—	1·9	—	—				
France	37	18	25	15	1,610	1,700	1,800	2,200
Gabon	20	—	5	5	436	800	800	1,200
Germany	0·5	0·5	1	3	26	uncer-tain	250	250
India	3·4	25·8	0·8	22·5				
Italy	—	1·2	—	1				
Japan	1·1	6·6	—	—	9	4	30	30
Korea	—	2·4	—	—				
Mexico	5	1	—	—				210
Niger	40	10	20	10	1,250	1,200	1,200	2,200
Portugal	6·9	—[e]	—[e]	—[e]	89	115	115	130
Spain[i]	10	93·5	8·8	98	60	144	144	340
Sweden	—	300	—	—				
Turkey	2·6	0·5	0·4	—				
Yugoslavia	4·2	2·3	—	15·2				
Zaire	1·8	—	1·7	—				
Total (rounded)	1,190	810	1,140	980	18,461	19,183	25,600	44,100

NOTES

[a] All dollar figures are in 1975 American dollars and (except those for Canada, which refer to price categories) represent costs. In general the costs include not only direct costs of mining, milling and extraction, but also that of capital spent in providing and maintaining the production unit; exploration costs are not included. The United States figures are based on a forward-cost concept that excludes sunk cost and profit. In no case do the figures here refer either to true economic cost of production or market price, which is of course affected by supply and demand factors as well as cost.

[b] Uranium that occurs in known ore deposits of such grade, quality and configuration that it could be recovered within the given production cost range by means of currently proven mining and processing technology. Estimates of tonnage and grade are based on specific sample data and measurements of the deposits and on knowledge of ore-body habit.

[c] Uranium, surmised to occur in unexplored extensions of known deposits or undiscovered deposits in known uranium districts, which is expected to be discoverable and could be produced in the given cost range. The tonnage and grade of Estimated Additional Resources are based primarily on knowledge of the characteristics of deposits within the same districts.

[d] Does not include 140,000 tonnes uranium as a by-product from phosphates and copper production, which might be recovered before the year 2000. The following additional potential resources of greater uncertainty are indicated by the United States:

major producers. France, Niger, Gabon and, to a lesser extent, Spain, Portugal and Argentina produce significant quantities from a much smaller resources base.

The isotope U-238 that comprises the vast majority of natural uranium is not without importance for reactor fuel cycles, since, if sufficient numbers of fast neutrons are available in the reactor core, the fissioning of U-238 can contribute to the energy production. More important, U-238 can be transformed into fissile Pu-239 by the capture of a neutron and subsequent radioactive decay. This conversion occurs whenever U-238 is present in a reactor core, and in some reactors subsequent plutonium fission provides a significant portion of the energy. If the residual plutonium is recovered from the irradiated fuel and recycled into the reactor core, the net result is the effective use of additional U-238 as reactor fuel. The amount of plutonium available for such recycling depends on the design of the reactor and its fuel. Plutonium breeder reactors are specifically designed to produce large amounts of plutonium. Since a breeder reactor by definition produces more fissile material than it consumes, a plutonium breeder economy can therefore in effect draw on all the U-238, as well as the U-235, as reactor fuel.

Reactors can also use the fissile isotope U-233 as an energy source. Although U-233 does not occur naturally, it can be produced from Th-232, essentially the only naturally occurring thorium isotope. In a thorium–uranium fuel cycle, neutron capture and radioactive decay produce U-233 from thorium in the same way that Pu-239 can be produced from U-238. Thorium is therefore a potentially important resource for future reactor fuel cycles. A true

thorium breeder can be operated totally on thorium and the U-233 produced. If the reactor is not that efficient in its use of neutrons, fissile material must be added to the U-233 in the fuel, and either U-235 or plutonium could be used for this purpose.

A true thorium breeder would be able to draw on essentially the total thorium resource base. To date little exploration has been done for minable thorium deposits, but from what information is available (largely about deposits associated with other minerals) the extent of the world's thorium resources seem to be as large as, and possibly larger than, uranium resources. India, Norway, the United States, Canada, Brazil and Australia all have large known reserves, and smaller deposits have been identified in several other countries.

The following description of the fuel cycle will deal primarily with uranium, since it is the critical mineral for fuel cycles currently in use, and for most of those under development. Following removal from the mine, uranium ore is treated by mechanical and chemical methods until a concentration of 70–80 per cent or more of uranium oxide (U_3O_8) is reached. This process is called milling. Concentrated U_3O_8 (called yellowcake) leaves the mill and is shipped to a chemical conversion plant.

The next step in the fuel cycle depends on the type of reactor in which the uranium is intended to serve as fuel. Reactors using natural uranium require conversion to either uranium metal or uranium oxide (UO_2), while those using enriched uranium require conversion to uranium hexafluoride, the chemical form needed for enrichment by gaseous diffusion or any other enrichment technology in current use. Enrichment for

---

possible resources < $30 per lb:
1,270,000 tonnes uranium
speculative resources < $30 per lb:
590,000 tonnes uranium
e Estimates of resources in this range have not been made and are therefore unknown. Exploration to date has concentrated on proving high-grade resources.
f The 350,000 tonnes uranium total uranium resources for Africa has been apportioned as a best estimate to the various resource categories, although reservations have been expressed concerning the accuracy of the split figures.
g Categories are by reference to *price*, not cost.
h Estimates in this price range are preliminary, restricted only to principal deposits, and are thus very conservative.

i Includes some 80,800 tonnes uranium reasonably assured and 63,800 tonnes uranium estimated additional resources in lignites in the cost range $15–30 per lb U_3O_8, for which the availability is uncertain.

Source: Organization for Economic Co-operation and Development, Nuclear Energy Agency and International Atomic Energy Agency, *Uranium Resources, Production and Demand* (Paris: OECD, 1976), except for United States – derived from Energy Research and Development Administration press release, April 12, 1976 – and Canada – derived from Energy, Mines and Resources, Canada, *1975 Assessment of Canada's uranium supply and demand* (Ottawa: Information EMR, 1976).

117

most reactors increases the U-235 concentration to a level of 2 to 4 per cent, known as low-enriched uranium. The high-temperature gas reactor and reactors used for ship propulsion require U-235 concentration over 90 per cent – which is weapons-grade material. After enrichment the uranium must be converted to a chemical form appropriate for reactor fuel, either uranium oxide (UO_2) or uranium carbide (UC). Thorium must also be converted to an oxide (ThO_2) or carbide (ThC) before being made into fuel, and plutonium is used only as the oxide (PuO_2).

Uranium oxide fuel elements are fabricated by compacting uranium oxide powder into small fuel pellets, stacking a number of pellets into a thin-walled metal tube or cladding, sealing the tube (thus completing a 'fuel rod') and bundling a number of rods together to form a fuel element (also referred to as a fuel assembly or a fuel bundle). When recycled plutonium is used with uranium, plutonium oxide powder is mixed with uranium oxide powder before fabricating pellets. Any facility for fabricating a mixed uranium and plutonium oxide fuel must contain pure plutonium compounds and is therefore a potential point of diversion from the fuel cycle. Further, unless such a facility is co-located with a re-processing plant this material must be shipped from one to the other.

The fuel for high-temperature gas reactors consists of so-called BISO particles of fertile thorium oxide mixed with recycled U-233 oxide (early models used carbide) in burnable carbon coatings and so-called TRISO particles of weapons-grade, high-enriched and medium-enriched uranium carbide in carbon and unburnable silicon carbide coatings. These particles, about the size of fine sand, are mixed in suitable proportions and formed into fuel rods using a graphite matrix as a binder. The rods are then fixed in graphite blocks for insertion into the reactor. Gas-cooled reactors of British and French design use metallic uranium fuel in a metallic cladding, similarly embedded in a graphite block.

As already mentioned, during reactor operations U-238 is converted into Pu-239 by neutron capture and beta decay. In fact subsequent neutron capture by the plutonium leads also to the creation of Pu-240 and higher isotopes of plutonium. Figure 2 (p. 12) indicates the change in plutonium isotope concentration as a function of reactor burn-up time for a pressurized light water reactor (LWR) fuelled with 3·3 per cent enriched uranium fuel and for a CANDU heavy water reactor. It is noteworthy that the relative concentration of Pu-240 and higher isotopes increases with time relative to Pu-239 concentration. This explains why the quality of plutonium for weapons purposes declines as burn-up time increases.

After removal from a reactor core, spent fuel is stored for at least 140–180 days at the reactor site to let the level of radioactivity decline to manageable levels. It can then be sent to a reprocessing plant to await reprocessing, or to other temporary storage facilities. (In the United States and some other countries the present lack of alternative storage has resulted in a build-up of spent fuel at reactor storage pools.) The purpose of chemical reprocessing of spent fuel is to package radioactive wastes into a form chemically and physically suitable for long-term storage and to retrieve reusable materials. From a uranium–plutonium fuel cycle these are highly purified plutonium and uranium, the value of the latter being dependent on the U-235 and U-236 content. Spent fuel from LWRs can be expected to contain uranium which has a slightly higher U-235 concentration (0·8–0·9 per cent) than normal uranium, and in this case it may be worth about as much as the plutonium in the fuel.

Uranium and plutonium are separated by a process called plutonium and uranium recovery by extraction (PUREX), and current reprocessing plants produce pure plutonium that is usable for weapons or a plutonium compound that is readily reducible to metallic form. Fuel rods containing thorium employ a somewhat different process (THOREX) and yield thorium and uranium. Some of the uranium may have sufficiently high U-233 or U-235 content to be usable for explosives.

The radioactive wastes produced in reprocessing plants include heavy actinide nuclei that are very long-lived and fission products that, for the most part, are much less so. Both must be isolated from the environment for as long as they retain appreciable radioactivity. Embedding the waste material in a chemically inert glass and permanent deposit in stable, dry geological structures are under active study in several countries as ultimate solutions to the still unresolved problems of reactor waste storage.

118

III. NUCLEAR POWER TECHNOLOGY

The degree and ease with which an indigenous commercial nuclear industry provides a country access to weapons materials depends on the choice of reactor design and the extent to which all components of the fuel cycle are domestically available. The two reactor types now in widespread use and available on the international market are light-water reactors and CANDU heavy-water reactors. Two additional designs, the liquid-metal fast breeder reactor and the high-temperature gas reactor are in the advanced development stage and might begin to become available within the next decade. In addition, gas-cooled graphite-moderated reactors are in use in several countries, and steam-generating heavy-water-moderated reactors are under development in Britain; however, neither is likely to be a significant factor in international commerce. The United States Navy has a light water cooled, thorium cycle reactor design under development that it hopes can be made into a breeder. Gas and molten salt cooled breeders are also in the early stages of investigation.

In this section, we first compare the extent to which the fuel cycles of the most important reactor types can be used as a source of weapons materials and then examine in some detail the two most sensitive aspects of the fuel cycle: spent fuel reprocessing and uranium enrichment.

Comparative Analysis of Nuclear Fuel Cycles[1]

Since for all important reactor types the quantity of materials flowing annually through the fuel cycle for a commercial sized reactor is large compared with the requirements for making one or several weapons, the following analysis of weapons proliferation implications is not concerned with detailed materials balances.[2] Full fuel cycle diagrams for the most important reactor types will be found in Appendix A. Table 2 on p. 17 summarizes their salient features.

Light Water Reactors

Light water cooled and moderated reactors (LWRs) dominate the nuclear industry now, and will continue to do so into the next century. Well over 100 LWRs are now operating in 15 countries for the purpose of generating electric power, and over 200 are under construction or on order,

For notes, see p. 49.

including the first LWRs for about 16 countries. Firms or government enterprises in the United States, the Soviet Union, France, West Germany, Sweden, Italy, and Japan currently build LWRs of the pressurized water (PWR) or boiling water (BWR) variety. While American firms still dominate the export market, their leadership has been eroded in recent years, as French and German vendors have become active. Italian and Japanese firms have not yet entered the export market.

The equilibrium fuel cycles for LWRs with and without plutonium recycle that are given in Appendix A do not distinguish between the two reactor types. At the level of generality relevant here, there is little difference between them; the enrichment level for uranium fuel is somewhat lower for BWRs, but in either case it is only 2 or 3 per cent – far too low for explosives use. However, a country with its own enrichment facilities could, in the absence of safeguards and assuming the political will, use the commercial facility to produce weapons-grade uranium. The cost and degree of difficulty in doing so depends on the enrichment technology available.

The range of burn-up times for LWRs varies greatly from one reactor to another. The range is roughly 15,000 megawatt (thermal) days per metric ton (MW d/te) to 34,000 MW d/te, with newer reactors tending toward the higher figure. In the absence of recycling, the fissile proportion (mostly Pu-239 and Pu-241) of plutonium in the spent fuel can be as high as 85 per cent with low burn-up or as low as 70 per cent with high burn-up (see Figure 2). Such percentages are not so low as to preclude the plutonium's use for explosives purposes, but they are low enough to require sophisticated design and fabrication techniques, unless a very inefficient yield is acceptable. A country wanting to build a plutonium explosive is not likely to value such plutonium very highly. Any country wishing to produce better-grade plutonium from an LWR can do so simply by exposing the fuel to a lower burn-up: at 5,000 MW d/te the fissile content rises to about 90 per cent, and at still lower burn-up it goes even higher. But using a reactor in this way would involve frequent shutdowns for refuelling and would be very costly in terms of electric power not produced; it would also be easily detectable by safeguards mechanisms.

119

Figure 2: Plutonium Isotope Concentrations for LWR and CANDU Fuel as a Function of Burn-up Time

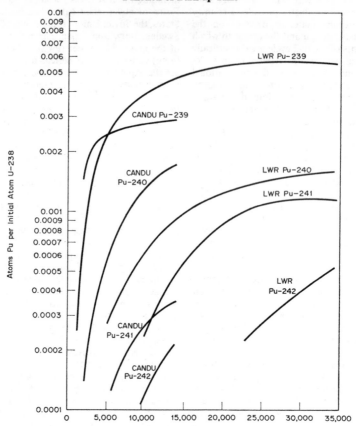

Megawatt Days per Tonne Fuel

Whether intended for explosives or for reactor use, plutonium must be separated from the other components of spent fuel in a chemical reprocessing plant. However, it is conceivable that spent fuel might be reprocessed without plutonium recovery. This might be done to recover unutilized, partially enriched uranium and to reduce the volume of wastes to be disposed of.

A country that imports its enriched fuel and refrains from reprocessing its spent fuel would not have access to weapons materials from an LWR fuel cycle. If it exported the spent fuel for

reprocessing it would, of course, have such access only if the plutonium were returned for use. Fabricating it into mixed oxide fuel before the return would increase the difficulty of gaining access to the plutonium, but not very significantly. An individual LWR cannot be made self-sustaining simply by recycling the plutonium produced and adding natural uranium. Either enriched uranium or additional plutonium produced in another reactor would be required.

It is possible in principle to use a thorium–uranium cycle in LWRs. In fact, the United States

120

Navy has a programme that it hopes will demonstrate not only the feasibility of doing so but also that the conversion ratio can be made to be greater than one – that is, that a true breeder can be produced. Since U-233 can be used for weapons purposes, and since reprocessing would be an essential component of such a fuel cycle, this cycle would be advantageous from the point of view of non-proliferation of weapons only if reprocessing occurred outside the user country and the U-233 produced were denatured with U-238 to the point where it could no longer be used for explosives. However, such addition of U-238 would mean that plutonium would be produced when the fuel was used. This could be disposed of or used by weapons states. Addition of U-238 would also reduce the conversion ratio by about 0·1, precluding a true breeding cycle. The feasibility and economics of this fuel cycle design deserve further study.

Heavy Water Reactors[3]
The pressurized heavy water reactor (PHWR) is the second most popular type today. The international market is now the exclusive domain of Atomic Energy of Canada Ltd, with its CANDU design; the department of Atomic Energy of India is building its own reactors, based on CANDU, but has no known plans as yet to enter the international market. Commercial-scale PHWRs are operating in Canada, India, Pakistan and Argentina. Canada and India are actively building new plants, and Canada has to date, agreed to sell one reactor each to Argentina and South Korea.

Reliance on heavy water as a moderator permits the use of natural uranium for fuel and obviates the need either to build enrichment facilities or to purchase enrichment services from others. Burn-up is low, because there is simply not enough U-235 in natural uranium to maintain criticality after 8–10,000 MW d/te. This burn-up in an LWR would produce plutonium with close to 90 per cent fissile content, but the lower U-235 concentration in CANDU fuel results in more neutron interactions with Pu-239 than occur in an LWR. The result is greater fissioning of Pu-239 and greater conversion to Pu-240. The overall result is a lower fissile content for the plutonium in CANDU fuel than LWR fuel of the same burn-up. Depending on the actual burn-up time, CANDU fuel has about 70–80 per cent fissile

content, about the same range as high burn-up LWR fuel. CANDU does, however, produce more plutonium per unit of electricity generated than does an LWR.

To increase the availability of CANDU reactors for electricity generation they are fuelled while in operation, by pushing fuel bundles through individual, horizontal fuelling channels. If this feature were exploited to move some fuel through the reactor rapidly, it would experience lower burn-up and therefore contain better-quality plutonium: i.e., plutonium with a high fissile content. There are, however, two reasons why using some fuel channels to produce lower burn-up fuel would be quite costly. First, operating experience suggests that, because of the busy schedule of the fuelling machine under normal operations and the extent of its down-time, faster refuelling of several particular channels could only be done at the expense of maintaining normal reactivity in the rest of the core. The result would be a reduction in power output. Second, unless depleted uranium fuel were employed, presence in one or more channels of fuel that, because of more rapid refuelling, had a higher than design U-235 concentration would produce local hot spots in the core. To reduce the risk of fuel failure, the power level of the whole reactor would have to be lowered.

While there is no firm data on the extent of these problems, it seems quite likely that an attempt to use a commercial CANDU reactor to produce any reasonably interesting quantity of high-quality plutonium would lead to a rather significant loss of power output. This does not prevent a country from using a CANDU to make high-quality plutonium, but it does suggest that it is not very likely. Building a small specially designed plutonium production reactor would be much less expensive. Moreover, any use of a CANDU reactor for this purpose and subsequent diversion of the irradiated fuel would very likely be detected by an operating safeguards system, which must be rather different to systems for LWRs because of the continuous fuelling feature.

Plutonium can only be removed from CANDU spent fuel by reprocessing. While this reprocessing would be cheaper per kilogram of fuel than for higher burn-up LWR fuel, there is less recoverable plutonium per kilogram and the uranium is depleted in fissile isotope relative to natural uranium. At current uranium prices, it is not economically attractive to reprocess CANDU fuel for recycle in a CANDU reactor (Figure A3 in Appendix A shows the simple once-through fuel cycle). If a market developed for plutonium to be used in LWRS or fast breeders, reprocessing and sale of plutonium might be profitable, but the uncertainties of the economics are very large. Canada does not now reprocess spent fuel and her plans to develop the capability for plutonium recycle are contingent, in part, on the quantity and price of domestic uranium supplies. A pilot plant for mixed-oxide fuel fabrication is now under construction to permit tests of CANDU reactors operated with fuel containing small quantities of plutonium.

The Canadian nuclear designers are very interested in a thorium fuel cycle for CANDU as a means of stretching their domestic fuel supply. They believe that a conversion ratio of close to $1\cdot0$ could be attained and that the fuel cycle would therefore be very nearly self-sustaining, apart from a one-time start-up charge of plutonium or highly enriched uranium. The frequency of reprocessing and refuelling would be reduced if other fissile material were added to the thorium–U-233 fuel. At anything like current prices for uranium and fuel cycle services a mixed thorium–plutonium fuel seems most economically attractive, though this is, of course, not a self-sufficient fuel cycle. Weapons-grade U-233 is produced in a thorium fuel cycle, but if it were removed the fuel cycle could not be sustained unless it were replaced by plutonium or uranium highly enriched in U-235. A pure thorium or thorium–plutonium cycle may be slightly more worrisome from a weapons proliferation perspective than a recycled plutonium one, since it offers the possibility of production of high-quality U-233 from rather low-quality plutonium.

High-temperature Gas Reactors[4]
The prognosis for the high-temperature gas reactor (HTGR) is quite uncertain. Of the three prototype plants that began operations in the mid-1960s, the 40 megawatt electric (MWe) Peach Bottom facility in the United States, the 20 MWe *Dragon* facility built in Great Britain by the Organization of Economic Co-operation and Development and the 15 MWe AVR reactor in West Germany, only the last is still operating. The 342 MWe Fort St Vrain demonstration plant in Colorado went critical in 1974 and, start-up

problems solved, began commercial operations during 1976; all orders for subsequent HTGRS from General Atomic, the American vendor, have now been cancelled, however, and the company has suspended sales efforts. The HTGR's future in the United States now depends on decisions being made in the company and in the government. In Germany interest remains high.[5] A 300 MWe demonstration plant is under construction in West Germany and is expected to begin operations in 1978.

The HTGR is helium cooled and graphite moderated. It would rely on a Th/U-233/U-235 or, conceivably, a Th/U-233/Pu fuel cycle. Current plans assume the former mode, and that is the fuel cycle presented in Figure A4 in Appendix A. Highly enriched uranium is required as part of the fuel, and this – if diverted – could be used for explosives. Once fabricated into fuel, however, it is quite difficult to remove. The TRISO particles containing the highly enriched uranium are coated with silicon carbide, which neither burns nor dissolves in acid, and they must be physically crushed by large and sophisticated machinery. The spent fuel contains both TRISO particles and carbon-coated BISO particles containing thorium and converted U-233. Except for some unavoidable mixing as the fuel is crushed and prepared for reprocessing, the U-235 and U-233 streams are kept separate in the reprocessing plant. After one pass through the reactor, the U-235 is too depleted to be useful for weapons. After a second pass the concentration is so low it is discarded.

After one pass through the reactor, and neglecting the effect of mixing, the uranium produced from thorium has concentrations of 86 per cent U-233, 12 per cent U-234, 2 per cent U-235 and traces of U-232 and U-236. Aside from the handling problem caused by penetrating gamma radiation from the U-232 daughters, this material would be very good for weapons purposes. Under equilibrium conditions of multiple re-cycles of the U-233, the relative uranium concentrations in this stream, again neglecting mixing, are 60 per cent U-233, 25 per cent U-234, 8 per cent U-235 and 7 per cent U-236. This material could be used for explosives, but considerably greater care and sophistication would be required than with relatively pure U-233. As a result of mixing of the U-233 and U-235 streams the actual fissile content is reduced.

Liquid Metal Fast Breeder
The salient aspect of a breeder reactor fuel cycle from the point of view of energy production is its ability to produce enough surplus neutrons to convert a fertile material into a fissile material at a rate faster than its own consumption of fissile fuel. A uranium–plutonium breeder would thereby permit the extraction of the otherwise largely unusable energy from U-238, the isotope that constitutes 99 per cent of natural uranium. Similarly, except for the need for plutonium or highly enriched uranium to initiate the cycle, a thorium breeder can be operated with total reliance on fertile thorium. This breeding concept was well understood from the earliest days of the nuclear era. In fact, the first nuclear-generated electric power was produced by the American Experimental Breeder Reactor I in the 1950s. The greater simplicity of other designs, the availability of ample uranium and uranium enrichment facilities and the desire of several countries to produce high-quality plutonium for weapons manufacture led to a slow development of the breeder in comparison to other reactor types. Now, however, the Soviet Union, France and Britain have demonstration-size plants operating, and others are under construction or planned in Japan, West Germany and the United States. A 600 MWe plant is now under construction in the Soviet Union and will be followed by a 1,500 MWe plant,[6] while France's 1,200 MWe *Super Phénix*, planned to be built with West German and Italian assistance, will begin operations possibly in the early to mid-1980s.[7] All these use liquid sodium as a coolant.

As with the HTGR, fuel reprocessing is essential to a liquid-metal fast breeder reactor (LMFBR) fuel cycle. The plutonium produced is of slightly better quality for weapons use than plutonium from an LWR or a PHWR, assuming that the irradiated fuel rods and blanket material are mixed during reprocessing. If the blanket material is reprocessed separately, plutonium that is over 90 per cent Pu-239 is available.[8] Thus the existence of such high-quality weapons material and the requirement to move plutonium through the fuel cycle make the LMFBR a reactor type with significant implications for nuclear proliferation.

Enrichment is not required for the fuel of an LMFBR once it is operating at equilibrium. Recycled plutonium serves as fuel, and natural or depleted uranium can be used for the blanket. But until equilibrium is reached highly enriched uranium or plutonium from a LWR or other converter reactor must be supplied.

Other Fuel Cycles
In the late 1950s and through the mid-1960s Britain and France developed and built a number of gas-cooled reactors (GCRs), using carbon dioxide coolant, graphite moderator and natural uranium fuel in Magnox or magnesium–zirconium claddings. The burn-up time was very short, less than 4,000 MW d/te in the British case and less than 5,000 MW d/te in the French, with considerably shorter times in the case of some reactors. The reactors, which could be fuelled while operating, were designed specifically to generate power and produce plutonium for nuclear weapons programmes, but were not competitive with other designs for purely commercial operations. Because of the unstable nature of irradiated Magnox fuel, storage over long periods of time is very difficult and reprocessing is desirable. Apart from single reactors bought from Britain by Italy and Japan and France by Spain, this type of reactor did not penetrate the export market. No more are now being produced, since France has turned to LWR technology, and Britain turned to advanced gas reactors in the mid-1960s.

The Advanced Gas Reactor (AGR), developed and now coming into use in the United Kingdom, also uses carbon dioxide coolant and graphite moderator but the uranium fuel is enriched to 2–2·6 per cent U-235. The burn-up time is about 18,000 MW d/te and the reactor produces plutonium of poorer grade than the GCR and not very different from that produced in an LWR. No AGRs have been, or are likely to be, built outside the United Kingdom, and Britain itself has decided to change to a steam-generating heavy water (SGHWR) design for future commercial reactors.

Britain began building a 100 MWe prototype SGHWR in 1963, but it was not until 1974 that the government decided to adopt this design for commercial power reactors. Six are now planned, each with an output of 660 MWe. Low enrichment (slightly over 2 per cent U-235) is used, and the reactor design requires heavy water as a moderator and boiling light water as coolant. The plutonium produced will again not be very

123

Table 2: Comparison of Implications for Proliferation of Equilibrium Fuel Cycles of Various Reactor Types

	Enrichment Required	Burn-up MW d/te	Fissile Content of Pu in Spent Fuel	On/off Power Fuelling	Reprocessing Needed/ Useful	Availability and Quality of Weapons Material
Light Water Reactor (no Pu recycle)	Low	16–28,000 for BWR 24–33,000 PWR	70% or higher	Off	No/Yes	With reprocessing, plutonium is available; its quality for weapons purposes could be made very good by operating with very low burn-up; enrichment facility could be used to produce weapons-grade uranium
LWR (Pu Recycle)	Low	25,000	About 55%	Off	Yes	Plutonium is reasonably good after one cycle through the reactor; after more than one cycle it is quite poor
CANDU Reactor	None	7–10,000	About 70%	On	No/Yes when U prices rise	With reprocessing, plutonium available from commercial operations is of roughly same quality as from LWR. Much better quality plutonium can be made at considerable economic cost
High-temperature Gas Reactor	High	95,000	No Pu	Off	Yes	U-235 93% going in; very good, but difficult to remove from TRISO particles; thorium–uranium reprocessing stream yields uranium that is usable with difficulty at equilibrium but better after one pass
Liquid-metal Fast Breeder	None	65–100,000	73% on average; over 90% from blanket	Off	Yes	Plutonium mixed together is reasonably good; blanket held separate is very good
Gas-cooled Reactor	None	3–5,000	Very high	On	No/Yes	Plutonium in spent fuel is good to excellent quality
Advanced Gas Reactor	Low	18,000	About same as LWR	On	No/Yes	Plutonium in spent fuel is about same quality as LWR; enrichment facility could be used to produce weapons-grade uranium
Steam-generated Heavy Water Reactor	Low	21,000	About same as LWR	Off	No/Yes	Plutonium in spent fuel is about same quality as LWR; enrichment facility could be used to produce weapons-grade uranium

124

different in quality from that produced in an LWR, and off-power fuelling makes the SGHWR easy to safeguard. Like the LWR it can be operated with recycled plutonium. The first British commercial facilities are not expected to be operating until 1981, and to date no interest has been expressed by other countries.

Several additional types of reactor are worth mentioning briefly. Italy and Japan are both building small, light water cooled, heavy water moderated reactors (LWCHWR). The Italian facility, rated at 35 MWe, will use natural or slightly enriched uranium, while the Japanese, rated at 200 MWe, will use a mixed-oxide fuel in which the uranium is slightly enriched. Three countries have gas-cooled heavy water reactors (GCHWR): Germany, whose 100 MWe version was closed down in 1974, France, whose 70 MWe reactor has been operating since 1971, and Czechoslovakia, whose 112 MWe facility achieved full power in 1973. The first two use slightly enriched uranium oxide fuel, while the last employs natural metallic uranium. The Soviet Union has built several light water cooled, graphite moderated reactors using two different designs, one relying on natural uranium–molybdenum alloy, and an advanced graphite moderated reactor is under construction. None of these reactor types seems likely to play a significant role in international nuclear trade.

Summary

The HTGR and the LMFBR fuel cycles require the use of weapons material in their fuel: highly enriched U-235 and U-233 in the first case, and recycled plutonium in the second case. If U-233 were diverted from the HTGR reprocessing plant after one irradiation, or if the blanket material of an LMFBR were reprocessed separately from core material, the weapons quality of both would be increased markedly. LWR, CANDU, GCR, AGR and SGHWR fuel cycles can produce plutonium for weapons if the spent fuel is reprocessed, though the quality of the plutonium produced is less than ideal for weapons purposes, except in the case of that produced in low-burn-up GCRs. In every case the quality could be improved by reducing burn-up time, but that would involve a significant economic penalty if a commercial power reactor were involved. LWR, AGR and SGHWR fuel cycles require low-enriched uranium for fuel, and in principle the enrichment plant could be used

to produce high-enrichment, weapons-grade uranium.

Facilities designed specifically to produce weapons-grade fissile material would be cheaper and more straightforward for a moderate weapons programme than reliance on any commercial reactor and associated fuel cycle. Two relatively simple facilities must be constructed: a small heavy water or graphite moderated reactor fuelled with natural uranium and operating at low pressure, and a small reprocessing facility for extracting plutonium from low-burn-up fuel. Besides their lower costs, use of separate facilities would avoid disrupting the large-scale technical and administrative operations involved in the generation of commercial electric power.

Chemical Reprocessing of Spent Fuel

A reprocessing plant is a point in the nuclear fuel cycle of commercial power reactors (and for most reactor types the only point) where nuclear material directly usable for weapons is produced during routine operation. On entering a reprocessing plant uranium and plutonium are contained in irradiated fuel rods that are extremely radioactive and difficult to handle; but on coming out both are highly purified and in convenient chemical forms. For most reactor types the purified uranium is so depleted in fissile isotopes that, like natural uranium, it is not directly usable for nuclear explosives, but the HTGR is the single exception. With sophisticated designs, sufficient quantities of uranium purified in a commercial HTGR reprocessing plant could be used to produce a low-yield nuclear explosive. Any plutonium emerging from a reprocessing plant could also be used for manufacturing explosives. As explained above, its quality for that purpose would depend importantly on the type of reactor in which it was produced and its period of irradiation.

Apart from some refinements introduced as a result of greater experience and to take account of the increased levels of radioactivity in high-burn-up fuel, the technology for separating uranium and plutonium from spent reactor fuel has not changed fundamentally since just after World War II. What has changed is the degree of diffusion of the technology and the expectation about its economic viability in a commercial light water reactor fuel cycle. A description of

125

reprocessing technology, a list of facilities and a discussion of their status is provided in Appendix B. In this section we will examine the difficulty involved in a state building its own reprocessing facility as part of an explosives programme, the status of reprocessing within the commercial nuclear fuel cycle and the possibility of diverting plutonium from a commercial reprocessing plant.

A Deliberate Explosives Programme
The United States made public the basic technology of reprocessing in 1955 as part of its Atoms for Peace Programme. By now this technology is readily available in the open literature and widely diffused. What is not easily accessible is the engineering know-how and operating experience gained by those who have actually built and run processing facilities. Nevertheless, working from what is available any state with some experience in building and operating complex chemical processes (oil refineries for example) would have little difficulty building a first pilot reprocessing plant able to accept fuel from a commercial reactor. India, for example, has built a small plant essentially on its own, and Argentina is in the process of expanding a small laboratory-scale facility that it built independently.

A plant specifically designed to extract plutonium for weapons from fuel irradiated in a plutonium production reactor would be easier to build in a number of respects. It need not, for example, recover uranium in a purified form, since this would be of no interest for explosives. The level of purity required of the plutonium and the level of efficiency in recovery could be lower than would be required for a commercial operation. Because the level of radioactivity and the concentration of some troublesome isotopes is less in the low-burn-up fuel than in fuel from a commercial reactor, shielding requirements and the complexity of the plant's chemistry could be diminished somewhat. With low-burn-up fuel aluminium can be used for the cladding material, obviating the need for complex machinery to break up the fuel, and, if health and safety standards less stringent than normally required in commercial operations were acceptable, the plant could be even further simplified. Finally, there exist plutonium extraction processes simpler than the PUREX process that would be entirely adequate

for separation of material for weapons. These include relying on oxalic acid to precipitate plutonium from a nitric acid solution and using beads of a readily available resin to extract plutonium from a nitric acid solution by ion exchange.[9] Taking all, or even some, of these potential simplifying factors into account, there seems little doubt that almost any state with a modest chemical industry could on its own build a reprocessing plant large enough to supply plutonium to a small explosives programme. A recent study has even concluded that a small facility could be built by many classes of non-state entities.[10]

The cost and time required to build a PUREX plant of the size and type suggested are quite uncertain. One reference point is the 50-tons-a-year plant built by India, which is about the size of a plant needed to support a modest weapons programme based on low-burn-up fuel. This is said to have cost $7 million at the time it was built and to have required four years to become operational. It does not seem unreasonable to estimate, therefore, that the cost of a small reprocessing plant built specifically to extract plutonium for an explosives programme would be of the order of $10 million to $25 million and that, depending on the country, it would take three to seven years to build it without outside assistance. This cost is clearly not prohibitive for any state, and, if foreign nationals with relevant experience could be hired, the time needed might be reduced. The conclusion must be that the ability to build the reprocessing part of a deliberate explosives programme is well within reach of a large number of states.

Commercial Reprocessing
In contrast to the relative ease and low cost of building a small reprocessing facility, optimized to recover plutonium for weapons from low-burn-up natural uranium fuel, the task of building and operating a commercial-scale reprocessing plant designed for high-burn-up oxide fuel is very demanding and expensive. Nonetheless, until recently the process of extracting uranium and plutonium from irradiated fuel and recycling them through the fuel cycle was expected to be profitable. That is, the value of the materials was expected to be higher than the cost of recycling. The LWR fuel cycle was designed with that

expectation in mind, and in the firm belief that sooner or later reprocessing and recycling would take place. Today that expectation is somewhat in doubt. The costs of reprocessing, waste management and mixed-oxide fuel fabrication appear to be too high, and the back end of the fuel cycle may well involve a net cost, and not a net credit, to the ultimate price of electricity – though in any event it will be small.

There are three options to consider for the back end of the fuel cycle: reprocessing and recycling uranium and plutonium; permanently disposing of spent fuel; and storing spent fuel for reprocessing in the future. By internalizing the cost of safeguards and environmental protection, an economic comparison of these alternatives becomes possible – at least in principle. A fourth option, reprocessing without recycling plutonium, is clearly unattractive.

The comparison of these alternatives is intrinsically uncertain today. The sources of uncertainty are fivefold.[11] First, there is very little experience of building reprocessing plants to handle LWR fuel. Second, there is ambiguity about what reprocessing entails; plants and plant designs can include or exclude such processes as conversion of uranium nitrate to uranium hexafluoride, conversion of plutonium nitrate to plutonium oxide, or waste solidification. Third, a variety of structural, health and safety regulations have changed in recent years, and their cost implications are by no means understood. Fourth, it is very unclear, at least in the United States, whether the use of plutonium in mixed-oxide fuels will be socially acceptable. Finally, there is almost no experience of geological or other permanent storage of high-level nuclear wastes, or of permanent or retrievable storage of spent fuel. Projections are merely extrapolations from an inadequate data base or the intrinsically uncertain results of design studies. All but the last of these uncertainties increase the risk for any entrepreneur contemplating entry into the reprocessing business, and therefore increase the expected cost of reprocessing services rendered by any operator that does not receive government subsidies.

Costs of plants have risen steeply in recent years. An optimum-sized plant of 1,500-tonnes per year capacity is currently estimated to cost from $500 million to $800 million.[12] Because reprocessing is so capital-intensive, its cost is very sensitive to this capital requirement, to the way in which this is financed, and to the expected rate of return, so that lack of precise knowledge about these factors makes cost estimation very difficult. Reprocessing costs are also somewhat sensitive to the size of the plant, because of moderately important economics of scale. Yet another important unknown is the cost of dealing with low- and high-level wastes, since both the regulatory environment and the technology for waste management are still very much in flux. Estimates of the costs for the back end of the fuel cycle – including temporary storage and shipment of spent fuel, reprocessing, safeguards allowance, conversion to plutonium oxide and uranium hexafluoride, and management of low- and high-level wastes – range from about $180 to well over $250 per kg of fuel, but the actual uncertainty is almost certainly much broader than this range would suggest.[13]

The value of the recovered materials is partly determined by the costs of natural uranium, conversion to uranium hexafluoride and enrichment. However, there are substantial penalties attached to the use of recovered fissile material, because of the presence of the neutron-absorbing U-236 isotope in the recycled uranium and the additional cost of fabricating and safeguarding mixed-oxide fuel compared with uranium fuel. The extent of these penalties is uncertain, though many estimates which take them into account conclude that the value of the materials recovered is less than the cost of obtaining them.[14] The excess of processing costs over materials value depends not only on the cost of enriched uranium and extent of the penalties but also on the speed with which the purified plutonium is recycled, since the cost of storing it is high.

Finally, a comparison must be made between this excess cost of the back end of the fuel cycle with recycling and the cost of either long-term storage of spent fuel or temporary storage. The cost of neither storage method is really known, since no facilities have yet been built to store large amounts of spent fuel as economically as possible. Estimates for long-term storage range from $50 to well over $150 per kg.[15] The economics of short-term storage depend not only on its actual cost but also on the future cost of reprocessing, the future value of the fissile materials recovered, the period of storage assumed and the discount rate used to make the calculation.

127

The conclusion from this very tentative review of uncertain data is that the economics of reprocessing compared to a throw-away LWR fuel cycle or retrievable storage of spent fuel is uncertain, but that the difference in cost is not likely to be large, given currently projected prices for uranium. With or without reprocessing, the back end of the fuel cycle is unlikely to account for more than 10 per cent of the total fuel-cycle costs and a few per cent of total electricity costs. Therefore, the decision on whether or not to include reprocessing in the LWR fuel cycle can, and probably will, be made primarily on non-economic grounds. For heavy water reactor fuel, on the other hand, reprocessing is unambiguously unfavourable at anything like current uranium prices. Although the cost of reprocessing the lower burn-up fuel is less, this is more than offset by the lower plutonium content per kg of fuel and by the fact that the uranium recovered is depleted in U-235 relative to natural uranium.

Several important non-economic issues are relevant. A state may prefer not to reprocess fuel and recycle plutonium: (a) because of the health and safety risks of working with and transporting this very toxic material, and (b) because of the risk of the theft and subsequent use by terrorists or other non-state entities. On the other hand, a state may be interested in reprocessing: (a) because the likelihood of reprocessing and recycling eventually becoming attractive for economic or energy-conservation reasons, or the likelihood of eventually relying on plutonium breeders is very high, and that therefore a plutonium stockpile and a capability to handle mixed-oxide fuels should be initiated at an early date; (b) because of the attraction of creating an industry that will permit the exercise of the weapons option quickly; and (c) because it desires to separate the rather small quantities of high-level radioactive wastes from the larger volumes of spent fuel and to dispose of the former permanently. In cases where the last is the primary concern, there should be no reluctance to rely on reprocessing services supplied by others. The decision on whether to reprocess spent fuel and whether to acquire domestic facilities to do it will be made according to somewhat different criteria in each country. Economic factors will be only one of several relevant considerations in the calculation.

Diversion of Plutonium

Plutonium can be diverted from the nuclear fuel cycle in several ways. A state willing to develop weapons overtly need only abrogate or disregard agreements it may have with other states or the IAEA and either use an existing reprocessing plant or build a new one. Covert diversion would be more difficult. Diversion of spent fuel would require a clandestine reprocessing plant. Diversion from an existing reprocessing plant, a mixed-oxide fuel fabrication facility or a transportation link would probably yield plutonium in a chemical form not optimal for weapons manufacture, though transforming it into pure plutonium would not be difficult. There is now considerable interest in co-locating mixed-oxide fuel fabrication facilities with reprocessing plants, or at least in mixing plutonium oxide with uranium oxide at the reprocessing plant.[16] Either of these would avoid the transport of plutonium itself or of plutonium compounds. While laudable as a means of impeding the theft of significant quantities of plutonium by terrorists or other non-state entities, these measures would have virtually no effect on states which might divert material in their own control.

All current and prospective reprocessing facilities in non-weapons states are or will be under IAEA safeguards.[17] (See Appendix B, pp.143-5 for a list of non-military reprocessing facilities.) These involve a combination of material accountancy, containment, surveillance and inspection in order to detect the diversion of significant quantities of material and, by creating the risk of detection, to deter it. This is not the place for a detailed discussion of the operation, cost or deficiencies of the safeguard procedures; suffice it to say that most people who have looked closely at the issue seem to agree that, while there is room for improvement in a number of areas, IAEA safeguards are an important component of any strategy to prevent or inhibit nuclear proliferation. However, diversion from a safeguarded reprocessing plant cannot be shown to be impossible. Very little actual experience has yet been gained of safeguarding reprocessing plants, and without much more experience the difficulty of diversion is just not known. The risks would certainly be diminished, though, if plants were designed to facilitate safeguarding and if the IAEA monitoring began with design and continued through construction.

There is no way to be totally confident of preventing diversion from a commercial reprocessing plant or to guarantee that it will never be used overtly for a weapons programme – only the absence of a plant will provide such assurance. Short of a willingness to use military, economic or political coercion, however, external states are not in a position to prevent almost any state with industrial capacity from acquiring a reprocessing plant of some sort. Refusal to export technology is not sufficient; as already argued, states can build small facilities on their own, given the commitment to do so. This raises the very difficult but important question of how to control the diffusion of nuclear technology to minimize the risks and possibility of proliferation. This will be the subject of Section IV of this Paper.

Uranium Enrichment
For many years concern about nuclear proliferation focused on plutonium as the fissionable material for weapons, rather than on U-235. This was because it was generally felt that separating plutonium from fission products and other actinides produced either in power or special-purpose reactors would be much easier and less expensive than obtaining uranium sufficiently enriched in U-235 to be useful for an explosive device. To a substantial degree this was because it seemed likely that uranium enrichment plants would almost necessarily be enormous, costing in the range of a billion dollars and requiring the use of very complex gaseous diffusion technology held secretly by those states that had developed it. Plutonium reprocessing plants, by contrast, could be much smaller, could be based entirely on information in the public domain, and could be built for a few millions or tens of millions of dollars.

In recent years there have been developments that may change the situation, and there appear to be more dramatic changes on the horizon. There are several alternative techniques that have been developed to the point where they may be economically competitive with the gaseous diffusion method for large-scale enrichment of uranium for nuclear power plants, and they will almost certainly be economically superior if the interest is in small quantities – particularly if it is to be highly enriched. In the light of these

developments, and out of concern that there could be a world-wide shortage of enrichment capacity, a number of nations may decide it is both feasible and desirable to have their own enrichment capability, so as to ensure fuel supplies for power reactors.

Whether or not there will be a shortage, and if so when, is highly uncertain. This will depend on the rate of growth in nuclear electric power generation, the addition of new enrichment capacity, how widely plutonium and unconsumed uranium that might be extracted from spent fuel are used, and the amount of U-235 left in the 'tails' during the enrichment process. An estimate of world supply and demand (excluding the Communist countries, apart from an estimate of Soviet export capacity) is given in Table 3 below. Enrichment capacity is measured in 'separative work units'. A 1,000 MWe light water reactor operating at 65 per cent capacity will need of the order of 100,000 SWU per year of enrichment service (for details, see Appendix C).

It will be apparent that if the projections of growth of nuclear power on which Table 3 is based are approximately correct there is not likely to be a shortage of enrichment capacity on a world scale until the mid-1980s. In fact, if anything the projections now seem high (they are based on a growth to 805 gigawatts electric (GWe) for the United States and 1,451 GWe for the rest of the non-Communist world by 2000).

In thinking about the possibility of nations using enriched uranium for explosives, it may be useful to consider three different approaches:

(a) Deliberately building a plant to produce highly enriched uranium (90–97 per cent U-235).

(b) Using a facility developed to produce enriched uranium for reactors to produce weapons-grade material for use in explosives.

(c) Diverting highly enriched uranium from a safeguarded enrichment facility.

In doing this there are basically four different kinds of technology which are of interest (their details are discussed in Appendix C): gaseous diffusion, which has been the process used for almost all uranium enrichment to date; the gas centrifuge process, well proved technically and beginning to produce small amounts of enrichment; two aerodynamic processes, one developed in Germany by Professor E. Becker, the other

129

Table 3: Enrichment Service Supply and Demand (millions of swu)

	1976	1980	1984	1988	1992	1996	2000
Supply							
plants in operation[a]	16·4	20·4	20·1	20·2			
plants planned and authorized	1·1	13·3	22·3	23·2			
	17·5	33·7	42·4	43·4			
Demand[b]		10·9	25·7	48·4	75·2	105·6	137·4	162·3
Surplus		6·6	8·0	−6·0	−31·8			
Cumulative surplus		30·3	57·5	67·5	−16·0			

[a] Includes assumed imports from USSR into non-Communist countries of 0·8 × 10⁶ swu in 1976 and 3 × 10⁶ swu per year thereafter.
[b] Based on 0·3 % tails assay, no plutonium or uranium recycle, and 72 % capacity factor.

SOURCE: *Enrichment Services Supply*, J. J. Steyn, Edison Electric Institute Nuclear Fuels Supply Study Program, Unclassified Final Report, Task IV, December 1975 (Rockville, Md: NUS Corporation, December 1975).

South African; and as yet unproved processes, based on the preferential excitement by a laser of one isotopic species as compared with another. The degree of enrichment that can be achieved in passing UF_6 gas through a single barrier in a gaseous diffusion plant is very slight. This process must therefore be repeated many times in order to produce weapons materials. A number of stages in series will also be required if enrichment is accomplished with centrifuges or one of the aerodynamic processes.

A Deliberate Explosives Programme
If a nation decides to go into the uranium enrichment business primarily in order to produce material for weapons, its requirements are likely to be small, at least initially – perhaps of the order of that required to run a single LWR, or even less, since one reactor (1,000 MWe) requires about as much separative work as would be needed for 50 or 60 weapons per year. For such a small enrichment effort there would be no great premium on economies of scale and little on minimizing power consumption (unless the programme were a clandestine one, and there were concern about discovery through looking at power distribution and consumption).

A continuously operating gaseous diffusion cascade would require 3,500–4,000 stages (the number depending on the tails assay), but for a modest weapons programme the stages would be small compared to those in existing plants. The Portsmouth, Ohio, ERDA plant has 4,080 stages

and can produce a weapons-grade product with 0·3 per cent tails, but it has a capacity of over 5 × 10⁶ swu per year, and even the British and French diffusion plants have capacities of the order of 500,000 swu. A plant with many fewer stages can be used to produce highly enriched uranium, but in that case the product from one run through the plant – say 3 per cent enriched product – would be used as feed for a second run and so on. A critical consideration in such an operational mode is the inventory of UF_6 in a cascade. In the case of a diffusion plant of 1,000 stages or so this is such that equilibrium is reached in a few weeks. If the time available for producing weapons-grade uranium were of the order of a year, therefore, processing with such a plant (or even, perhaps, one with fewer stages) would seem to be feasible. All things considered, however, gaseous diffusion technology is a relatively unsatisfactory and expensive choice for a modest weapons programme. It would require a substantial manufacturing capability and, in particular, a knowledge of how to make barrier material.

Centrifuges would almost certainly be preferred for several reasons. Of the order of 35 stages would be required for 90 per cent enrichment, and a minimum-size plant might involve as few as 1,000 centrifuges to provide a capacity of 5,000 swu per year – enough for a couple of weapons per year. Greater capacity would be obtained simply by adding centrifuges in parallel (or, if they were available, using larger capacity

Table 4: Comparison of Alternative Enrichment Technologies

	Diffusion	Centrifuge	Aerodynamic	Laser
State of the Art	Mature technology; little room for improvement; proven in large scale production; barrier technology classified	At the pilot plant stage; large-scale manufacturing processes not yet implemented; substantial growth potential; some details of technology classified	Technology thoroughly demonstrated; pilot plants not yet built; substantial growth potential. Becker nozzle technology in the public domain; South African process classified	Milligramme-scale separation achieved with U metal; no separation yet reported using UF_6; fundamental problems still to be solved; commercial scale separation probably 8-12 years off
Requirements for Production	Knowledge of barrier technology needed; requires large scale production of pumps	Mass production of precision equipment	Some precision machining capability needed; overall, requirements probably less than for diffusion or centrifuge	Probably minimal for process based on UF_6, once principles have been demonstrated; probably more difficult in the case of U metal
Stages Required in Ideal Cascade (0·3% tails)				
3% enrichment	1,086	10	600	Possibly only 1
90% enrichment	3,731	35	2,000 (at a cut of $\frac{1}{4}$ – see Appendix C)	Possibly only 1

131

Suitability for a Nuclear Power Fuel Cycle	Not likely to be economically competitive for small or modest programmes; may not be competitive at all if pilot plant experience with others is satisfactory	Will probably be preferred (lasers excepted) where power costs are very high	Will probably be preferred (lasers excepted) where power costs are low, especially for small or modest scale operations	Likely to be particularly desirable because it will probably extend uranium supplies greatly
Adaptability of facilities developed for a power programme (enrichment to 2–3% to weapons production	Least desirable; requires construction of additional stages or 'batch processing' which would be inconvenient and time-consuming because of large cascade inventory of gas	Much preferred to diffusion or aerodynamic processes because of possibility of increasing the number of stages by changing plumbing connections	Will require additional stages or 'batch processing'; latter is more feasible than with diffusion because of smaller inventory of gas in cascade	Will probably be best; process may lead naturally to highly enriched U
Suitability for a small or modest deliberate weapons programme	Unattractive because of large number of stages required; experience is with plants that are of large capacity	Very good; several plants now operating or planned of a scale interesting for weapons purposes	Unattractive compared to centrifuge but probably better than diffusion, especially considering greater feasibility of batch processing	Probably preferred
Possibility of diversion of materials from power programme to weapons construction	Not serious if enrichment is only 2–3%; serious for all three processes if enrichment for power purposes is to 90–97% (i.e. for HTGR's)			Probably most worrisome

centrifuges such as are being developed in the United States). However, the number of centrifuges required to produce 100,000 SWU per year would be very large – so large that mass production techniques for manufacture would be indicated. We lack information that would permit a reliable estimate of the cost of a centrifuge enrichment plant of very low capacity (i.e., capable of producing enough highly enriched uranium for a few weapons per year), but it is likely to be tens of millions of dollars. (The smallest plant for which we have an estimated cost is one of 272,000 SWU capacity – enough for some 100 weapons per year. The estimate in this case is $195 million.)

The Becker and South African aerodynamic processes are probably least demanding in manufacturing capabilities and capital requirements, and this would seem to be their major advantage over the centrifuge for small-scale weapons manufacture. However, they might be preferred to gaseous diffusion on other grounds as well. The number of stages required for a continuous process is only a fraction as great. And if batch processing were preferred, the situation would be much more favourable because cascade inventory of gas is much less, and equilibrium therefore attainable much more quickly: 16 hours for the South African process if the cascade is designed to produce 3 per cent enriched uranium and probably even less for the Becker process. The great disadvantage of higher power consumption compared with centrifuges, and even with diffusion, would not be likely to be important in a small weapons programme.

If one of the laser processes is developed to the point where the separation of kilogram quantities of uranium can be demonstrated, it will almost certainly be the preferred choice for the would-be nuclear power. It is likely to have the enormous advantage of producing very high enrichment in one or a few stages. Moreover, it will probably not require as much of an industrial base or capability for undertaking large-scale engineering enterprises as the other techniques. This is likely to be especially so in the case of a plant based on the use of UF_6. It is impossible at this time to make any meaningful predictions about likely costs for laser enrichment, but they could prove to be much less than for any of the other processes.

Power-based Programmes

It is perhaps useful to begin a discussion of the role of enrichment in power programmes by noting that from an economic perspective enrichment is a relatively small item in a very costly kind of enterprise: only about 5 per cent of the total cost of generating power. However, availability of enrichment service is critical once a nation has made a commitment to a large power programme using reactors that require enriched fuel. Despite this, there has been a reluctance to construct new plants, particularly in the United States, which is the supplier of most of the world's enrichment service. This is because projections of demand are uncertain, and the economics of the newer technologies (and in the case of lasers, even the feasibility) are not well understood. No one wants to be caught with a costly plant that can only produce separative work at a cost much greater than that which may be possible with a newer technology. This has contributed to the possibility of a medium-term shortage of capacity and to interest in the United States in government encouragement, possibly including guarantees, to those willing to construct new plants.

From what is known at this time it seems possible that the several technologies may all be important. Estimates of capital costs as a function of capacity are shown in Figure 3 for three of them. Since there has been no experience of the construction of production facilities based on nozzles and little experience of centrifuges, the estimates in these cases must be regarded as very approximate (and probably lower bounds). The estimates for small diffusion plants must also be regarded with scepticism, considering that they are based on long extrapolation of costs for large plants.

It will be noted that economies of scale appear to be more significant in the case of diffusion and nozzle processes than for centrifuges, which is consistent with the conventional wisdom. However, when one considers the cost of producing separative work, economy-of-scale arguments that might be made in favour of diffusion or nozzle processes have to be softened, the degree depending on the cost of electric power. If it is high, power costs will be a very large fraction of the total cost of separative work in the case of diffusion, and an even larger fraction for aerodynamic processes, and the cost of power is

133

Figure 3: Capital Costs for Enrichment

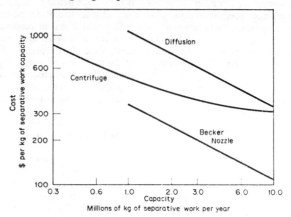

In the gaseous diffusion and centrifuge cases, costs are based on estimates for 9×10^6 SWU and 3×10^6 SWU plants respectively in 'A Feasibility Study of Gas Centrifuge Enrichment Facilities' (Electro Nucleonics, Inc., 1975), p. 17. Scaling for centrifuges is based on information from the same source (p. 14); in the case of diffusion plants it has been assumed that costs scale as the square root of plant size, which is consistent with information given in C. Frejacques and R. Galley, 'Enseignements tirés des etudes et réalisations françaises relatives à la separation des isotopes de l'uranium' (UN 3rd Peaceful Uses of Atomic Energy Conference), p. 330. Another source – R. L. Hoglund, J. Schachter, E. von Halle, 'Diffusion Separation Methods', in *Encyclopedia of Chemical Technology* (New York: John Wiley, 1965), p. 107 – suggests 0·6 power scaling. All costs are for late 1974.

Costs for the Becker nozzle process are based on information in E. W. Becker, W. Bier, W. Ehrfeld, K. Schubert, R. Schutte, D. Seidel, 'Present State and Development Potential of Separation Nozzle Process' (Institut für Kernverfahrenstechnik, KFK 2067, September 1974), p. 7, adjusted for inflation. Square root scaling has been used, which is consistent with the very limited information given in this source (p. 8).

likely to be almost independent of scale over the range of interest. The effect is illustrated in Figure 4 overleaf, assuming a cost of 25 mills per kilowatt-hour (kWh).

In considering Figure 4 the reader should bear in mind that rather large uncertainties underly the estimates. The most critical ones are the cost and reliability of centrifuges, the specific power consumption (kWh required per SWU) for the Becker nozzle process, and the scaling of capital costs for the diffusion and Becker processes below plant capacities of about 2 million SWU per year. Taking these uncertainties into account, and the fact that the curves are as close together as they are, suggests that only in exceptional circumstances will it be possible to make a strong case for or against any of the three processes. In the near term there may still be a case for

new diffusion plants for large-scale operations by nations with the ability to manufacture efficient barrier materials. It rests largely on the fact that it is a well-established technology. But the potential for improvement in the other technologies and the low power requirements for centrifuges, and probably for lasers, make it likely that not more than two or three more large diffusion plants will be built: the one under construction in France and possibly one more each in France and the United States.

On economic grounds the Brazilian choice of a nozzle process seems sensible. Brazil has enormous hydro-electric potential available at distances so remote from population centres as to make transmission unattractive, and this means power costs are in its case low and relatively unimportant. (Note that, if one assumes

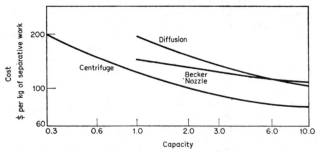

Figure 4: Cost of Separative Work

Costs are based on the same references as for Figure 3. It has been assumed that maintenance and operating costs, as well as financing costs, are proportional to capital costs. The curves in this diagram are computed by multiplying the capital costs from Figure 3 by 0·137, 0·230 and 0·156 for diffusion, centrifuge and the Becker nozzle respectively; the cost of power is then added in each case, assuming a cost of 25 mills per KWH and specific power consumption of 2,200, 220 and 3,560 KWH/kg SWU respectively.

power at 10 mills instead of 25 mills per kWh, the Becker process would appear to be preferable to either of the others over the whole range of capacities considered in Figures 3 and 4.) Demands for capital and the attractions of simplicity and ease of maintenance also argue against a centrifuge process. Some of the same arguments would seem relevant in the South African case; ease of maintenance, relatively low capital costs, and cheap power based on coal make its aerodynamic process a relatively attractive choice compared to centrifuges or diffusion plants. But construction of a large plant in South Africa, which seems likely, can be justified, at least for the near term, only on the assumption of a programme to export enriched uranium.

One can also identify countries – small ones with high levels of technical skill and power costs exceeding 25 mills per kWh – where the arguments might favour centrifuge-based enrichment. Assuming that they were built to produce uranium of low enrichment ($\sim$3 per cent U-235), however, plants based on centrifuges would also be the most worrisome from a proliferation perspective, lasers aside. As noted earlier, plants of any reasonable capacity will require enormous numbers of centrifuges – many in parallel in each stage of a cascade. Thus, there is the

possibility – very attractive from the perspective of rapidly producing highly enriched uranium – of rearranging the plumbing to increase the number of stages in the cascade by a factor of three or four, at the expense of reducing the throughput.

In the case of the diffusion and aerodynamic processes, production of highly enriched uranium would be dependent on manufacturing many additional stages or on operating the system in a non-continuous mode. The aerodynamic processes offer more potential for either alternative than gaseous diffusion: first, because the number of stages to be added would be much less and, second, because the inventory is much smaller, and the equilibrium time correspondingly less

In this consideration of power-based programmes we have not discussed lasers, because it is not yet possible to make meaningful economic comparisons. There is, however, one point that should be made. If laser separation turns out to be feasible, it will almost certainly turn out to be practicable and desirable to extract a larger fraction of the U-235 contained in natural uranium than is done in the case of the other processes. Assuming going to nearly nil tails, this means a 40–70 per cent increase in the energy extracted from natural uranium. The effect would be a very substantial expansion of uranium

135

resources; in addition, existing stockpiles of 0·2-0·3 per cent tails could presumably be reworked to extract most of the U-235 contained in them, thereby extending uranium resources somewhat further.

Diversion of Enriched Uranium

Assuming enrichment of uranium only for use in light water reactors, concern about diversion for weapons purposes would be minimal for all technologies, the only possible exception being the case of lasers. In that case, it is possible that the technology might develop so as to lead naturally to the production of highly enriched uranium, which would then be mixed with tails or uranium of natural enrichment to produce fuel for LWRs; there would then be the possibility of diversion of the highly enriched material for weapons purposes. On the other hand, if fuel were being produced for reactors that operate on highly enriched uranium (e.g., high-temperature gas reactors) one would have to be seriously concerned about diversion possibilities in all cases, and it is hard to see why one would be more worrisome than another.

Table 4 on pp.131-2 compares, in summary fashion, the alternative enrichment technologies discussed.

Interaction with Other Fuel Cycle Developments

For most nuclear power programmes, enrichment is likely to be a near- and medium-term requirement, because of the commitment to light water reactors.

In a few places – notably Canada – this will not be so, because of reliance on heavy water reactors which use uranium of natural composition (though they can beneficially use enriched fuel). A shortage of enrichment capacity, for whatever cause, would make HWRs more attractive, and this could be of importance in international trade. Consequently, if sellers of LWRs are to compete with vendors of HWRs, they may have to include guaranteed enrichment capacity (perhaps enriched fuel) as part of a package deal, or else provide an enrichment plant.

The need for enrichment can be alleviated somewhat by recycling plutonium, but in a pure LWR economy with recycling this will be a small effect: separative work requirements will drop by only about 20 per 'cent. In a mixed LWR–HWR economy the need could be further reduced if the plutonium from the HWRs were also fed into the LWRs. Finally, if and when breeders become an important element in the generation of nuclear power, there will be a further diminution (and ultimately perhaps elimination) of the need for enrichment. However, this is a distant prospect, at least in the case of the United States (it will be the 1990s before breeders become a significant factor in power production and after the turn of the century before they dominate LWRs). Moreover, it may well be that the expansion of breeder construction will be such that there will not be enough plutonium available for initial fuelling, in which case moderately or highly enriched U-235 will be needed to fuel them. In any case, it is almost certain that before breeders are a significant factor in power production, laser and perhaps other enrichment processes will have been developed to the point where a very large number of nations (and many sub-national groups) will be able to secure material for weapons purposes easily, quickly and cheaply by simply going into the uranium enrichment business without reference to power programmes.

One other development affecting the enrichment question has already been mentioned: interest in reactors using weapons-grade uranium as a fuel, of which the HTGR is an example. Although the prospects for sales of such reactors in the near term now seem very poor (see p. 14) the technology appears to be attractive, and it will be more so in the absence of plutonium recycling. This would be a particularly attractive choice for a nation that wanted the option to get into weapons manufacture quickly at a future date.

IV. CONTROLLING THE DIFFUSION OF NUCLEAR TECHNOLOGY

The preceding discussion has identified the ways in which the technology and materials of the commercial nuclear fuel cycle relate to the manufacture of nuclear explosives. There are three approaches to reducing the likelihood of non-nuclear states drawing on that technology to produce weapons: (a) banning the export of the most sensitive components of the fuel cycle – reprocessing and enrichment technology; (b) exacting assurances that such technology will not be used for weapons purposes; and (c) reducing the nuclear-power-related incentives nations may have to acquire such technology.

Individual nations could refuse absolutely to permit the export of enrichment and reprocessing technology to non-nuclear states and some (e.g., the United States) do so. However, it has not been possible to secure agreement by all nuclear supplier states to ban sales of these sensitive elements of the fuel cycle, because of the intense competition among reactor producers. Although the profits from the sale of an enrichment or reprocessing plant would rarely be large, it is tempting for reactor producers to offer them in a package deal that includes the sale of several reactors; it would be particularly tempting for those producers whose domestic reactor sales alone are too few for efficient production. The package deal between West Germany and Brazil that included a uranium enrichment plant and a fuel reprocessing plant illustrates the economic pressures on the vendor states and the opportunities for the purchasers. In short, the structure of the international nuclear industry today creates poor prospects for a complete ban on the sale of sensitive technology to non-nuclear states, and the situation is likely to get more difficult as additional nations become vendors of nuclear power facilities.

Moreover, a large number of countries (including many that are not fully industrialized) have, or will soon have, their own technical capability to build small, relatively primitive facilities to produce fissile materials and to assemble nuclear explosives. In particular, they could build plutonium production reactors and reprocessing plants – and might in time be able to build uranium enrichment plants, using some of the new enrichment technologies. These countries can probably reduce the lead time of a nuclear weapons programme by purchasing many of the necessary components from foreign sources or by hiring foreign technical personnel. Some could even build facilities of sufficient capacity for their nuclear fuel cycle to become independent of foreign suppliers of services. We therefore conclude that a ban on the transfer of sensitive nuclear technology would not prevent many states from developing nuclear weapons once they had decided to do so. It would, however, slow the progress of a weapons programme and might also have an influence on the decision process itself.

We turn next to the possibility of obtaining political or institutional assurances that 'sensitive technology' will not be used for the manufacture of explosives. Ideally, such assurances would include becoming a party to the Non-Proliferation Treaty or acceptance of international safeguards on all nuclear facilities, whether built domestically, acquired previously or resulting from the transfer in question.

At the very least the assurances might include:

(a) A pledge not to use the material produced by the transferred technology for the manufacture of nuclear explosives.

(b) An acceptance, with no option for termination, of international safeguards on all material, equipment or facilities transferred and on any replication (defined as broadly as possible) of the technology transferred.

(c) An agreement (i) not to transfer the technology to third countries unless they too accept the constraints on the replication, use and transfer of the technology, and (ii) to permit the original supplier nation to have a veto on any contemplated transfers to third parties.

We must recognize that technical changes made by the recipient nation could substantially alter the technology that was originally transferred. Thus, it might not be clear at what point the technology could be considered new, and so not subject to the terms of the original agreement. This ambiguity could be handled by specifying a length of time – the longer the better – during which there would be no question about coverage. The nuclear suppliers apparently concurred on such requirements in January 1976 and have used them in their recent agreements with purchasers.

Scepticism has developed about the usefulness of the 'assurances' approach, which permits continued sales of enrichment and reprocessing facilities, because some vendor states seem to have seized upon it merely to justify their commercial interests. Moreover, there can be no guarantee that assurances will prevent the misuse of transferred technology. In a world of sovereign states, commitments made by governments can be, and are, violated, particularly by new regimes that do not feel constrained by commitments made by their predecessors. But neither should we underestimate the importance of political commitments by sovereign states. They establish a norm of behaviour that is reinforced by internal governmental operating procedures. Safeguard arrangements, while not foolproof, strengthen the norm and raise the potential cost of violations. Moreover, bilateral political arrangements involve the supplier state's prestige in making sure that its customers do not violate agreements.

Reducing the incentives for nations to acquire the sensitive components of a nuclear power programme offers a third approach to reducing the likelihood of such a programme contributing to weapons development. In this connection it may be of some importance that enrichment and reprocessing services be available at reasonable prices. However, the costs of enrichment will be only 5–10 per cent of the total cost of generating electricity, and the cost of reprocessing even less. Although economies of scale and capitalization on the latest technology – the latter possibly particularly important in enrichment – may make it possible for the United States and other large industrially advanced countries to provide enrichment and reprocessing services at costs below those realizable by small operators, the advantage will rarely be decisive, and this will be true even if the supply is heavily subsidized. Assured supply and independence from foreign suppliers (whether prompted by economic considerations or for reasons of national pride or national security) and a desire to accumulate a plutonium inventory and gain experience in handling plutonium fuel in anticipation of a breeder economy will be more important than price.

Security of supply will be particularly important in the case of enrichment, because enriched uranium is required to fuel about 90 per cent of the world's power reactors. (The need can be obviated by relying, like Canada, on heavy-water-moderated natural-uranium reactors. But Canada's export capacity is limited, so this possibility is likely to have little effect in reducing incentives for other nations to build indigenous enrichment capacity.) The issue of assured enrichment service was particularly compelling in 1974, when it seemed likely that the United States (the principal source of separative work) would be unable to meet all demands for future delivery. With subsequent lower projections of demand, this concern is not now as acute as it has been.

In contrast to enrichment, reprocessing of spent fuel is not essential for the operation of any current commercial reactor. Indeed, it is clearly unattractive for heavy water reactors and at best marginal for light water reactors. Nevertheless, there are important motivations for states to acquire reprocessing plants, independent of any interest they may have in weapons development. We have mentioned two – the desire for independence and an interest in breeders. The latter may be especially attractive to nations with a large commitment to nuclear power but limited uranium resources. Indeed, France, Britain, Germany and the Soviet Union have substantial breeder development programmes and could well have their first commercial breeders operational in the next decade. The rate of diffusion of breeders to other countries, and especially to the less developed ones, is highly uncertain. But those countries that have an interest in acquiring breeders as soon as they are feasible (including perhaps Brazil, Iran and Taiwan) will want to reprocess at least some of their spent fuel in order to accumulate plutonium and to gain experience in working with it as a fuel.

There are other reasons for interest in reprocessing. While recycling plutonium and uranium is not economically attractive today, it may be so in the future. Most projections of demand and supply indicate that currently known uranium reserves, exploitable at less than about $100 per lb, are likely to be exhausted before the turn of the century and that currently estimated additional reserves, if they indeed exist, will be committed under long-term contract before then. Unless these projections grossly underestimate the future availability of uranium, prices will rise, supply will become tighter, and the economic value of reprocessing and recycling will increase. Recycling uranium and plutonium would also reduce the dependence of uranium-short states on foreign suppliers by about 20–30 per cent. Finally, waste-disposal considerations might also be factors in motivating states to acquire reprocessing facilities. While retrievable storage for long periods of time is feasible – and several

138

countries are actively investigating the best means to store large quantities of spent fuel – others (e.g., Germany), have decided that reprocessing should be accomplished with little delay, so that the final waste products can be put into permanent geological storage.

Concerns about security of supply of enrichment and/or reprocessing services can be alleviated through government guarantees and long-term contracts. However, increasing the total supply of the world's enrichment and reprocessing capacity is likely to be more effective. The construction of facilities in a number of nuclear countries, or in non-nuclear ones where the likelihood of diversion for weapons production is small, may be particularly desirable in order to avoid giving full market control to only a few nations. The creation of multinational (perhaps regional) or international facilities to provide enrichment and/or reprocessing services might also, with careful siting and strong international guarantees, alleviate much anxiety about security of supply. Providing an ownership stake in such facilities might also help to satisfy some of the political concerns that might otherwise motivate states to build their own plants.

Concern about security of enrichment services might be further reduced by supplying user countries with sufficient enriched uranium to last seven or ten years. Then, if enrichment services became unavailable for political or other reasons, a nation would have sufficient time to initiate construction of its own enrichment facility. Some states might be willing to bear the cost of stockpiles themselves; for others, however, the carrying charges on fuel stockpiles would probably have to be borne in one way or another by those nations interested in dissuading them from acquiring indigenous capabilities. Fortunately, such costs would be small when measured either against the cost of electric power or of defence programmes. Linking the supplies of natural uranium and enrichment services under long-term contracts at reasonable prices might provide still another possibility for reducing the incentive for uranium-short nations to acquire their own enrichment plants. Such arrangements might offer greater security in obtaining fuel than relying on imported natural uranium and on indigenous enrichment plants. There are some indications that natural market forces will generate movement in this direction. South Africa, a major uranium exporter, is building an aerodynamic enrichment plant with some West German assistance, and Australia, potentially a very large uranium exporter, is considering building a centrifuge plant with help from Japan.

Linking the supply of reprocessing services to waste disposal might contribute to inducing nations not to build indigenous reprocessing facilities. There are probably a number of states that would be willing, and perhaps even enthusiastic, about others doing their reprocessing for them *if* the reprocessor would also accept responsibility for disposal of the waste products. The problem is that few nations are likely to be willing to accept others' wastes. Moreover, even if such arrangements could be worked out, there would still be a question about the disposition of the plutonium that had been extracted from the spent fuel. The reprocessor could, of course, retain purified plutonium in exchange for cash or enriched uranium, but if external reprocessing were followed by immediate shipment of pure plutonium back to the state of origin, this would hardly contribute to the prevention of proliferation. Proposals have been made for returning the plutonium to the nation of origin in a form not easily usable for weapons. One possibility would be to ship only fuel elements in which plutonium oxide is mixed intimately with uranium oxide; another would involve adding an intense gamma-ray-emitting substance, or refraining from removing it during reprocessing. But neither alternative would present a serious obstacle to any nation that otherwise has the capability to make nuclear weapons. For countries insisting on gaining experience in handling mixed-oxide fuels or in preparing for the operation of breeders, an alternative would be the return of plutonium to the state of origin only as needed for use in reactors and under strict safeguards.

In conclusion, opportunities are available for reducing the motivation of states to acquire sensitive facilities. Also, political and/or economic pressure can be applied to discourage countries from acquiring such facilities, as the United States has recently demonstrated in inducing South Korea to forgo purchase of a reprocessing plant from France. The effectiveness of such pressure, which may be great in the short term and negative in the long term, has not been analysed here.

Notwithstanding the best efforts of supplier countries, we can expect that some countries will persist in wanting their own facilities, and the nuclear suppliers will then be left with the choice of refusing to sell sensitive facilities or of selling them with safeguards. Which choice will be more effective in inhibiting weapons proliferation will depend on the willingness and capacity of the country in question to develop such facilities on its own (or acquire them from a willing supplier), as well as on the weight attached to the commitments made to the supplier. In the case of the less-developed countries a ban might be quite effective. In the case of more advanced developing countries – and these concern us most now – a ban on sales would be less effective, since they can build small reprocessing plants on their own. For such countries the possession of sensitive facilities as components of a nuclear power programme might reduce the lead time and economic costs of a weapons programme and make it easier to generate a larger and more diversified one than might otherwise be possible. However, they could make weapons no matter what the nature and extent of their nuclear power programmes. Their decisions about weapons acquisition will derive from assessments of their own security interests and political relationships. If acquisition called for renouncing or violating existing agreements and institutional arrangements, such as IAEA safeguards, political costs could be high.

In the final analysis, it would be illusory to think that nuclear weapons proliferation could be severely limited by imposing controls on the sale of nuclear power facilities. The fundamental problem remains: minimizing the motivation nations have to acquire nuclear weapons altogether. This involves issues far beyond the realm of a nation's interest and involvement in the development of nuclear power to generate electricity.

APPENDIXES

APPENDIX A: FUEL CYCLE DIAGRAMS

Figure A1: Equilibrium Fuel Cycle for Light Water Reactor Without Plutonium Recycle

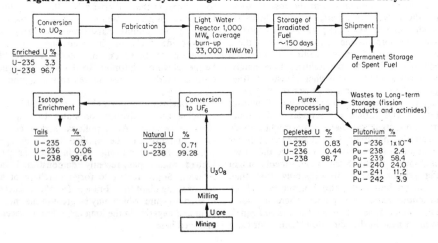

Figure A2: Equilibrium Fuel Cycle for Light Water Reactor with Plutonium Recycle

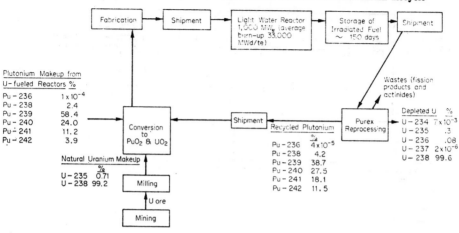

This figure indicates natural uranium used in the fuel. If enriched uranium were used, the quantities of plutonium in the make-up could be reduced.

Figure A3: Fuel Cycle for CANDU Heavy Water Reactor

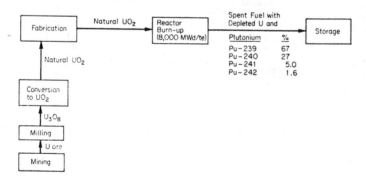

141

Figure A4: Equilibrium Fuel Cycle for High-temperature Gas Reactor

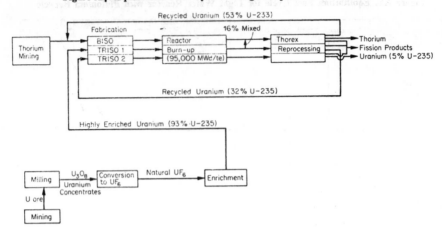

Figure A5: Fuel Cycle for Liquid-metal Fast Breeder Reactor

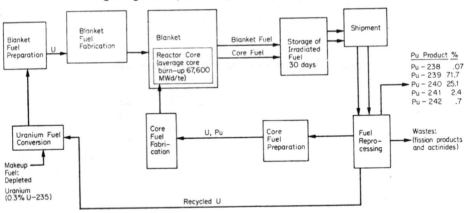

This appendix provides a description of reprocessing technology and a report on the status of reprocessing facilities around the world.

Brief Description of Reprocessing Technology

Although several processes can be, and have been, used for chemical reprocessing of spent fuel,[18] a solvent extraction process called Plutonium and Uranium Recovery by Extraction (PUREX) is now, with minor variations, universally employed for uranium or uranium–plutonium fuels. A dry fluoride volatility process looks rather promising but has not yet been demonstrated on a large scale. The mixed thorium–uranium fuel of HTGRS requires a somewhat different process called THOREX.

All processes must deal with a number of difficult common problems. The radioactive nature of the materials handled and the toxicity of plutonium necessitate heavy shielding, remote or semi-remote handling, complex and duplicated equipment and piping, stringent standards for fabrication and inspection of equipment, and thorough clean-up of liquid and gaseous effluents to minimize radioactive discharge. As a result, the capital cost of a commercial chemical reprocessing plant is much higher than that of a non-nuclear facility of comparable size and process complexity; one estimate goes as high as five times as much.[19] To minimize the ever-present risk of accidental accumulation of a supercritical mass of fissile material and consequent release of radioactive materials, great care must be taken in the design and operation of the plant. Rigorous accountability must be maintained at all times. Safeguards can be applied to a reprocessing plant in order to deter and detect diversion, but their intrusiveness and the time required to shut down, start up and re-establish chemical equilibrium when inventory is taken (8–13 days for the Nuclear Fuel Services plant[20]) make their application quite difficult and costly.

PUREX

The principal steps of the PUREX process are shown diagrammatically in Figure B1 below. To allow the short-lived fission products to decay and the level of radioactivity to decline significantly, spent fuel elements are kept in storage for at least 150 days for LWRs (at least 30 days for LMFBRs), with the actual period depending on the detailed design and operating practice of the reprocessing plant and the extent of irradiation of the fuel. Storage for 150 days allows all gaseous fission products except Krypton-85 to decay to inconsequential levels, reduces the activity of 8-day Iodine-131 to manageable levels, and eliminates Neptunium-239 and U-237. LWR fuel elements entering a reprocessing plant after that time would still have 4·5 million Ci of radioactivity and 20 kW of decay power per ton if a burn-up of 33,000 MW d/te is assumed; given a shorter burn-up, the content of fission products would be lower, and the reprocessing consequently easier. With longer storage times before reprocessing, the operation could be simplified somewhat, and the storage time required before concentrated wastes could be solidified would be reduced. Storage times of two or more years may well become standard for at least some reprocessing facilities.

The first step in reprocessing is decladding – the removal of the fuel element casing. For steel or zircalloy cladding this is done by mechanical shearing or sawing. Fuel and cladding are then treated with hot nitric acid, dissolving the oxides of uranium and other elements but leaving the cladding essentially unreacted. The cladding is removed from the solution, treated further, packaged and disposed of in a manner appropriate for materials containing small amounts of plutonium. Chemicals are then added to the aqueous solution selectively converting the plutonium to a tetravalent state. These steps together are called the head-end of the reprocessing operation. One plant can be rendered fairly versatile by the provision of several head-end facilities, appropriate to different types of fuel, all feeding into the same chemical separation equipment.

Chemical separation is effected by solvent extraction. A counter-current flow of tributyl phosphate in an inert hydrocarbon solvent, usually normal dodecane, removes the PuO_2 and the UO_2 preferentially from the aqueous solution, leaving the fission products and other actinides behind. The plutonium is then reduced to its trivalent state and separated from the uranium by transfer back into aqueous solution. The separated uranium and plutonium streams

143

are then further purified. The intense radiation of high burn-up fuel leads to serious solvent degradation in this part of the process, and several techniques are being tested to circumvent this problem of the PUREX process by reducing the contact time between the solvent and the radioactive materials. The absence of the solvent, and therefore of this contamination problem, is a major advantage of the fluoride volatility process, and makes it particularly attractive for very high burn-up fuel from LMFBR. Another variation from current practice that is now being studied is separating the uranium and plutonium from the radioactive wastes without separating them completely from each other. A uranium and plutonium mixture would then be recycled, obviating the necessity for compounds of pure plutonium to move within the fuel cycle.[22]

The final output of the reprocessing plant can be the nitrates of uranium and plutonium, or these can be converted to more convenient chemical forms. In fact plutonium would probably leave the plant in oxide form and uranium would probably be shipped as uranium oxide or uranium hexafluoride. To be reused in an LWR, the latter could be put through an enrichment plant. The plutonium can be stored or reused immediately by mixing it with uranium in a mixed-oxide fuel.

Very high levels of purification can be achieved by this process. The Nuclear Fuel Services plant achieved a decontamination factor (ratio of impurity content of feed to impurity content of product) of 5×10^7 for uranium and 2×10^8 for plutonium. Average recovery levels of 99·2 per cent for uranium and 98·5 per cent for plutonium were achieved there.

The gaseous effluent from reprocessing plants contains radioactive Kr-85 unless it is scrubbed by means of expensive cryogenic absorption, not yet in use anywhere. The non-gaseous waste product, a solution containing trace amounts of uranium and plutonium, radioactive fission products and other actinides, is stored in large

Figure B1: Principal Steps in Fuel Reprocessing by PUREX Process

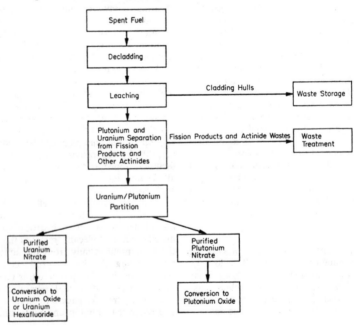

Figure B2: Principal Steps in Reprocessing Fuel from High-temperature Gas-cooled Reactors

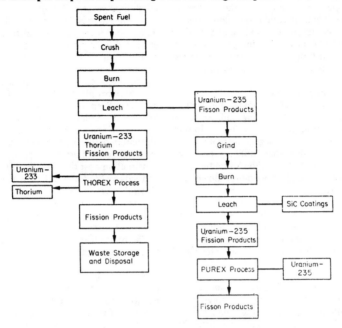

holding tanks on the site of the reprocessing plant. Because large volumes of this waste are produced and the storage tanks may eventually leak, government regulations in the United States now require that waste be stored in liquid form for no more than five years. Wastes must then be concentrated, solidified, packaged in stainless steel, and shipped within ten years for long-term storage. In some processes glass-forming chemicals, such as borax, alumina and silica, are added to increase the stability of the solid. Future regulations may further require that the small volume of actinides whose half-lives are of the order of 100,000 years should be separated from the larger volume of fission products whose half-lives are of the order of 1,000 years or less.

THOREX[23]

The steps for reprocessing fuel from HTGRs are schematically shown in Figure B2 above. Spent fuel assemblies would be crushed, burned to remove the graphite coating on BISO particles and

then leached (see p. 10 for a description of BISO and TRISO particles). The leaching dissolves all thorium-bearing ash and U-233 from BISO particles, some U-235 from broken TRISO particles and some of the fission products. This solution is treated by the THOREX process. Remaining TRISO particles, protected from burning by their silicon carbide coating, are separated by filtration, ground to break their coating and leached with nitric acid a second time to dissolve the U-235 and fission products. This solution is treated by a simplified PUREX process that, because of the negligible amount of plutonium present, lacks the plutonium separation steps.

The THOREX process separates thorium and uranium from fission products and from each other. As in the PUREX process, tributyl phosphate in normal dodecane is used to extract the uranium and thorium from the aqueous solution containing the fission products. Since thorium is exclusively tetravalent, it cannot be separated from uranium by changing its valence, as is done

145

with plutonium in the PUREX process. It is therefore separated by exploiting the difference between the chemical equilibrium constants for formation of complexes of uranium and thorium with tributyl phosphate. In this process, losses of uranium and thorium are expected to be less than 0·1 per cent and 0·2 per cent respectively.

The Status of Reprocessing

As indicated in Table B1, reprocessing facilities of some sort are available, being built, or under active consideration in sixteen countries. In only a few cases, however, has large-scale reprocessing taken place for other than military purposes. Plants in Belgium and the United States that have operated in the past are now closed down, and only in Britain and France is commercial reprocessing currently under way. While the technology may be well understood therefore, the industry is still struggling to become established. In many cases the commissioning of a new plant has been delayed or interrupted because of technical problems or regulatory uncertainty.

The first reprocessing facility was built during World War II at Hanford, Washington, to produce plutonium for the Manhattan Project. This initial facility, using a chemical precipitation process, was replaced after the war by solvent extraction plants at Hanford and Savannah River, Georgia. These plutonium production reprocessing facilities are designed to handle fuel elements fabricated of natural uranium metal, clad with aluminium.[24] The Idaho Chemical Processing Plant at the National Reactor Testing Station is used as a production facility, an engineering-scale process demonstration facility and an operational facility to reprocess naval reactor cores.[25] The Metal Recovery Plant at Oak Ridge National Laboratory was the initial pilot plant for the THOREX process.

The American commercial LWR reprocessing industry was initiated in 1966 by the Nuclear Fuel Services facility at West Valley, New York. In nearly six years of operation it recovered not the designed 300 tonnes per year but only 630 tonnes in total,[26] and in 1972 it closed for major rebuilding and enlargement. It now seems unlikely that it will reopen. Efforts to begin operating General Electric's 300-tonnes-per-year pilot plant at Morris, Illinois, using a new process based partially on solvent extraction and partially on

fluoride volatility, were abandoned in 1974, after three years of trying and an investment of $64 million, because of technical problems and design inadequacies.[27] Reconstruction has been estimated to cost more than $130 million and to require four or more years from a decision to begin.[28]

The 1,500-tonne-per-year Allied General Nuclear Services plant at Barnwell, South Carolina, has also been delayed because of regulatory uncertainty. Delays and the addition of ancillary facilities to convert plutonium nitrate solution to plutonium oxide and to solidify high-level wastes have now driven estimates up from the original construction cost of $70 million to $600 million and above.[29] Financial assistance from the Federal government is being sought to help the company deal with these escalating costs. Start-up is not expected before 1978 and may well be delayed further.

The only other commercial LWR reprocessing facility under active consideration in the United States is a 1,500-tonne-per-day plant of Exxon Nuclear at Oak Ridge, Tennessee. An application was sent to the Nuclear Regulatory Commission in early 1976.[30] Planning had been in progress for the construction of an HTGR demonstration reprocessing facility, large enough to service ten to twenty reactors, which was once expected to be built in the 1980s by government and industry and to be operating by the early 1990s. However, the great uncertainty about the future of the HTGR reactor industry in the United States has put this plan in doubt.[31] A demonstration reprocessing plant for LMFBR reactor fuel is anticipated for the 1980s or 1990s.[32]

Much of the delay and cost escalation for the American reprocessing industry is directly attributable to regulatory changes and delays. The rules concerning construction specifications, plant siting and safety, transportation of nuclear fuel, waste storage and physical protection have all changed while the Barnwell plant has been under construction; the major uncertainty still remaining is the acceptability of using mixed-oxide fuel in LWRs. A decision from the Nuclear Regulatory Commission is now expected in 1977 but may be delayed beyond that.[33] Assuming a positive decision and the absence of (quite likely) additional delays because of court challenges or congressional action, the industry might be close to normal commercial operations by the early

146

1980s. But no facilities beyond the Barnwell plant will be operational before the mid-1980s. New investment from private industry will probably await not only a clarification of the regulatory environment but also a demonstration of the profitability of existing ventures. In the meantime, both the annual output and the accumulation of spent fuel will continue rising. American demand for reprocessing services has been projected to be 4,000–5,000 tonnes per year by 1985.[34] Interim storage of spent fuel has already become a bottleneck, but plans to provide additional facilities external to individual reactor sites are now moving ahead gradually.

The prospects of the commercial reprocessing industry are better outside the United States.[35] France has operated two natural uranium metal plants for many years and is now converting one to accept low-enriched uranium oxide fuel. Operations began in May 1976 and full capacity of 800 tonnes per year is expected by 1982.[36] Design work has begun on a larger uranium oxide facility expected to be completed in the mid-1980s. A small pilot plant for LMFBR fuel is also operational.

Uranium metal reprocessing has been carried out at Windscale in the United Kingdom for 24 years. In 1968 a 400-tonne-per-year head-end plant was added to accept oxide fuel. It operated for a short time but was closed down because of technical difficulties; it is being refurbished and is expected to enter small-scale commercial operation in the late 1970s. A new 1,000-tonne-per-year plant is under consideration for the mid- to late 1980s to service the domestic market and, pending a decision on social acceptability of importing foreign fuel for reprocessing, the overseas market. Britain has a long tradition in international sales of reprocessing services, having accepted fuel from the gas-cooled reactors in Italy and Japan and smaller amounts of fuel from Switzerland, Germany, Spain, Sweden, Canada and Belgium.[37]

Under the plans of the Anglo-French-German joint company, United Reprocessors, that is co-ordinating the growth of uranium oxide reprocessing capacity in the three countries, a 1,500-tonne-per-year facility is being planned for operation in Germany by 1986.[38] Significant political difficulties are anticipated in selecting a site, however. In the meantime, Kernbrennstoff-Wiederaufarbeitungs-Gesellschaft mbH (KEWA), the German partner in United Reprocessors, is operating a 40-tonne-per-year uranium oxide pilot plant at Karlsruhe. A small graphite fuel pilot plant is also under construction in Germany and is expected to begin operation in 1977.

Several other facilities are shown in the table below. The Eurochemic pilot plant at Mol in Belgium operated for eight years but closed down in 1974. A Belgian group is considering expansion of this plant to 300 tonnes per year and reopening it in the late 1970s. Italy had planned to build a large commercial facility by the mid-1980s, but these plans are now reported to be shelved. Two small pilot plants are operational in Italy, one for thorium–uranium fuel and the other for uranium oxide or uranium metal. Sweden has under consideration an 800 tonne-per-year facility anticipated for the early 1980s.[39] Two metal and low-enrichment uranium oxide facilities have been built in India; one is in operation, the other is now being tested with non-radioactive fuel, and there is also a small laboratory-scale thorium–uranium facility. A 200-tonne-per-year uranium oxide facility in Japan has been tested and shut down for alterations; commercial operation will be delayed beyond early 1977.[40] Plans for a commercial-scale plant adjacent to the pilot plant are running into considerable opposition. In Japan, as in Germany, a utility must demonstrate contractual commitments for reprocessing services before a construction permit for a nuclear power plant will be issued. The Japanese have therefore been seeking contracts in Britain and France for the 1980s.[41] Spain has a small pilot plant in operation, Argentina and Yugoslavia have laboratory-scale facilities, Argentina's having been shut down for expansion and redesign. Taiwan is building a laboratory-scale metal fuel facility. Brazil has contracted with Germany for the purchase of a small plant. The Republic of Korea has recently been dissuaded by the United States from concluding an agreement with France for the purchase of a pilot facility.[42] Whether the French sale of a plant to Pakistan will be completed is now in some doubt.

147

Table B1: Non-military Reprocessing Facilities

Country	NPT Party	Facility	Fuel Type	Design Capacity	Safeguard	Status
Argentina	No	Ezeiza Nuclear Facility	Metal (research reactor fuel)	Lab scale	Yes	Shut down, but being reactivated for operation in 1977; may include redesign for low-enriched UO_2 fuel
Belgium	Yes	Eurochemic, Mol	Metal and UO_2, low-enrichment and metal high-enrichment	60-85 tonnes low-enriched, 1·25 tonnes high-enriched per year	Yes	Start-up 1966; shut down 1974
Brazil	No		UO_2 low-enrichment		Yes	Purchase from Germany
Britain	Yes	Dounreay	MTR and fast reactor fuel	Small pilot plant	No	In operation
		British Nuclear Fuels, Windscale (United Reprocessors)	Natural U metal	2,000 tonnes/year	No	In operation
			Low-enrichment UO_2 head end	Small-scale commercial	No	Operated 1969–73; shut down for modification; will reopen late 1970s with refurbished head end to feed into natural uranium separation plant, depending on availability of capacity
			UO_2 low-enrichment	1,000 tonnes/year	No	Start-up mid-1980s for expected domestic and overseas requirements
France	No	Cogema, La Hague (United Reprocessors)	Natural U metal	800 tonnes/year	No	Start-up 1967
			Low-enrichment UO_2 head end	800 tonnes/year	No	Start-up May 1976; 800 tonnes/year by 1982
		Cogema	Low-enrichment UO_2	1,000 tonnes/year	No	Under consideration
		Cogema, Marcoule	Natural U metal	1,000 tonnes/year	No	Start-up 1958 for military purposes; will take over commercial role from La Hague
			LMFBR	5 tonnes/year pilot plant	No	Operational

Country	NPT Party	Facility	Fuel Type	Design Capacity	Safeguard	Status
W. Germany	Yes	KEWA (United Reprocessors)	UO$_2$ low enrichment	1,500 tonnes/year	Yes	Planning stage; start-up 1986 or later
		KEWA Karlsruhe	Breeder and UO$_2$	200 kg/day pilot plant	Yes	In operation since 1971
		KFA Jülich	Graphite	2 kg/day pilot plant	Yes	Start-up 1977
India	No	Trombay	Thorium/uranium oxide	Lab scale	No	In operation
		Trombay	Metal and UO$_2$	350 kg/day	No	In operation
		Tarapur	Metal and UO$_2$	100 tonnes/year	No*	Being cold tested
Italy	Yes	Eurex-1, Sallugia	UO$_2$ and metal	Small pilot plant	Yes	In operation
		ITREC, Rotondella	Thorium/uranium	Small pilot plant	Yes	In operation
		Unnamed	UO$_2$ low enrichment	500 tonnes/year		Start-up 1985; plans temporarily shelved
Japan	No	PNC Tokai-Mura	UO$_2$ low enrichment	200 tonnes/year	Yes	Tested, closed for alterations; commercial operations late 1977 or beyond
		PNC Tokai-Mura	Metal	Small plant	Yes	In operation
Pakistan			UO$_2$ low enrichment		Yes	Purchase from France uncertain
Spain	No	Centro Juan Vigón, Madrid	Metal	Small pilot plant	Yes	In operation
Sweden	Yes		UO$_2$ low enrichment	800 tonnes/year	Yes	Under consideration
Taiwan	No	Nuclear Energy Research Institute	Metal	Lab scale	Yes	Being built

Country		Facility	Fuel	Capacity		Status
United States	Yes	Nuclear Fuel Services, West Valley	UO$_2$ low enrichment	300 tonnes/year	No	Operated 1966–72; closed for expansion and rebuilding
		General Electric, Morris	UO$_2$ low enrichment	300 tonnes/year	No	Inoperable in present form
		Allied General Nuclear Services, Barnwell	UO$_2$ low enrichment	1,500 tonnes/year	No	In construction; operation expected 1978 or after
		Exxon Nuclear, Oak Ridge	UO$_2$ low enrichment	1,500 tonnes/year	No	Application pending
		ERDA and General Atomic, Idaho Falls	HTGR fuel	Demonstration scale	No	Under consideration
		ERDA	LMFBR fuel	Demonstration scale	No	Under consideration
Soviet Union	Yes				No	Facility in operation
Yugoslavia	Yes	Boris Kidric Metal Institute		Lab scale	Yes	In operation

* Will be safeguarded when reprocessing American-supplied fuel.

There follows a brief description and technical assessment of the several enrichment methods that are now feasible and/or promising.[43]

Gaseous Diffusion

Virtually all of the enrichment of uranium that has occurred has been accomplished by the gaseous diffusion method developed during the Manhattan Project, and it has naturally become the reference standard against which other techniques are compared. Enrichment is accomplished by pumping UF_6 gas through a porous barrier. If the holes are the right size, $^{235}UF_6$ molecules move through more readily than $^{238}UF_6$ molecules. However, the degree of enrichment is very slight, being proportional to the square root of the ratio of the molecular weights of the two molecules.* This means that in order to achieve significant enrichment the process must be repeated many times. Thus, a gaseous diffusion plant requires many stages which are arranged in a cascade, as indicated in Figure C1 opposite. If the plant operates so that the tails assay is 0·20 per cent U-235 about 1,300 stages are required to produce uranium enriched for use in LWRs (~3 per cent U-235). Since the amount of product is only a small fraction of the input (18 per cent in the example given), the stages at the top of the cascade should be smaller than those at the input point; indeed in an ideal cascade each stage would be different in size, but for practical reasons it is usual to use three sizes. To minimize consumption of power, the isotopic composition of the two streams feeding each stage should be the same. This condition is met by pumping about half the gas that enters each stage through the barrier.

This requires that an enormous amount of work be done. It is usually measured in 'separative work units' (SWU).† The separative work required as a function of the degree of enrichment and the tails assay is shown in Table C1 below, along with the number of stages required, assuming an ideal cascade and a feed of natural uranium (i.e., UF_6 containing 0·711 per cent U-235).

Costs of separative work are about $60 per SWU, but can be expected to rise. As a reference point, it might be noted that to provide fuel for a 1,000 MWe light water reactor requires about 100,000 SWU per year (assuming 0·25 per cent tails), and if one assumes that a nuclear weapon requires a minimum of 10 kg of highly enriched uranium, the requirement is about 2,000 SWU per weapon (again assuming 0·25 per cent tails).

The three gaseous diffusion plants of the United States have a total capacity of 17·2 million SWU per year and require 6,100 MW of power to operate them.[44] The capacity is to be expanded to 27·7 million SWU per year by about 1981 by means of installing improved barrier material, modifying compressors and piping and uprating about half the stages to operate at higher pressure. These last changes will require

---

* The separation factor α is defined as $y(1-x)/x(1-y)$, where y is the $^{235}UF_6$ fraction in the gas enriched in $^{235}UF_6$ and x is the $^{235}UF_6$ fraction in the depleted gas. For the gaseous diffusion process $\alpha = 1·0049$.

† Notwithstanding that a SWU is a measure of work, it has the dimensions of mass, being proportional to the amount of gas pumped through a barrier. Throughout this paper SWU refer to 'kilograms of separative work'. Literature on the subject is occasionally confusing because of the use, without clarification, of metric tons as the unit of separative work.

Table C1: Separative Work as a Function of Enrichment and Tails Assay

Product Assay (% U-235)	Tails Assay (% U-235)	Separative Work (kg SWU/kg product)	Stages in Ideal Cascade ($\alpha = 1·0049$)
3	0·2	4·31	1,276
	0·3	3·42	1,086
	0·4	2·85	952
90	0·2	227	3,912
	0·3	193	3,731
	0·4	170	3,597

Figure C1: A Cascade of Gaseous Diffusion Stages

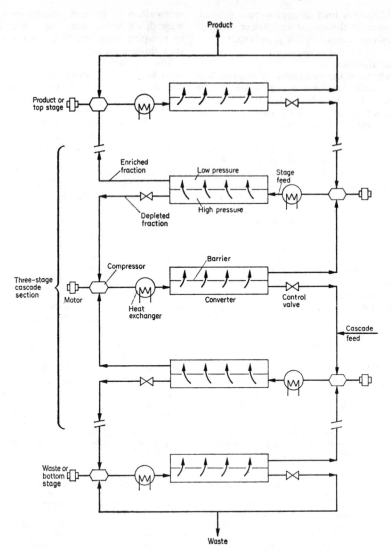

Table C2: Status of Processes for Enriching Uranium

Location	Capacity (millions of kg separative work per year)	Year
GASEOUS DIFFUSION PROCESS		
Operating		
Oak Ridge, Tennessee	4,730	
Paducah, Kentucky	7,310	
Portsmouth, Ohio	5,190	
Total US ERDA	17,230	
Siberia	7–10	
Pierrelatte, France	0·4–0·6	
Capenhurst, Britain	0·4–0·6	
Lanchow, China	?	
Under Construction		
Improvement and uprating of US ERDA plants	10·5	1977–81
EURODIF, France	3·0	1979
to	10·70	1981
Under Consideration		
UEA, Dothan, Alabama	9·0	1983
COREDIF, France (may use centrifuges)	9·0	1985
GAS CENTRIFUGE PLANTS		
URENCO plants (British, Dutch, German):		
Capenhurst, Britain	0·025	1973
Almelo, Holland	0·400	1976
	2·0	1982
	10·0	1985
United States (3 proposals)	9·0	1987
BECKER NOZZLE PROCESS		
Germany (now shut down)	0·002	1972
Plant for Brazil		
SOUTH AFRICAN PROCESS		
UCOR (planned)		1975 (part-operational)
		1984 (operational)
	5·0	1986 (full capacity)

SOURCES:
Manson Benedict, 'Fuel Cycle for Nuclear Reactors: Uranium Enrichment and Reprocessing' (paper presented to the International Symposium on Nuclear Power Technology and Economics, Taipei, Taiwan, 13–20 January 1975), and notes for lecture 1M-4, 1975, Principles of Nuclear Fuel and Power Management (Nuclear Engineering 22. 98S), MIT; additional information from S. A. Levin, 'Remarks on World-Wide Uranium Enrichment Capacity Plans Outside of the United States' (paper presented to Panel on Enrichment Session, ANS-CNA Joint Topical Meeting on Commercial Nuclear Technology Today, Toronto, 30 April 1975, Union Carbide Corporation Report No. K-OA-2707); Wilcox and Bradbury, *op. cit.*; A. J. A. Roux and W. L. Grant, 'Uranium Enrichment In South Africa' (paper presented to the European Nuclear Conference, Paris, April 1975).

greater power, so that the total input for the complex will be 7,400 MW. Provision for additional heat removal will also be needed.

The Soviet Union, Britain, France and China have also built diffusion plants, and additional ones are planned for France and are under consideration for the United States. The capacities of plants that have been built, and of some that are proposed, are indicated in Table C2 on p. 45.

The key to the successful development of the gaseous diffusion process was the development of a suitable barrier. That now used is much improved over the material developed during the Manhattan Project, but details remain classified. The manufacture of suitable barrier material would probably be the most difficult technical problem that newcomers interested in building gaseous diffusion plants would have to solve.

Gas Centrifuges
Separation of uranium isotopes, again using UF_6, is also now being accomplished on a very limited scale using gas centrifuges. The heavier molecules concentrate at the periphery and the lighter ones near the axis. By establishing a counter-current flow of UF_6 parallel to the axis, say with $^{235}UF_6$ flowing downward near the axis (in a vertical centrifuge) and $^{238}UF_6$ flowing upward near the periphery, it is possible to make the gas pro-
gressively richer in U-235 near the bottom and richer in U-238 near the top (see Figure C2). The separation factor in this case depends on the acceleration at the periphery of the centrifuge (which depends on the radius and the rotation rate) and on the length of the centrifuge, increasing with both. Separation factors are very much larger than in the case of diffusion plants, and this means that enrichment can be accomplished with very many fewer stages. It has been suggested by Donald G. Avery, of Urenco, that 'a centrifuge cascade requires in the region of 10–12 stages to achieve the U-235 concentration required for a plant to produce nuclear fuel'.[45] This implies a separation factor in the range of 1·4–1·5.

Pilot plants with capacities of 5,000–14,000 SWU per year are now operating in Britain and the Netherlands, while 200,000 SWU per year plants are being built in both countries and larger ones are planned. Since the capacity of each centrifuge will be somewhere in the range of 2–10 SWU per year, scaling up to large-size plants will require adding many stages in parallel – with the European developed centrifuges, of the order of a million centrifuges will be required for a commercial plant of a size that would produce as much separative work as each of the American gaseous diffusion plants. There is no doubt about the technical feasibility of the centrifuge approach and that it will require much less power per unit of separative work than the diffusion method ($\sim \frac{1}{10}$ as much). What is in doubt is the expected life of the centrifuges – and the commercial viability of the process is a strong function of the failure rate. The United States has also had a substantial centrifuge programme, critical details of which are classified – though it is known that the American centrifuges are of very much larger capacity, apparently at least ten times as large as the European ones. There have been reliability tests with satisfactory results and development of mass production technology is now underway.[46] Feasibility studies suggest that the technology has now been developed to the point where it must be considered as at least seriously competitive with, if not superior to, gaseous diffusion, and three organizations have made proposals to the Energy Research and Development Administration for the construction of 3–4 million-SWU plants. Japan and Australia are also developing the technology.

Figure C2: A Counter-current Centrifuge

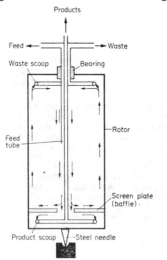

154

Figure C3: Cross-section of Separation Nozzle System Used to Date in Commercial Implementation of Separation Nozzle Process

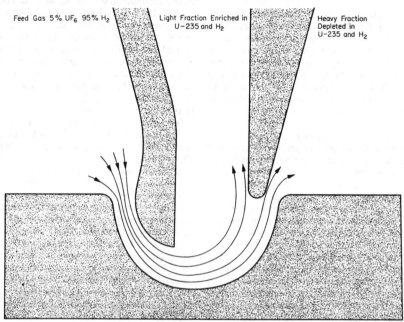

Feed Gas 5% UF$_6$ 95% H$_2$

Light Fraction Enriched in U-235 and H$_2$

Heavy Fraction Depleted in U-235 and H$_2$

Since large capacity can be achieved only by adding many stages in parallel, in contrast to the possibility of increasing stage size virtually without limit in gaseous diffusion plants (and in the aerodynamic process discussed below), economies of scale in manufacture will be less for centrifuge-based enrichment than for other methods.

Aerodynamic Enrichment Techniques
A third approach for separating uranium isotopes, the Becker process, has been developed in Germany. In this case the UF$_6$ is mixed with hydrogen or helium. The mixture of gases is passed over a curved surface at supersonic velocities and then separated into two streams by a knife edge (see Figure C3). The U-238 collects near the concave surface and the U-235 (and the hydrogen and helium) is concentrated nearer the centre of the curvature.

The separation factor achievable depends on pressure, expansion ratio, the fraction of UF$_6$ in

the gas mixture and the placement of the knife edge. One conceptual design has a factor of 1·0148 but this involves a uranium 'cut' of a quarter – i.e., placing the knife edge so that the light fraction contains only a quarter of the UF$_6$ (see Figure C3). With this 'cut' the cascade arrangement is more complex than that shown in Figure C1: the product from each stage feeds the third stage above it, rather than the next one up. The number of stages needed is thus twice that needed with a cut of a half. To produce 3 per cent enriched fuel requires about 700 stages for 0·2 per cent tails (or 570 for 0·377 per cent tails, which is the actual design). Prototype stages have been built and operated, and it is now planned to build first a pilot plant and then a large plant in Brazil.

With the necessity for repeatedly compressing large amounts of hydrogen (or helium) as well as UF$_6$, the power requirements are large – presently about 50 per cent greater per SWU than for diffusion, but capital costs are likely to be

155

less than for either gaseous diffusion or centrifuge plants.

The South Africans have also developed an aerodynamic process for enrichment, but have not disclosed details. It is apparently similar in some respects to the Becker process, and it is also characterized by high power requirements. A pilot plant is partially operational and a plant of 5 million SWU capacity is planned, to be operational in the mid-1980s and possibly to be expanded to 10 million SWU capacity.

Laser Enrichment Techniques

The remaining processes of great current interest are those that depend on the selective excitation of either U-235 atoms or $^{235}UF_6$ molecules (in both cases in the gas phase) by a sharply tuned laser. The gas is then irradiated with another light source, which need not be so sharply tuned. This causes ionization or a photochemical reaction in the excited atoms or molecules but not in those atoms or molecules that are not in excited states. In principle, these methods have enormous advantages over those discussed earlier. Nearly complete separation may be achievable in a single stage, and the energy requirements will be very low – two or three orders of magnitude lower in the case of UF_6 than for diffusion. (It is unlikely that the savings in energy will be as large in the case of uranium metal, because vaporization of the metal will consume a substantial amount of energy.)

But there are also formidable difficulties that must be solved. In the case of the metal, very high temperatures are required to obtain reasonable vapour pressures, and this raises serious materials problems. In practice, vapour pressures may have to be held so low that there will be problems in scaling up to plant sizes that will be commercially interesting. Obviously, if separation is to be achieved, the U-235 ions must be separated from neutral gas consisting mostly of U-238 before charge exchange can occur. This has been accomplished in experiments in which U-235 ions are deflected by electrical and magnetic fields and milligram quantities of product highly enriched in U-235 have been obtained. An alternative to vaporizing uranium metal to obtain uranium atoms has recently been demonstrated. It involves forming a uranium-organic compound, urocene, and decomposing it at 460°K.[47] This, or a similar approach, may get around some of the serious problems involved in the atomic uranium process. Recently Exxon Nuclear Company has announced plans to construct a $15 million experimental test facility for uranium enrichment based on lasers, to begin operating in 1978–79.

In the case of UF_6 the richness of the spectrum and the overlap between $^{235}UF_6$ and $^{238}UF_6$ lines seemed likely to make clean separation difficult. The problem is greatly complicated by the fact that at temperatures at which UF_6 has reasonable vapour pressures so few of the molecules will normally be in the ground state (~ 0.5 per cent at room temperature), and for those molecules in excited vibrational states the absorption lines will be slightly displaced, with overlap of $^{235}UF_6$ lines by $^{238}UF_6$ lines. It has recently been disclosed that it is possible to obtain gas at reasonable pressures with nearly all the molecules in the ground state. This is done by expanding a mixture of UF_6 and an inert gas, such as helium or nitrogen, through a nozzle, which produces cooling of the UF_6 without nucleation and coagulation.[49] The same report also discloses that it has been possible to use a laser source to resolve the spectrum into lines characteristic of U-235 and U-238. This means that some of the difficult obstacles to laser separation using UF_6 have now been solved, at least in principle. There may still be a problem in finding an infra-red laser of adequate power, an ultra-violet laser of useful efficiency and power output to dissociate the vibrationally excited UF_6, and a chemical reaction that will permit separation of molecules enriched in U-235. So far there are no reports in the unclassified literature of successful separation using lasers and UF_6, but it is our judgment that feasibility is likely to be demonstrated fairly soon. If this problem is solved, there will still be engineering problems: i.e., developing an operational process based on the scientific developments.

156

NOTES

[1] Reactor data is derived from 'World List of Nuclear Power Plants', *Nuclear News*, February 1976, pp. 52–64; *Nuclear Engineering International*, April 1976 Supplement. See also fuel/cycle diagrams in Appendix A.

[2] For fuel cycle flow charts, including materials balances, the reader is referred to Thomas H. Pigford and Kiat P. Ang, 'The Plutonium Fuel Cycles', *Health Physics*, 29 (October 1975) pp. 451–67 and US Atomic Energy Commission, *Reactor Fuel Cycle Costs for Nuclear Power Evolution* Wash-1099 (December 1971).

[3] This discussion is based on Hugh C. McIntyre, 'Natural Uranium Heavy-Water Reactors', *Scientific American*, 233 (October 1975), pp. 17–27; A. J. Mooradian and O. J. C. Runnalls, 'CANDU – Economic Alternative to the Fast Breeder', AECL-4916, September 1974; S. Banerjee, E. Critoph and R. G. Hart, 'Thorium as a Nuclear Fuel for CANDU Reactors', *The Canadian Journal of Chemical Engineering*, 53 (June 1975), pp. 291–6; E. Critoph, S. Banerjee, F. W. Barclay, D. Hamel, M. S. Milgram and J. I. Veeder, 'Prospects for Self-Sufficient Equilibrium Thorium Cycles in CANDU Reactors', AECL-5501 (March 1976); S. R. Hatcher, S. Banerjee, A. D. Lane, H. Tamm and J. I. Veeder, 'Thorium Cycle in Heavy Water Moderated Pressure Tube (CANDU) Reactors', AECL-5398 (June 1976); S. R. Hatcher, 'Fuel for Nuclear Power in Canada: Options Beyond the Year 2000', *The Canadian Business Review*, 2 (Autumn 1975); and on conversations with employees of Atomic Energy of Canada Limited, to whom the authors are indebted for their assistance.

[4] This discussion is based on V. S. Boyer, J. P. Gibbons, T. A. Johnston, R. J. Hoe, D. K. Feldtmose and W. C. Orotleff, 'Fulton Station HTGR', *Nuclear Engineering International*, August 1974, pp. 635–9; R. C. Dahlberg and L. H. Brooks, 'Core Design Characteristics and Fuel Cycle', *Nuclear Engineering International*, August 1974, pp. 640–6; R. E. Walker and T. A. Johnston, 'Fort Saint Vrain Nuclear Power Station', *Nuclear Engineering International*, December 1969, pp. 1069–73; R. C. Dahlberg, R. F. Turner and W. V. Goeddel, 'Core Design Characteristics', *Nuclear Engineering International*, December 1964, pp. 1073–7; R. C. Dahlberg, R. F. Turner and W. V. Goeddel, 'HTGR Fuel and Fuel Cycle Summary Description', GA-A12801 (Rev), 21 January 1974; and on conversations with Colin Heath of General Atomic Co., to whom the authors are indebted for his assistance.

[5] *Nuclear News*, June 1976, pp. 79–80.

[6] Simon Rippon, 'BN 600 Status Report', *Nuclear Engineering International*, June/July 1975, pp. 551–5; and 'Prototype Fast Breeder Reactors Operating in Europe and the USSR', *Nuclear Engineering International*, June/July 1975, pp. 545–50.

[7] Sieb Ellens, 'European LMFBR Programmes – Progress Subject to Political Pressures', *Nuclear Engineering International*, June 1976, p. 37.

[8] V. Gilinsky, 'Fast Breeder Reactors and the Spread of Plutonium', (Santa Monica, Calif.: Rand Corp., RN-5148-PR, March 1967).

[9] For a description of these and other relatively easy methods for extracting plutonium see O. J. Wick (ed.) *Plutonium Handbook: A Guide to the Technology*, Vol. II. (New York: Gordon and Breach, 1967).

[10] Statement of Theodore B. Taylor before the Subcommittee on International Security and Scientific Affairs of the Committee on International Relations, US House of Representatives, 28 October 1975.

[11] M. Sharefkin, 'The Simple, Uncertain Economics of Multinational Reprocessing Centers', in Abram Chayes and W. B. Lewis (eds), *International Arrangements for Nuclear Fuel Cycle Facilities* (Cambridge, Mass.: Ballinger, 1976) provides an excellent discussion of these uncertainties.

[12] Walton A. Rogers, James A. Pickard and John W. Vallence, 'The Throwaway Fuel Cycle' (paper presented to the Atomic Industrial Forum Fuel Cycle Conference – 75, Atlanta, 20 March 1975), p. 3; The Fuel Cycle Task Force, *Nuclear Fuel Cycle* (Washington: Energy Research and Development Administration, ERDA-33, 1975), chart 9; B. Wolfe and R. W. Lambert, 'The Back End of the Fuel Cycle' (paper presented to the Atomic Industrial Forum Fuel Cycle Conference – 75), p. 12; 'Germans and British Step Up Reprocessing Investment Plans', *Nucleonics Week*, 15 May 1975, p. 13.

[13] Sharefkin, *op. cit.*

[14] Exceptions are 'Nuclear Fuel Cycle Closure Alternatives' (Allied-General Nuclear Services, April 1976), and the 'Generic Statement on the Use of Recycle Plutonium in Mixed Oxide Fuels in Light Water Cooled Reactors' (US Nuclear Regulatory Commission, 1976), in which a substantial net benefit is found for reprocessing. This disappears, however, if a U-236 penalty and a more realistic estimate of the capital cost of new facilities are included, and less rapid increases are assumed for the price of natural uranium and enrichment.

[15] L. J. Colby, Jr., 'Fuel Reprocessing in the United States: a review of problems and some solutions', *Nuclear News*, January 1976, pp. 68–73, provides estimates of $50–100 per kg if cost is related only to heat content and $130–300 if it is related to volume.

[16] 'Nuclear Blending Reviewed as Means against Diversion', *Nuclear News*, February 1976, p. 47.

[17] International Energy Agency, *Annual Report 1 July 1974–30 June 1975*, Annex F_1: Nuclear Installations Under Agreements Approved by the Board of Governors and Expectations Concerning NPT Signatories'.

[18] See Manson Benedict and Thomas H. Pigford, *Nuclear Chemical Engineering* (New York: McGraw Hill, 1957), Chapter 8; John F. Hagerton, *The Atomic Energy Deskbook* (New York: Reinhold, 1963), pp. 140–4.

[19] J. M. Costello and D. M. Levins, 'Reduction in Capital Costs of Fuel Reprocessing Plants' (paper prepared for Ainse Engineering Conference, Lucas Heights, NSW, 19–21 August 1974), p. 2.

[20] J. P. Duckworth, (Plant Manager for Nuclear Fuel Services Reprocessing), lecture at MIT, 22 July 1975.

[21] This discussion is based upon Manson Benedict, 'Fuel Cycle for Nuclear Reactors: Uranium Enrichment and Reprocessing' (paper presented to the International Symposium on Nuclear Power Technology and Economics, Taipei, Taiwan, 13–20 January 1975), pp. 3.9–3.19; Hagerton, *op. cit.*, pp. 192–3.

[22] *Nuclear News*, February 1976, p. 47.

[23] Discussion based upon Benedict, *op. cit.*, pp. 3.19–3.24.

[24] Hagerton, *op. cit.*, pp. 191–3, 219–20, 492–3.
[25] US Atomic Energy Commission. *National Reactor Testing Station*, pp. 17–19.
[26] J. R. Clark, 'Modifying the West Valley Reprocessing Plant', *Nuclear Engineering International*, February 1976, pp. 27–31.
[27] Robert, Gillette, 'Nuclear Fuel Reprocessing: GE's Balky Plant Poses Shortage', *Science*, Vol. 185 (30 August 1974), pp. 770–1.
[28] 'G. E. Decision of MFRP to Await NRC Policy', *Nuclear News*, September 1975, p. 59.
[29] Rogers, Pickard and Vallence, *op. cit.*, p. 2; Jeffrey A. Tannenbaum, 'White Elephant? Big Plant to Recycle Nuclear Fuel is Hit by Delays, Cost Rises', *Wall Street Journal*, 17 February 1976, p. 1.
[30] *Nucleonics Week*, 5 February 1976, p. 12; *Nuclear News*, March 1972, p. 59.
[31] Energy Research and Development Administration, *A National Plan for Energy Research, Development and Demonstration: Creating Energy Choices for the Future*, ERDA-48, Vol. 2 (Washington: USGPO, 1975).
[32] *Ibid.*, p. 153.
[33] *Nuclear News*, December 1975, p. 17.
[34] Bertram Wolfe and Ray W. Lambert, 'The Back End of the Fuel Cycle' (paper presented to the Atomic Industrial Forum Fuel Cycle Conference – 75, Atlanta, Georgia, 20 March 1975), p. 5; Benedict, *op. cit.*, p. 3.8.
[35] The discussion of non-US reprocessing facilities is based largely upon Simon Rippon, 'Reprocessing – What Went Wrong?', *Nuclear Engineering International* February 1976, pp. 21–7; G. Rossney, 'Reprocessing in Europe', *Ibid.*, April/May 1976, pp. 20–1; US Senate. Committee on Government Operations, 'Foreign (Free World) Fuel Reprocessing Capabilities', *Facts on Nuclear Proliferation*, 94th Congress, First Session, December 1975, p. 27 (data provided by Energy Research and Development Administration). Other sources are indicated where appropriate.
[36] *Nuclear Engineering International*, July 1976, p. 8.
[37] *Nuclear Engineering International*, Dec. 1975, p. 989.
[38] *Nuclear News*, June 1976, p. 63.
[39] *Nuclear Engineering International*, July 1976, p. 23.
[40] *Nuclear Engineering International*, June 1976, p. 12.
[41] *Nuclear News*, May 1975, p. 63.
[42] Richard Halloran, 'Seoul Officials Say Strong US Pressure Forced Cancellation of Plans to Purchase a French Nuclear Plant', *New York Times*, 1 February 1976, p. 11; *Nucleonics Week*, 5 February 1976, p. 4.
[43] This section draws heavily on material brought together by Manson Benedict for the symposium cited in note 21 and for a 1975 summer course at MIT.
[44] These figures are for October 1975. William J. Wilcox and J. T. Bradbury, 'Enrichment – The Current Status at Oak Ridge, Portsmouth and Paducah', Union Carbide Doc. No. K-L-6353 (paper presented to the American Nuclear Society Winter Meeting, San Francisco, November 1975).
[45] *Science*, Volume 183 (29 March 1974), p. 1272.
[46] F. B. Baronowski, 'US Gas Centrifuge Program Nears Production Status', *Information from ERDA*, Washington, DC, 24 April 1975, No. S-6-75.
[47] Deborah Shapley, 'Chemistry – A Means to Simpler Uranium Enrichment?' *Science*, Vol. 190 (14 November 1975), p. 645.
[48] *Nuclear Engineering International*, April/May 1976, p. 15.
[49] C. Paul Robinson and Reed J. Jensen, 'Some Developments in Laser Isotope Separation Research at Los Alamos' (paper presented to the American Physical Society Meeting, New York, 2–5 February 1976).

LIST OF TABLES AND DIAGRAMS

Index

ARAMCO (Arabian-American Oil Company) : and French attempt at special oil trade with Saudi Arabia, 59

Abu Dhabi, vii, 8

aerodynamic process of uranium enrichment, 129-36, 155-6

Afghanistan, 28

Alaska: development of oil resources in, 7

Algeria: development of economic powers of, 24; and NPT, 76; and oil production cutbacks, 18-9; and oil trade with USSR, 55

Arab Maritime Petroleum Transport Company, 15

Arab-Israeli dispute: and IEA, 50; and Israel's nuclear status, 82; in 1973 oil crisis, 66; and oil as weapon, 1, 3, 4, 7, 7-8, 10-12, 33, 37, 38

Argentina: Canadian nuclear assistance to, 100; economic aspects of nuclear power in, 100; and NPT, 76, 77; nuclear reprocessing facilities in, 147, 148; and Treaty of Tlatelolco, 80, 100; uranium in, 117

Atomic Energy Commission, 94

Atomic Energy of Canada Ltd. : aid to Argentina, 100; aid to India, 84-5, 89-90; aid to Pakistan, 92; and international market, 121

Australia: nuclear power in, 93; thorium reserves in, 117; uranium reserves in, 115-7

BP (British Petroleum): and 1973 embargo, 61; nationalisation of by Iran in 1951, 63; source of oil supplies, 60

Bahrain: Iran's claim to, 27

balance of power: and oil as weapon, 20

Baruch Plan (1946), 76

Becker, Professor E., 129, 133

Belgium: current energy requirements of, 42; energy policy of, 11; nuclear reprocessing facilities in, 147, 148; vulnerability of to disruption in oil supply, 49-50

Berlin, 79

biological warfare, 79

Brazil: and NPT, 76, 77; nuclear reprocessing facilities in, 148; thorium reserves in, 117; and Treaty of Tlatelolco, 80; uranium enrichment in, 134-5; vulnerability of to disruption in oil supply, 50, 52

British National Oil Corporation, 61

CCD (Committee of the Commission on Disarmament) 104

CENTO (Central Treaty Organisation) 28

CFP (Compagnie Francaise des Petroles): and 1973 embargo, 61

COMECON (Council for Mutual Economic Assistance) 53

Canada: assistance in nuclear technology to Argentina, 100; assistance in nuclear technology to India, 84-5, 89-90; assistance in nuclear technology to Pakistan, 92; current energy situation in 41-2; and development of Soviet oil production, 54; enriched uranium needs of, 136; oil production in, 5, 37; oil requirements of, 57; state owned oil companies in, 61; thorium reserves in, 47; uranium reserves in, 114-7; vulnerability of to disruption in oil supply, 49-50

CANDU, see heavy water reactor car: and oil conservation, 45

centrifuge enrichment plant, 2, 154-5

centrifuge technology, 85, 101, 129-36

Chile: and Treaty of Tlatelolco, 80

China: coal production in, 53; gaseous diffusion plants in, 154; and India, 91; and Iran, 27; and NPT, 76, 77; nuclear role

160

of, 104; and nuclear-free zone in Asia, 95; oil production and consumption in, 53, 56, 72; and Persian Gulf politics, 35; and Treaty of Tlatelolco, 95, 104

coal, production of: in China, 53; in communist countries, 53; in France, 44; in Germany, 44; in Northern Europe, 42

communist countries: energy requirements of, 53-6

conservation: of oil, 7

Convention on Biological Warfare, 79

Czechoslovakia: and nuclear technology, 78

Denmark: state ownership of oil companies in, 61; vulnerability of to disruption in oil supply, 49-50

detente, 79

denterium oxide,˙ see heavy water reactors

diffusion (gaseous) process of uranium enrichment, 129-36, 151-4

EEC (European Economic Community) : energy policy of, 11; oil stocks of, 41; and oil weapon in Arab-Israeli conflict, 10

Eastern Europe: coal production in, 53; oil production and consumption in, 53, 72

economic growth: in Iran, 26; in Iraq, 31; in Saudi Arabia, 31-2

economic power : derived from oil power, 24-5

economic vulnerability (according to energy ˙dependence) : of communist countries, 53-6; of developing countries, 50-3; and IEP, 64; of industrial nations, 41-50, 63; international aspects of, 63-8

Egypt: and NPT, 76; and 1973 oil embargo, 8

electricity: cost of related to uranium enrichment, 133-4; nuclear based and weapons manufacture, 119-25; and oil conservation, 45

Euratom (European Atomic Energy Community) 98

Europe: current energy requirements of, 42; and oil embargo of 1973, 66; oil requirements of, 57; oil stockpiles in, 48, 49

Exxon, 60, 61, 156

Faisal, King, 7, 32

France: current energy requirements of, 42; energy policy of, 11; gaseous diffusion plants in, 154; and NPT, 76, 77, 96; nuclear reprocessing facilities in, 148; oil arrangement with Saudi Arabia, 59; and Suez Canal, 59; uranium reserves in, 117; vulnerability of to disruption in oil supply, 43-5

Gabon: uranium reserves in, 117

gas, production of: in Northern Europe, 42; in USSR, 54

gaseous diffusion, 129-36, 151-4

grain market: and oil market, 6

graphite: use in nuclear reactors, 83-4, 101

Great Britain: current energy requirements of, 42; and development of Soviet oil production, 54; energy policy of, 11; gas centrifuge plants in, 154; gaseous diffusion plants in, 154; and NPT, 77; and North Sea oil, 42; nuclear reprocessing facilities in, 147, 148; oil embargo against, 4; oil import dependence of, 40; oil trade with Iran, 59; in Persian Gulf, 27; and Suez Canal, 59

guerilla activity, 21

heating: and oil conservation, 45

heavy water reactor: fuel cycle diagram for, 141; fuel for, 83-4; gas cooled, 125; light water cooled, 125; and nuclear fuel cycle, 121-3, 140-2; and reprocessing of nuclear fuel, 128; and safeguards, 101; steam generated, 123-5; and uranium enrichment requirements, 136

high temperature gas reactors: and enriched uranium, 136; fuel cycle diagram for, 142; process of, 122; and PUREX, 145-6; and THOREX, 145-6

Holland, see Netherlands

IAEA (International Atomic Energy Agency) : and commercial aspects of nuclear development, 100-3; role of in safeguards for NPT, 77-8, 93, 95-9, 106, 128

IEA (International Energy Agency) 16, 42n, 47, 49-50

IEP (International Energy Programme) 48-50, 58, 64-8, 71

163